Ethics in Higher Education

Ethics in Higher Education

PROMOTING EQUITY AND INCLUSION THROUGH CASE-BASED INQUIRY

EDITED BY

Rebecca M. Taylor and Ashley Floyd Kuntz

HARVARD EDUCATION PRESS
Cambridge, MA

Paperback ISBN 978-1-68253-700-8

Library of Congress Cataloging-in-Publication Data is on file.

Published by Harvard Education Press,
an imprint of the Harvard Education Publishing Group
Harvard Education Press
8 Story Street
Cambridge, MA 02138

Cover Design: Endpaper Studio
Cover Image: enjoynz/iStock via Getty Images

The typefaces in this book are Myriad Pro and Sabon

Contents

Foreword

Every day, legislators, administrators, and teachers make decisions, some of which will have lasting consequences for individual students or even whole education systems. The discomfort surrounding these hard choices is understandable, and decision makers sometimes imagine that their burden would be lifted if only they had more or better data. Of course, other things being equal, more and better data *will* help. But data do not—indeed cannot—drive decisions. All decisions are grounded in values: to know whether one decision is better than another, we need to know what the overall aims are and what values the agent should be pursuing. Thinking well about aims and values is difficult enough. Thinking well about aims and values in complicated contexts that do not allow for ideal outcomes is harder still. Debates about higher education often invoke normative concepts; there is no shortage of appeals to equity, diversity, social justice, excellence, academic freedom, inclusion, or liberal education, to mention just a few. But these concepts are contested—each is understood differently by different people. How they should guide action in specific circumstances, especially when they are in tension with one another, is often hard to discern. We do not, as a sector, have rich and inclusionary intellectual resources for learning from one another about where we differ and where we agree about the concepts, let alone how to apply them. And it can be hard to make progress when debate stays at the level of abstract philosophical deliberation about values, undisciplined by directing attention to the kinds of decisions people really have to make.

This is the lacuna that Rebecca M. Taylor and Ashley Floyd Kuntz—and their collaborators and contributors—begin to fill with *Ethics in Higher Education*. The seven case studies at the center of this book have been carefully wrought to draw attention to the ways in which different values come into tension in realistic, if fictionalized, case studies of specific decision points. Each case identifies an individual or collective decision maker, provides sufficient information for the reader to have a sense of the conflicts the decision maker faces, and provokes reflection on both the choice to be made and the values that should guide it. Chapters focus on the tensions between intellectual diversity and inclusion on campus; what norms should govern faculty use of social media; how institutions should balance different interests in responding to sexual misconduct; what responsibilities colleges have to students caught up in the criminal justice system; questions about funding for higher education; how to weigh priorities in deciding on candidates for leadership at a historically Black college or university (HBCU), and the tensions and dilemmas that surround colleges' relationships with their surrounding communities.

None of these cases allows for an easy answer. Each brings out genuine conflicts in values, and reasonable people are bound to disagree about how to weigh those values in the particular circumstances. But we can make better choices about what values to prioritize and, ultimately, what to do through careful airing and consideration of different perspectives. Deliberative collective reflection on values and on how to weigh them against each other in contexts where the salient features are clearly brought to the forefront improves our decision-making capacity, both collectively and individually, because such reflection among good-willed, reasonable, and well-informed people generally (though not always) yields progress.

To facilitate this kind of deliberation, the volume brings together commentators across several boundaries. Different roles—teacher, or institutional leader, or student service professional, or enrollment management professional, or legislator—enable people to see some features of the situation more clearly, while probably obscuring other features. As a teacher and an administrator, respectively, the two of us suspect that administrators sometimes find it difficult to discount the significance of very loud voices that falsely claim to represent wider constituencies, whereas faculty members sometimes find it difficult to appreciate—or even to access—the perspectives of, say, student services personnel or enrollment managers. So the volume brings administrators, faculty, and college leaders into dialogue with one another.

The commentators also cross disciplinary boundaries. All of economics, sociology, philosophy, anthropology, political science, and policy studies have distinctive resources to bring to bear; they also all have disciplinary knowledge gaps. As a philosopher and an economist, we humbly suggest that philosophers tend to naivete when it comes to institutional detail and economists tend to myopia when it comes to ethical nuance. Well-designed dialogue across disciplines will bring the actually salient issues to the fore and enable a richer and more productive deliberation than practitioners of any particular discipline can manage by themselves. And, importantly, the commentators bring different ethical perspectives to the problems: these are offered in a spirit of, and as a resource for, mutual learning, as they must be for progress to be made.

The set of commentaries on each case provides ideas and perspectives that will help the readers to formulate their own judgments about the case, reflect better on what values and principles inform those judgments, and be better prepared to enter a dialogue with colleagues and other stakeholders when approaching the decisions they have to make. We believe that the value of the intellectual and ethical resources developed here is not limited to decisions about the particular areas of higher education singled out by the seven cases. Whatever your areas of responsibility, we think that the method of reflection displayed, as well as the substantive ethical ideas deployed, will prove helpful. We hope that this excellent volume will be read widely and that readers will not be satisfied with simply consuming it, but will use it to provoke and structure wide-ranging discussions across disciplines and institutional roles on their campuses.

—Harry Brighouse and Michael McPherson

CHAPTER 1

Advancing Collaborative Ethical Inquiry in Higher Education

REBECCA M. TAYLOR AND ASHLEY FLOYD KUNTZ

One of the greatest sources of tension on US college campuses in recent years has been advancing equity and inclusion while also protecting individual and institutional freedoms. In 2020, colleges and universities faced new and renewed challenges amid the COVID-19 pandemic, anti-Black racism, and deep political unrest at the national level. College students, faculty, and higher education professionals across the country have challenged institutional racism on their campuses, police brutality against people of color, decisions to open or close campuses in response to the pandemic, federal immigration restrictions impacting international students, and college investments in the fossil fuel industry and prison labor. They have called out their institutions forcefully and often. In response to internal conflict and public scrutiny, campus leaders frequently attempt to quell potential controversy by issuing public statements that reaffirm institutional core values. Yet these statements are often made in a climate of urgency and fear of public backlash that can obscure the complex ethical dimensions at stake.

With this volume, we invite readers to pause and carefully consider pressing ethical issues in higher education, both those that have attracted national attention and those that may have been eclipsed by more attention-grabbing flashpoints. Although higher education law or campus policies may dictate what colleges and universities *must* do in some of these situations, they do not tell us what institutions *should* do. Determining what should be done is an ethical imperative. This volume presents a collection of normative case studies and commentaries from multidisciplinary scholars and practitioners that examines pressing ethical issues facing colleges and universities and considers ways in which institutions can enact their core values in the face of practical constraints.

IDENTIFYING PRESSING ETHICAL ISSUES IN HIGHER EDUCATION

In recent years, student activists brought national attention to Middlebury College, Auburn University, the University of California, Berkeley, and many other campuses when they protested against conservative speakers who, they argued, were peddling racist ideas. Alongside the increase in progressive student activism, conservative student groups have turned to the courts to push for greater freedom of expression on campus. In this climate of political polarization, colleges and universities are facing new calls from the political right to increase *intellectual diversity*. In 2019, South Dakota became the first state to pass a bill mandating that public universities protect intellectual diversity—defined as diversity in ideological and political viewpoints. In contrast, a Yale University committee tasked with making recommendations for faculty diversity and inclusivity appealed to the value of intellectual diversity in calling for greater disciplinary and interdisciplinary representation on tenure and promotion committees and greater diversity of racial and gender representation among the faculty. These divergent uses of the term "intellectual diversity" raise the question: What responsibilities do colleges and universities have to protect and even foster each of these forms of intellectual diversity?

In addition to debates about intellectual diversity, the limits of *free speech on social media* for faculty and students are being tested. In 2014, the University of Illinois at Urbana-Champaign withdrew a job offer to Professor Steven Salaita after a string of fiery tweets he posted against the Israeli government drew outcry from university donors, among others. Attention to the implications of faculty speech on social media for other institutional aims and values is growing, and in 2018, Kansas became the first state to address faculty speech on social media directly in a comprehensive policy. Faculty are not alone in facing scrutiny. Amid the Black Lives Matters protests and counter-protests in 2020, incoming students saw admissions and athletics offers rescinded due to racist comments they had made on online platforms. Cases like these can pose complex ethical challenges for college administrators when individuals' rights to freedom of expression come into conflict with other core institutional values, notably equity and inclusion on campus.

Beyond the contexts of speech and intellectual diversity, colleges and universities also encounter ethical tensions as they determine how to respond to admitted students' misconduct and whether to exclude applicants with prior records of arrest or conviction in the criminal legal system. For much of the past decade, higher education leaders across the US have been responding to highly visible instances of *sexual misconduct and assault* on their campuses. Given the widespread perception that existing legal structures and practices are insufficient for handling such claims, colleges and universities face increased pressure to fill this gap. Unfortunately, federal policy is currently, at best, ambiguous. The Department of Education under Betsy DeVos rescinded Obama-era guidance on Title IX in 2017 and issued new rules aimed at providing more protection for those accused of sexual harassment or assault in 2020. Shortly after President Joe Biden took office in 2021, his administration initiated a comprehensive review of the Trump-era regulations, sparking renewed debate about the proper role of colleges and universities in supporting survivors of sexual misconduct and violence on campus.

Concerns about how to balance the importance of inclusion, equity, and safety also emerge when considering *higher education access for people with histories of arrest or conviction*. Otherwise-qualified applicants may be denied admission based on past involvement in the criminal legal system, and many more are deterred from applying by the presence of criminal background questions on applications. The Ban the Box campaign has called for the removal of questions about criminal background from both employment and college applications. In response, the Common Application removed its universal criminal background question for the 2019–2020 application year. And after facing restrictions for decades, incarcerated people's eligibility for Pell Grants was restored in December 2020. These changes have occurred along with growing recognition of racial and economic injustice endemic to the criminal legal system in the US. Colleges and universities face important, underexamined questions regarding their role in redressing these societal inequities, including their responsibilities to include and support students with current or past involvement in the criminal legal system.

Further questions of access and inclusion arise with regard to tuition policies. Campaigns for *free college tuition* have gained momentum in recent years and reemerged as a campaign issue in the 2020 presidential election. A majority of Democratic candidates, including then-candidate Joe Biden, advocated making either two or four years of college available for free. And although support for free college proposals was higher in 2020 among Democrats than Republicans, a majority of young Republicans also supported these proposals.[1] Despite growing public support, questions about how tuition policies can best promote equity and access remain. Whereas supporters argue that free tuition policies will advance these goals, some critics argue that these policies actually harm those students with the most financial need by redirecting scarce resources to middle-class students. This prominent political debate raises important ethical questions for higher education leaders and scholars to consider.

Both within and beyond the free tuition debate, the *contemporary significance and sustainability of historically Black colleges and universities* (HBCUs) has emerged as a vital consideration as advocates call for policies that support both public and private HBCUs. The 2020 election of Vice President Kamala Harris, a graduate of Howard University, has renewed public attention to the exceptional historical and contemporary contributions of HBCUs and to how these institutions can best position themselves for the future. During a period in which colleges across the country are struggling financially in the face of enrollment declines and the unique challenges of the COVID-19 pandemic, HBCUs must also contend with the racial wealth gap that may restrict their financial resources in ways not experienced by predominantly White institutions (PWIs). HBCU leaders face both universal and unique choices as they determine how to maintain their institutions' distinctive missions while also creating sustainable funding models.

Finally, colleges and universities across the country face the ethical imperative of building *sustainable and just relationships with their local communities*. Institutions of higher education exist within and impact their communities in myriad ways: from community colleges partnering with local industries for workforce development, to elite schools in urban communities contributing to rising housing costs in surrounding neighborhoods, to liberal arts colleges creating service-learning courses that expand the boundaries of the classroom into community organizations, to public land grant institutions benefiting from land expropriated from Indigenous peoples. Developing just community relationships may require that colleges elevate community interests above their own. Yet doing so may put institutions at odds with the demands of students, parents, and donors. These decisions raise vital questions about the societal role and responsibilities of higher education institutions that warrant close attention.

USING NORMATIVE CASE STUDIES

The topics introduced above highlight just a few of the higher education contexts in which challenging, ethically laden choices arise. In this volume, we examine these seven contexts in a series of case studies and commentaries. We approach these issues using a form of collaborative, multidisciplinary ethical inquiry pioneered by Meira Levinson and Jacob Fay, but not yet applied to the context of higher education. Levinson is currently leading the way in advancing educational ethics as a recognized field of inquiry. In two prior volumes, Levinson and Fay introduced a model for normative case-based inquiry.[2] By applying this model to the context of higher education, we aim to foster collaborative dialogue that bridges traditional disciplinary and professional silos. We hope that this approach will help college and university leaders, scholars, and practitioners develop a deeper understanding of the ethical issues they encounter and build capacity to navigate these issues in ways that promote educational justice and other core values.

The use of case studies in ethical inquiry has a long history both in teaching and research. Such cases traditionally center on narrowly framed ethical dilemmas—that is, dilemmas about what *should* be the case or what central actors *should* do in light of considerations of ethics. These cases may be either fictional or nonfictional. In contrast to other forms of case studies (e.g., in qualitative research or practical professional training), these are unique in focusing squarely on ethical questions. Ethicists and applied philosophers from education, business, law, and medicine have used narrative cases to ground inquiry into value conflicts that emerge in practice. Within education, case-based approaches to ethics have been incorporated into curricula for undergraduate students and pedagogical tools for training teachers and higher education professionals.[3]

Among these examples of ethics case studies in education, the theoretical frameworks that guide the methods of analysis vary. In this volume, we advance an analytical approach that is not bound by the constraints of traditional moral theorizing. Traditional approaches in K–12 educational ethics apply abstract theories—consequentialist theories that prioritize benefit maximization and nonconsequentialist theories that prioritize virtues, care, or respect for persons—to analysis of narrative cases. In this top-down model, training in traditional moral philosophy is necessary to analyze ethics cases. In contrast, a bottom-up approach to educational ethics begins with particular practical realities, identifies ethical ideals or goals that stem from these realities, and then determines courses of action to advance these practically grounded ideals or goals. This latter approach is arguably best undertaken collaboratively by individuals whose professional and personal perspectives position them to contribute a diverse set of relevant insights to the practical scenario in question.

The model for normative case-based inquiry developed by Levinson and Fay that we employ embraces a bottom-up approach—one rooted in the importance of not only philosophical theory but also empirical evidence and practical expertise. Levinson and Fay define normative case studies as: "richly described, realistic accounts of complex ethical dilemmas that arise within practice or policy contexts, in which protagonists must decide among courses of action, none of which is self-evident as the right one to take."[4] By incorporating varied scholarly and professional perspectives on a particular normative case study, the resulting ethical analysis and recommendations for action may represent a deeper understanding of the ethical context and more robust proposals for ethical responses.

Our approach to case construction and analysis applies this collaborative, multidisciplinary approach. In this volume, we have included a set of empirically grounded, socially contextualized normative case studies that focus on complex, ethically laden choices facing a wide array of higher education actors—policy makers, governance boards, upper-level administrators, student and academic affairs professionals, faculty, and students. In selecting topics to represent in this volume, we chose some because they are pressing topics that are drawing widespread public and scholarly attention and others because they center important ethical questions for higher education that have yet to receive the level of attention in mainstream higher education circles that we believe is warranted. For each of these topics, our goal is to raise awareness of its ethical import and to seek clarity about what ethical responses look like.

DEVELOPING THE NORMATIVE CASE STUDIES

Each of the normative cases in this volume is coauthored by scholars with multidisciplinary expertise. In developing the cases, we reviewed media coverage, legislative and policy reports, social science research, and our own professional experience pertaining to the core topic. Case authors analyzed these sources of evidence to identify the scope of ethical issues within the topic area and the central value tensions at stake. Each of the case studies was workshopped at one or more scholarly convening at various stages of development, deepening the opportunities for the cases themselves to reflect a diverse array of disciplinary, professional, and experiential lenses.

Our case design approach diverges from that of traditional philosophical thought experiments and some ethics case methodologies, which tend to control for social and ethical complexity in order to pose narrow questions with two clear sides. Traditional approaches may help develop clarity on the particular narrow question posed and may elicit closer connections and contrasts between case responses. However, in real educational contexts, ethical questions rarely have this neatness. Rather, the ethical questions that arise are myriad and complex—informed by the particular social contexts of the individuals, communities, and institutions involved. The socially contextualized normative cases that we developed are not intended to represent a topic area in a universally generalizable way. Rather, each represents just one set of ethical questions within the topic area that are particular to the social context described in the case.

It is our view that practical ethical analysis in education should reflect this realistic complexity for both *methodological* and *pedagogical* reasons. For ethical inquiry in higher education to have validity, it should account for the variety of contextual features that inform ethical courses of action. This approach not only provides a better foundation for valid ethical analysis but also better reflects the types of scenarios that educators and professionals will encounter, leading to the development of stronger tools for ethics education. We hope this volume prepares current and future higher education professionals to navigate the messy ethical issues they will encounter and the multifaceted decisions they will have to make in practice.

Six of the seven cases present empirically grounded fictional narratives that incorporate rich social context. Each concludes with a set of ethical questions. While some include narrowly framed questions about whether or not the actor(s) should take a particular course of action, many introduce a range of questions about a variety of opportunities for ethical courses of action, and all include broader, open-ended questions about the values at stake and how they should guide the actors' approaches to navigating the ethical context presented. We endeavor to pose questions that represent the complex reality of practical ethical decision-making and the scope of agency that actors may have.

The remaining case takes a different, non-narrative approach. For this case (chapter 5), the authors linked relevant historical and contemporary context from the US criminal legal system to emerging conversations surrounding college admission and student success for people with prior arrests and/or convictions. This case format encourages readers to consider the ethical questions that arise for a wide array of higher education institutions as they determine whether and how to provide educational opportunities for both currently and formerly incarcerated (or *justice-involved*) people.

After initially considering grounding some of the case studies in real examples, we opted to fictionalize the narratives we include for both ethical and methodological reasons. Methodologically, we find that fictionalized accounts have the benefit of focusing ethical analysis on the details presented in the case itself, given that no further outside information is available, in contrast to a real-world example. This approach gives commentators and readers a common foundation from which to address the questions raised. Ethically, in the process of developing the volume, we learned about the potential harms of using nonfictional examples of individuals who have been at the center of cases that gained national attention. The use of real cases pulled from contemporary publicly available media sources is not uncommon in ethics, but we decided against this approach. These are serious events that are very real to the people involved, and presenting them as fodder for academic analysis and class discussion may be ethically fraught. Soliciting consent and participation from those involved in real cases may help mitigate these ethical concerns. However, using fictionalized narratives provides another option to represent realistically complex scenarios without risking potential harms to individuals involved in real cases.

Finally, it is important to note that the topics we include represent only a small subset of the contexts in which ethical questions arise in higher education that bear on equity, freedom, and inclusion. Many important topics are not addressed, including affirmative action policies, issues of access and accommodations for students with disability labels, and just treatment of college athletes, in addition to the countless interpersonal ethical choices that educators, students, and administrators face daily. We hope to engage in and see more scholarly attention to the myriad ethical issues that arise in higher education in the future.

ANALYZING THE CASE STUDIES

Each case in the volume is analyzed through a collection of commentaries from scholars and practitioners who represent a diverse array of disciplinary and personal backgrounds, career stages, and professional roles. The scholars include both philosophers and empirical researchers (e.g., educational sociologists, psychologists, anthropologists, and historians), who apply their expertise to identifying philosophically and empirically informed recommendations for ethical action. The practitioners include student and academic affairs professionals as well as administrators and community leaders. By incorporating analytical commentaries from a range of relevant disciplinary, experiential, and practical perspectives, we aim to model a collaborative approach to ethical inquiry in higher education.

In navigating ethical conflicts in practice, challenges often arise as differently situated individuals give varying levels of attention to different features of the situation. The commentary format we use aims to represent this feature of ethical decision-making realistically. Each commentator analyzes the case study through their unique lens, focusing on the particular ethical dimensions most salient to them. Differences in the details selected by each commentator are apparent within each chapter. Readers will notice variations in how authors refer to racial and ethnic identity constructs, as well as the centrality of philosophical, empirical, and practical insights in their responses. At the same time, some chapters reveal shared assumptions or core values among the commentators, despite their varied professional and personal perspectives. The commentaries are intended to challenge readers to consider not only how ethical dilemmas are resolved but also how they are framed.

By reflecting on these commonalities and differences, readers can achieve greater understanding of the ethical dimensions of each case. Our intention is that, taken together, the commentaries will guide readers in identifying and thinking through the complex ethical dimensions of each case and present them with tools to develop their own perspectives. Of course, it is important to recognize that the commentaries included in each chapter do not represent a comprehensive analysis of every ethical dimension of or perspective on the case in question. We encourage readers to engage critically with the case studies and each of these perspectives, considering both what is offered and what is missing.

USING THIS VOLUME

This volume includes seven chapters, each comprising a normative case study and six analytical commentaries. We present these chapters in an order that highlights common themes and connections between the various topics. However, each chapter can also stand alone, and they may be read in any order. We encourage readers to use this volume as a flexible tool to guide inquiry. In the concluding chapter, we provide additional recommendations for ways the cases and commentaries might be used in a variety of educational and professional settings.

Chapter 2 raises ethical questions regarding intellectual diversity on campus through a narrative that asks how the President's Diversity Council at a public university in the Southwest should respond to community and student protests surrounding a campus talk by a political speaker known for drafting anti-immigration legislation. Chapter 3 asks how a dean should respond to challenges to the tenure case of a Black woman scientist based on her social media activism. Chapter 4 centers a Title IX committee at a small liberal arts college in rural Appalachia determining how to implement the new 2020 federal regulations on handling cases of sexual assault and misconduct on campus. Chapter 5 presents the current state of higher education access for justice-involved students within the context of the broader criminal legal system in the US and asks what responsibilities institutions of higher education have to these students. Chapter 6 asks how the student representative to the board of trustees in a state considering enacting new legislation to create a free tuition program should weigh in on the proposed program. Chapter 7 focuses on the decision facing the presidential search committee at a private, religious historically Black college in the Southeast as they consider the candidates' competing visions for how to respond to fiscal concerns, students' call for greater inclusion of queer and other nonconforming students on campus, and the dual pandemics of COVID-19 and anti-Black racism. Chapter 8 presents the newly hired director of an initiative aimed at advancing the public good through community partnerships at a small Midwestern college as she tries to determine the best way to advance sustainability and justice. Finally, chapter 9 reflects on themes that emerge throughout the case chapters and offers recommendations for educators, scholars, and practitioners on how to use the volume to advance ethical policies and practices.

Taken together, we aim for the cases and commentaries included in this volume to address the following central questions: (1) How should colleges and universities respond through policy or practice to ethical issues surrounding equity, freedom, and inclusion? and (2) What new possibilities for ethical policies and practices may be imagined through multidisciplinary analysis of normative cases? In addition to addressing the need for more scholarly attention to ethics in the context of higher education, the volume is designed to facilitate its use as an educational resource for training higher education professionals, providing a valuable tool for both higher education graduate programs and practicing professionals.

CHAPTER 2

Controversial Speakers, Intellectual Diversity, and Inclusion on Campus

ASHLEY FLOYD KUNTZ, REBECCA M. TAYLOR,
AND DANIEL P. GIBBONEY JR.

This case imagines senior leaders at a flagship public university responding to student and community protests, legislative pressure, and faculty concerns surrounding a controversial speaker on campus.

For the past several months, tensions had been building at Southwestern State University.[1] In August, the board of regents expressed concern that students were receiving a one-sided, politically liberal education. At issue was a recent survey of the faculty showing that registered Democrats outnumbered registered Republicans by 16 to 1 at the flagship campus. With pressure from the state legislature, the board urged the university to do more to protect intellectual diversity on campus, calling for more diverse ideological representation among the faculty and more opportunities for students to engage with conservative policies and principles both in and out of the classroom. Many faculty viewed this pressure as a threat to academic freedom and countered that voter registration was not an indicator of how they approached teaching. In the words of one faculty member interviewed by the local newspaper, "Chemistry is chemistry. There isn't Republican chemistry and Democrat chemistry. There's just chemistry." The issue continued to dominate conversations on campus, but by October, media attention had died down and campus seemed to be returning to business as usual.

Then word spread that Curt Lyle—the controversial architect of several hardline immigration-related policies—had been invited to speak on campus by the College Republicans, and tensions flared again. University policy stipulated that student organizations were free to invite speakers to campus without requiring sponsorship by an academic unit; they were simply required to notify the Division of Student Affairs of the invitations and to arrange security, if needed, with campus police. Consistent with this policy, the College Republicans had invited Lyle and advertised his speech—"Immigration and Democracy"—with flyers and through social media postings. Doing so quickly captured the attention of both the campus and broader community.

Mr. Lyle had built his national reputation by helping state legislatures draft immigration-related policies, several of which had been deemed unconstitutional by federal courts. He had also been a vocal opponent of the DREAM Act and the Deferred Action for Childhood Arrivals (DACA) policy.

As word spread that he was coming to speak at Southwestern State, the university's La Raza Association, with the support of the American Indian Student Alliance and the Black Student Union, began organizing a protest.[2] Additionally, a statewide Hispanic coalition planned a community protest. Rhetoric on social media heated up, and the campus chapter of a national conservative association committed to "training students to promote freedom" began organizing a group of counter-protestors.

Learning of the planned protests, the College Republicans reached out to campus police and asked for additional security. On the day of the event, student and community protestors blocked the entrance to the speaker venue, carrying signs and chanting loudly. Those wishing to hear Mr. Lyle engaged in their own counter-protests and attempted to breach the wall of protestors and enter the venue. Before long, a fistfight erupted between two community members. Ultimately, campus police decided to clear the area and close the venue, resulting in Mr. Lyle being unable to speak.

Between local media coverage and videos posted to social media sites, news of the protests and counter-protests spread quickly, creating a public relations firestorm for Southwestern State. University President Nancy Tucker issued a brief statement reaffirming the university's commitment to promoting a culture of respect and civility, ensuring public safety, and allowing free speech. Yet many members of the campus community took issue with what they perceived as the university's relative silence on the events and began drafting their own statements, which helped contextualize the controversy over Mr. Lyle's visits.

In interviews with the press, members of the College Republicans described what they perceived as a biased campus climate in which they felt intellectually and socially isolated and unsafe voicing their political viewpoints. They argued that the faculty were overwhelmingly liberal and that outside speakers like Curt Lyle were their main avenue to learn about conservative political viewpoints on campus. Though they recognized Mr. Lyle as controversial, they argued that as a prominent Republican policymaker and rising star in the Republican Party, he was a suitable speaker for College Republicans to invite to campus. When asked what concerned them most about the events surrounding Mr. Lyle's visit, the students pointed both to what they saw as the violation of their and his free speech rights and to unfair restrictions on the types of topics deemed worthy of intellectual discussion on campus. One of the event organizers stated it this way: "We don't feel comfortable discussing conservative political ideas in our classes, and now the spaces we've created outside of class to have these conversations are also being threatened. Southwestern State says it cares about inclusion, but we can tell you that doesn't apply to conservative ideas, and we think that's wrong."

Glenda Jefferson, chair of the state legislature education committee, weighed in as well. In a public statement, she expressed concern that Southwestern State seemed to be an inhospitable climate for conservatives. She argued that the protests were proof that the campus lacked intellectual diversity and claimed that faculty were indoctrinating students in liberal viewpoints. Ms. Jefferson vowed that her committee would further investigate whether the university was living up to its responsibility to protect open inquiry and free speech.

Student leaders from La Raza and the other student organizations that co-organized the protests saw the issue differently. They issued their own statement situating Mr. Lyle's invitation in a broader context of mounting tensions on campus. They pointed specifically to two incidents that had occurred the prior semester. In the first, a Latino student who was attempting to enter an athletic event was asked by campus security to produce identification; when the student objected because other students were not being asked to provide ID, a police officer physically pressed him against the wall. The incident was caught on video, and the officer was placed on leave, but no further action was taken. In the second incident, racial slurs were painted on the door of the largest multicultural sorority on campus; no one was apprehended, and the sorority was forced to incur the cost of removing the graffiti. Members of the sorority expressed feeling unsafe on campus after the incident, not knowing whether each person they passed on campus might be the culprit or how pervasive those racist attitudes were within the student body.

Latine, American Indian, and Black students recounted numerous examples of being subjected to stereotypes and microaggressions by faculty, staff, and peers at Southwestern State. Contrary to claims that faculty were too liberal, these students complained that faculty didn't go far enough to ensure an inclusive educational environment. They described an overall chilly climate on campus, in which prejudicial comments from peers were often left unchecked in class discussions and faculty were often just as lacking in cultural sensitivity as students.

Joining forces, the student leaders consulted their student affairs advisers in the Office of Student Multicultural Programs and crafted a list of demands. First among them was the addition of a core curriculum requirement for an ethnic studies course. Citing data from the Anti-Defamation League documenting an alarming rise in hate crimes on college campuses across the country, the students wrote, "There has never been a more crucial moment to ensure that all Southwestern State students are educated about diverse histories and cultures and that they better understand how race and racism have undergirded political systems and contributed to systemic stratification and oppression." Second, the students charged the university with diversifying the campus community. Although Southwestern State was located in a state that is 30 percent Hispanic or Latino and 3 percent American Indian, they noted that just 10 percent of the student body and only 2 percent of the faculty identified as Hispanic or Latino and that students and faculty who identified as American Indian represented less than 1 percent.

Finally, the students called on the university to revise its invited speaker policies to align with the institution's academic standards and stated commitment to diversity, equity, and inclusion: "Consider the invitation for Mr. Lyle to speak from our perspective. The First Amendment gives him the right to speak, but that doesn't mean he *should* speak here. His policies have caused real harm to the Latine community, and federal courts have ruled that these policies are unconstitutional. He has the right to speak, but so do we, and we believe the university has a role to play in setting some parameters for who is an appropriate speaker. This is an academic institution, and not all ideas are worth debating. Student groups should be required to obtain co-sponsorship from an academic department. Additionally, the Office of Diversity and Inclusion should review all student-sponsored speaker events. It's not enough to say Southwestern State is committed to inclusion; we want campus leaders to consider the impact of speakers and ideas on students of color, undocumented students, DACA students, and students from mixed immigration status families. Mr. Lyle's ideas might be tossed around as an intellectual exercise for some, but for us, his ideas have very real consequences—families separated, friends deported, educational opportunities denied. At a minimum, the university should have given further consideration to the invitation for him to speak."

In response to the mounting firestorm, President Tucker called an emergency meeting of the President's Diversity Council. Behind closed doors, senior administrators debated what to do, given the demands and perspectives of students, faculty, staff, and the broader community. Dr. Lourdes Olivera, vice president for diversity and inclusion, opened the discussion, "Dr. Tucker's letter to the university community was right to remind us of our core mission and values and our responsibility to create an inclusive learning environment, but the question remains how we can best do that."

The provost, Dr. Hannah Jansen, expressed frustration about the demands that had been voiced, noting that the idea of an ethnic studies requirement had been raised during the last revision of the Core Curriculum, but faculty had not supported it. Moreover, in light of state budget cuts and a competitive market, she felt that her hands were tied in terms of diversifying the faculty. Other members of the council jumped in to question the focus on racial and ethnic diversity of the campus community and wanted to do more to support diverse ideological viewpoints, especially in light of the survey showing such a disproportionate number of registered Democrats on the faculty. Dr. Frank Owen, professor of economics and chair of the Faculty Senate, added, "Some state legislatures are considering intellectual diversity bills, and South Dakota passed one in 2019. I think we'd be wise to consider an institutional policy supporting intellectual diversity and making it clear that our campus is fully committed to free speech in all its forms, offensive and otherwise. We need to ensure that faculty hiring committees aren't biased against conservative candidates, either."

Dr. Jansen interjected, "But how would you do that in practice? As provost, I do not feel it is appropriate to establish a political litmus test for faculty hires. I'm concerned that our board and legislators like Representative Jefferson are intruding into faculty members' privacy. It's a slippery slope, and part of my job is to hold the line on academic freedom. We don't ask people about their religious affiliation, and likewise, we don't ask new hires their party affiliations. Even if we did, what would this tell us?"

The vice president for student affairs, Dr. Blair Jones, echoed her sentiments and expressed frustration that the university was being depicted as not living up to its values of free speech and diversity of thought. Inviting Curt Lyle to speak, he argued, was a clear example of how committed the institution was to ideological diversity. After all, his division went above and beyond to try to allow Mr. Lyle to speak; they didn't bar the College Republicans from inviting him, and they even incurred substantial security costs in an attempt to ensure public safety.

At this point, Dr. Olivera reminded the group that academic freedom and free inquiry are not the only values that are central to the university's mission; they are also committed to diversity, inclusion, and equity. "I fear we're taking too narrow of a view of intellectual diversity. It isn't just about party affiliation or political ideology or who speaks on campus," she said. Alluding to her work advising many of the student groups involved in the protest, she challenged her colleagues to keep in mind that some students—and faculty and staff—enter Southwestern State with less privilege due to systemic racism and bigotry:

> I can't speak to the experience of conservative students in the classroom, but I can tell you that students of color on this campus often keep their knowledge and perspectives to themselves. Just yesterday, a student stopped by to tell me about how her professor never even mentioned the deportation of Mexican Americans during a lecture on the Great Depression. When she tried to raise the issue, her professor just looked clueless, and a white student jumped in with a comment that steered the conversation in a totally different direction. It was like she wasn't even there, even though she had really valuable insight to contribute. Part of diversity of thought is diversity of *thinkers*; we haven't done enough to diversify our student body and faculty ranks, and the people of color we do have on campus often don't feel as if their perspectives are welcomed. That's the issue here.

It was clear to everyone on the President's Diversity Council that Mr. Lyle's visit had exposed fissures within the campus community, ones that raised important questions for senior leadership about the importance of diversity of thought at Southwestern State. Faced with a conflict between core institutional values of open inquiry and inclusion and feeling pressure from the legislature to protect and/or enhance intellectual diversity, senior leaders considered their next steps. Should Dr. Jones revise policies concerning student group speaker invitations? If so, what should the new university policy entail? What approach should Provost Jansen take in responding to the concerns of students, student affairs administrators, and faculty? Should she prioritize diversifying the racial and ethnic composition of the faculty? Building support for an ethnic studies requirement? Promoting more ideologically inclusive classrooms? Protecting academic freedom? Finally, what type of public response should President Tucker make to the various stakeholders expressing discontent with the intellectual climate at Southwestern State?

COMMENTARY

Return, Neutrality, Inclusion, or Transformation? Rethinking Intellectual Diversity in Higher Education

SHEEVA SABATI

This fictional case reflects the very real fractures that have surfaced in universities across the United States and is also reflective of our national political context. There is so much at stake beyond the urgent questions we are prompted to consider in terms of the curriculum, campus hiring policies, academic freedom, and event guidelines. What, then, constitutes an ethical response?

As a starting point, leaders must critically contextualize the kinds of intellectual "diversity" that are being called for. What assumptions are at the root of each position? Who benefits from each framing and how? Toward these ends, I unpack the varying calls for diversity that are invoked in this case and organize the positions that the characters present into four primary categories: (1) return, (2) neutrality, (3) inclusion, and (4) transformation.[3] Although fictional, this case illuminates important historical, cultural, and political contexts that shape universities, providing an opportunity to consider how we might reconceptualize ethics and accountability.

DIVERSITY AS RETURN

Diversity as return advocates for intellectual diversity by calling on values such as "free speech in all of its forms, offensive and otherwise" as its rationale. Within a political landscape in which white supremacists have been increasingly emboldened to enact racial terror, or where the government cages immigrant children in detention centers, the desire to protect "offensive" speech takes on acute meaning.[4] Here, the language of diversity is appropriated to "return" to a time where all speech—especially those ideas, policies, and practices that condone race-based stratification and violence—are not only acceptable, but encouraged as part of the purportedly rational political debate.

Those who co-opt the language of diversity for return may ascribe to the position that the American Dream has been encroached on by non-white immigrants, and so there must be a return to the core values of the country (*think*, "Make America Great Again").[5] Its defenders aim to protect their perceived entitlements to wealth, power, and privilege; as such, they might defend the violence of historical and contemporary racial economic policies as circumstantial, necessary, and normative. The return position ultimately re-entrenches political and economic power for groups who have historically accumulated wealth and power. We're told here that Curt Lyle, the College Republicans' guest speaker, has crafted several hardline immigration policies. Political pundits like Lyle frame issues like immigration through inflammatory rhetoric that blames socially othered communities for the problems that, in fact, their very own policies have created.

In response to the return position, leaders might respond by affirming the unique commitments to truth and education that universities are supposed to center. Not all forms of speech—especially those based on the fundamental dehumanization of racialized communities—are scholarly positions that deserve university resources, a point already raised by the Black, American Indian, and Latinx student leaders in the case.

NEUTRALITY, NOT DIVERSITY

This second position doesn't claim to take a stance on intellectual diversity, but tacitly asserts *neutrality* as the antidote to politically charged situations. Those who uphold this position—for example, the faculty member who asserted to the local newspaper that "Chemistry is chemistry"—understand themselves as not implicated in questions of power and socially produced inequities.

Still, these questions factor into academic disciplines that frame themselves as neutral or apart from the problem. For example, why is it that socioeconomic status, gender, race, and other forms of "difference" inform what sort of K–12 educational opportunities young people have and whether they have access to college, let alone to pursue undergraduate or doctoral studies in chemistry and to eventually land a tenure-track job as a chemistry professor? In a society where unequal access to education has been historically ensured, neutrality does not interrupt the ways in which power and resources are unevenly distributed.

DIVERSITY AS INCLUSION

Those who advocate for an *inclusionary* approach engage diversity as only an issue of representation. They may use the language of diversity as a benevolent, performative act that makes no material commitments to disrupt and dismantle the harmful structures, cultures, and practices that require interventions of diversity in the first place. Regardless of intent, the impact of this approach leaves in place the current structure that produces inequity and only seeks to include more people in the system, always at the expense of another group deemed marginal.

The existing academic and cultural context of Southwestern State might be characterized as advocating for an *inclusive* approach to diversity. This comes through in the *return* contingent's charge that the campus provides a "one-sided, politically liberal education," a characterization leveraged as a critique. Still, the many examples raised by the students of color—such as the "chilly" campus climate, the "unchecked" classroom discussions, and the limited curricular perspectives—demonstrate how mere *inclusion* of students of color on campus does not dismantle the harmful educational contexts.

The inclusion approach is based on superficial change. It is a convenient position for those who find the return position less than palatable, but who have not critically interrogated how they, themselves, benefit from the status quo organization of higher educational institutions in terms of the curriculum and culture of whiteness. Those who take on the position of inclusion may be willing to accept diversity insofar as it doesn't radically reshape their relative proximity to privilege.

DIVERSITY AS TRANSFORMATION

The *diversity as transformation* position is willing to candidly confront the role of universities in entrenching social and economic inequalities. Here, the concept of diversity is oriented toward transforming the distribution of power and economic stability within and beyond institutions of higher education, without attachment to one's own inherited proximities to privilege or power. It includes learning how universities are not only implicated in, but have been formative in, supporting the scholarship and political work of thinkers who promulgated racial knowledges and justified racial violence through the language of science, objectivity, and race-based definitions of rationality.[6] Transformative approaches center the demands of systematically marginalized and historically excluded members of a campus community toward the long-term work of changing institutional cultures, such as those articulated by students of color at Southwestern State.

Transformative intellectual diversity requires knowledge systems that denaturalize all that has become naturalized: borders, prisons, poverty, debt, hyper-wealth concentration, war, settler colonial nation-states, unfettered extraction of more-than-human life, and much more. It understands that what counts as "ethical" cannot be divorced from the racial and colonial contexts that continue to shape institutions of higher education, but rather must actively address, dismantle, and reimagine them.

Sheeva Sabati, PhD, is an assistant professor in anti-racist education leadership and policy studies at California State University, Sacramento. She utilizes critical race and anti-colonial feminisms to examine the social foundations of US higher education and reframe the ethical responsibilities of (public) universities.

COMMENTARY

Courageous Leadership: A View from the Middle

LAURA DINEHART AND HEATHER RUSSELL

University administration is challenging. In the face of controversy, we often keep opinions private and share dissent only in oral (not written) communication. Administrators' personal values can certainly conflict with their public response or non-response. Yet what activists remind us is that *silence is consent*. Systemic change requires university administrators to question and evaluate our systems and practices continuously. Real change will require courageous leadership.

PERSONAL VALUES

A figure like Curt Lyle, with an anti-immigrant platform, would be particularly controversial at our institution. As senior associate deans at Florida International University (FIU), we work at the largest Hispanic-serving institution (HSI) in the country. Approximately four hundred to five hundred of our students are Dreamers, and the Republican-dominated state legislature continues to support tuition waivers for undocumented students, even as they vote overwhelmingly in alignment with the national Republican platform. FIU is not immune to hosting controversial figures, including government officials. Betsy DeVos, Mike Pence, and Donald Trump have all visited FIU, and all support anti-immigrant positions and policies. Protestors were present at each visit. For us, therefore, the clash of value propositions at Southwestern State University outlined in the case study are neither theoretical nor unfamiliar.

Personally and ideologically, we would view a speech by any controversial anti-immigrant activist as a direct form of aggression toward our campus community. A major challenge for administrators at Southwestern State is the degree to which *all speech*, irrespective of administrators' own closely held values, is protected by the First Amendment. Complex decisions around so-called hate speech, including how it is defined, can result in unanticipated consequences for those fighting for equality and inclusion. But the solution is not simply to behave, as administrators, as though our hands are tied. We argue for creative solutions to help maintain a campus life within which anti-immigrant, racist, anti-LGBTQ+, sexist sentiment is unable to roam unchecked.

OPPORTUNITIES FOR CHANGE

Our role at FIU is largely academic, focused on supporting faculty and students. We see ourselves as well-connected and sensitive to faculty issues while also able and willing to communicate top-down university initiatives. Nonetheless, the view from the middle often feels quite frustrating. Decisions made by senior administrators, and in this case trustees, are not meant to be negotiated by most university administrators. Instead, midlevel administrators are tasked with adhering to upper administration's communication directives while simultaneously being compelled to facilitate community buy-in. Sometimes the top-down and bottom-up views are wholly incommensurate, and this is perhaps where courageous leadership enters.

Conventionally, Southwestern State's leadership approach is marred by silence, inaction, and deficit thinking. The Division of Student Affairs' speaker policy is top-down and warrants a much deeper fleshing out of the ideological interests of all stakeholders. Campus security's involvement in racist incidents remains unaddressed. Faculty are not *expected* to create an inclusive educational environment. The provost's argument regarding the costliness of diversity recruitment is a logical fallacy and an excuse for inaction. President Tucker's "brief statement" is inadequate and lacks courage. How might senior college administration respond differently to student, faculty, and stakeholder concerns?

Even an administration legally obligated to allow hate speech on campus can concomitantly work arduously to limit its scope. While speech is protected at government institutions, universities do have the power to define the parameters of such speeches, including where and when they take place and the imprimatur of support offered. University administrators can surround hate speech with counternarratives—speeches, events, exhibitions—alternative perspectives marked by the university's stated mission and values and curated precisely to challenge hate speech and the policies informed by such speech. Exclusion is antithetical to democracy, and universities should continuously work toward clipping its tentacles.

COURAGEOUS LEADERSHIP

Actions matter. Diversity and inclusion in higher education must be intentional and actionable. A values-driven university administration that leads intentionally is itself a counternarrative to hate speech. We offer, as examples, intentional initiatives designed to enhance diversity and inclusion on campus. At FIU, the Office to Advance Women, Equity and Diversity (AWED) was established in 2016 by the provost. Currently, all colleges and departments have ostensibly developed diversity and inclusion plans. Departments are encouraged to identify measurable outcomes (e.g., increasing diversity in faculty hires). Made possible by a National Science Foundation ADVANCE grant, all search and screen committees undergo STRIDE training (Strategies and Tactics for Recruitment to Increase Diversity and Excellence), and each committee appoints a trained diversity advocate. Additionally, AWED offers bystander training to raise faculty consciousness of biased behavior and/or microaggressions and of strategies to mitigate racial and gender bias. Although not mandatory, these trainings and associated programs have unquestionably raised the level of cognizance of diversity and inclusion in hiring and the importance of fostering more hospitable departmental climates.

Still, there is a long way to go. As hiring supported by the ADVANCE grant works to diversify the faculty, FIU's research office supports hires by sharing with the colleges the research-related startup costs (e.g., labs) typical of new faculty. The research office, however, will only support cost sharing for new faculty with transferable external funding. Often, junior faculty, women in STEM, and/or faculty of color have not been "approved" hires under this condition. Herein is a classic case of internal university policies working at cross-purposes and the implications of offices like AWED (whose funding is almost entirely grant-based) being established without real capital backing. To address this challenge, our dean also established a Distinguished Postdoctoral program to identify and place early-career faculty with highly productive mentors, with an eye toward supporting them to win grants and then hiring them into tenure-track lines once they do. At the time we are writing, an Afro-LatinX biologist just joined FIU as our newest hire—a small victory, though hardly enough.

These relatively low-cost strategies serve to challenge the provost's assertion in this case that diversity in recruitment is necessarily costly and therefore not worth pursuing. Diversification of faculty does not just happen—pipelines need to be established and recruitment of faculty of color needs to be ongoing, not just once a year when hires are approved.

We highlight these cost-effective tactics even as we believe strongly that more resources are needed to ensure that institutions are not merely paying lip service to diversity, but instead creating a "diversity of thinkers" as advocated by Southwestern State's vice president for diversity and inclusion. We recognize that institutions must invest in creating student of color pipelines from K–12 through the PhD. We are aware that the racial demographic of senior leadership at the fictional Southwestern State likely mirrors that of countless other institutions—predominantly white and male. We believe that Southwestern State's suggestion of a mandatory ethnic studies course, although an initial step, is limited in scope compared with a radical revision of its curriculum. We note with regret that the President's Diversity Council in the case includes only the chair of the Faculty Senate. We urge senior leadership to adequately support and/or tap into the faculty engaged in ethnic, racial, gender, and sexuality studies to help them work toward solutions. If such expertise is absent, administrators should seek it out in targeted diversity hires. Only then—and with ongoing intentionality—will practices aimed at enhancing the "diversity of thinkers" engender more diversity of thinking to help drive lasting change.

Dr. Heather Russell is a professor of English and dean of the School of Environment, Arts, and Society at Florida International University. She earned her PhD in English from Rutgers University and specializes in African diaspora literature and theory, postcolonial theory, Anglophone Caribbean cultural studies, and African American literature.

Dr. Laura Dinehart is an associate professor of early childhood education and dean of the School of Education and Human Development at Florida International University. She earned her PhD in developmental psychology from the University of Miami and specializes in early academic and developmental predictors of academic achievement.

COMMENTARY

Toward an Academically Grounded University

Janine de Novais

The case asks us compelling questions about what the university provost's response should be: "Should she prioritize diversifying the racial and ethnic composition of the faculty? Building support for an ethnic studies requirement? Promoting more ideologically inclusive classrooms?"

I am tempted to answer, "All of the above." All those proposed solutions would be helpful. Better yet, those solutions should already be in place. That they are not speaks to the fact that Southwestern State is, like most universities, a predominantly white institution (PWI). PWIs are a function of white supremacist historical and contemporary practices that are intolerable in a multiracial democracy, especially one that has yet to atone for its origins in the genocide of Native Americans and the enslavement and racial apartheid imposed on Black Americans. Too often, debates about free speech stubbornly eschew those sociohistorical realities that contextualize them. This is, basically, cheating. It is cheating because students of color are a minority on predominantly white campuses; they are taught an overwhelmingly Eurocentric curriculum by an overwhelmingly white faculty. Moreover, many of those students have experienced the persistent "whiteness of schooling" since kindergarten. Therefore, those students' experiences of and advocacy around freedom of any kind, including of speech, should be considered distinct from the freedom of speech experienced by the white majority. The overwhelming whiteness of most colleges ensures that students of color never experience the belonging that should be integral to learning. It causes those students to experience a hostility that can vary in degree but is always present. It ensures that students of color do not have the kind of the freedom that their white peers have.

ACADEMIC GROUNDING AS THE FOUNDATION OF IDEOLOGICALLY INCLUSIVE CLASSROOMS

For this essay, I will focus more narrowly on the proposed solution that I find most useful because it is most proactive: *promoting ideologically inclusive classrooms*. In my courses on race, I use an approach that I call Brave Community.[7] I define this as a process through which students draw from *academic grounding*—the mix of content and culture that distinguishes a learning space from other social spaces—to build intellectual courage about the questions that they ask and the intellectual distance they are willing to travel. This is the "brave" part. At the same time, those students exhibit more interpersonal empathy—the "community" part.

At the start of any course, I explicitly connect the academic content (about race) that we will be learning with the academic culture—or ways of being—that best supports that learning. I explain that reliance on course content and factual evidence, as well as on respectful interpersonal engagement, are required for learning about race in meaningful ways. This academic grounding is our foundation. Once my students begin to trust and rely on academic grounding, they become more intellectually brave. They ask harder questions and can better sit through the discomfort that learning often brings. At the same time, they are more empathetic toward peers doing the same work.

The academic grounding, bravery, and empathy that my students and I engage through the Brave Community approach are required for us to navigate the rough waters of teaching and learning about race in a racist society. We each enter the room with distinctive racial identities and experiences, and the Brave Community approach offers us a way to establish solid, common ground. When I begin every course by setting the stage for academic grounding, I am establishing two crucial premises: (1) that our classroom is a space where learning will rely on academic content that meets standards of accuracy and ethics, and (2) that learners within that space will have codependent rights and duties. That is, one student's intellectual bravery depends on another student's empathy.

The focus on academic culture allows students to take risks and be brave in their learning, knowing that others will receive them with empathy. The focus on academic content allows my classroom to be inclusive of debate across the political spectrum while disallowing white supremacist views. These views are not censored. They need not be censored. They simply do not withstand academic scrutiny. Are white supremacist views factually true and ethically sound? They are not. If they are not, they do not belong in a Brave Community classroom (or any classroom worth its name). Not because they cannot or do not "exist." They do exist, and the First Amendment protects them. However, they *do not belong* in an academically grounded space, a learning community, a classroom.

DEFINING AND PROTECTING UNIVERSITIES AS ACADEMICALLY GROUNDED SPACES

People who teach about race in order to help students understand and confront racism have, by default, a need for approaches like Brave Community that explicitly set the stage for the work ahead. We understand that in a racist society, teaching and learning about issues of race, culture, and inequality require intentionality and pedagogical consideration. What the Brave Community approach allows me to do with my students—that Southwestern State does not do—is identify explicitly that we are in an academically grounded community. My students and I understand that we are in a space that, because it is geared toward learning, involves academic content (accurate, factual, evidence-based) and academic culture (collegial inquiry, discussion, evidence-based, respectful disagreement).

Instead of saying that a speaker's white supremacist views do not belong in the university because they fall outside of the bounds of academic content and culture, universities like Southwestern State say that the speaker is not welcome *because the students of color are upset*. This reaction is irresponsible. To use a simple example: most science departments would not host climate denialists, not because their views offend climate activists, but because those views are academically discredited. Those speakers are protected by the Constitution to express inaccurate, anti-scientific views, but those views do not belong in a science department. Our racist society thrives on pretending racism and white supremacy are not cut-and-dried issues, but they are. They are ideas that do not withstand the slightest rigorous intellectual scrutiny and confrontation with existing data. So, too, with Curt Lyle's rhetoric and policy ideas.

Universities must stop pretending that beautiful statements on diversity, equity, inclusion, and academic freedom are substitutes for pedagogy. It is time that administrators and faculty take responsibility for the fact that universities should be, foremost, academically grounded spaces. They are collections of classrooms before they are anything else. As such, they must have clear standards for what falls within the bounds of academically grounded inquiry. They must engage their students explicitly and authentically in constructing a shared understanding of what such inquiry is, what it affords us, and what it requires of us. If they wait to do it reactively, after a Curt Lyle comes to campus, they will be doing too little, too late.

Janine de Novais is a sociologist interested in race, culture, and critical pedagogy. She is assistant professor at the University of Delaware's College of Education and Human Development.

COMMENTARY

Courage, Commitment, and Conflict: Higher Education and the Battle over Speech

EDWARD L. QUEEN

DUTIES AND VALUES PLURALISM

This case presents an opportunity to reflect on values pluralism and variations in role responsibilities or duties from individual to individual and institution to institution. By *values pluralism*, I do not mean values relativism, but a simple recognition that there are numerous goods in the world and we cannot realize all of them. In higher education, a school may emphasize the fine arts, engineering, a particular population or geographic region, or even a faith tradition. All of these are legitimate value choices for an institution, and none would, or at least should, gainsay that. Simultaneously, an institution may bear certain duties resulting from its general or specific nature. Among the primary duties of an institution of higher education is just that—education. A school that fails to effect its educational mission has failed in its duty. It has behaved unethically.

In terms of duties, Southwestern State—as a state school—has legal constraints that private institutions do not. It operates under the same First Amendment free speech guarantees as any other government entity. As early as 1943, Justice Robert Jackson wrote: "That they [i.e., schools] are educating the young for citizenship is reason for scrupulous protection of Constitutional freedoms of the individual, if we are not to strangle the free mind at its source and teach youth to discount important principles of our government as mere platitudes."[8] If elementary schools bear this duty, how much more ought colleges and universities—who educate more mature and independent students, many of whom we have granted the right to vote?

BAD SPEECH AND WHO DECIDES

We must confront the extent to which we grant individuals and groups with power, regardless whence that power emanates, the ability to determine what speech adults can hear. When placed in the hands of the state, this power always has been used to constrain voices of challenge and dissent—those demanding the vote, legal equality, and even knowledge about contraceptive options.

Aiming to limit only bad and dangerous speech, hurtful or harmful speech, is no answer. Those in power always use that argument. College administrators have used it to prevent student challenges to school policies, to limit social and political protest, and to punish faculty deemed too "controversial." Legislators have used it punish state schools for hiring faculty with views deemed too liberal, "communist," or anti-racist.

No one ever wishes to limit good speech or, more precisely, what one deems good speech. The issue is not whether there is good and bad speech. There is. Some speech not only is wrong, but is evil, wretched, beastly. The fundamental ethical issue is to whom do we grant the power to determine what speech is acceptable? Do we grant it to those in power, the police, the mob, to those who may be inconvenienced or made uncomfortable by the speech?

Allowing college administrators to sacrifice free speech for other values poses numerous problems. Any statement of value and substance is bound to make someone uncomfortable, if not threaten fundamental beliefs. Students enter higher education with such varying experiences, backgrounds, perspectives, and political and social views that it would be impossible to accommodate all of them. As a consideration in decision-making, personal offense is markedly subjective and, arguably, infinite. We must think critically and deeply about the consequences of suppressing some voices based on such subjective criteria and to whom we delegate the duty of adjudicating between competing subjectivities. Without the courage to make those decisions explicitly and clearly, college administrators today are no better than they were in Thorstein

Veblen's time when he decried them as "itinerant dispensar[ies] of salutary verbiage."[9]

This returns us to the question of duties. Do institutions of higher education owe students an environment in which they feel comfortable? Certainly, they have a duty to strive to ensure students are physically safe, and even public institutions, such as Southwestern State, have no duty to allow speech that directly threatens individuals. But ensuring comfort is a different issue. The question of what environment a college has a duty to create is an important one. It forces us to examine the extent to which education ought to challenge the intellectual, social, and cultural views held by students and the degree to which students ought to be allowed, encouraged, and even directed to be their own agents.

In this instance, the speaker was invited by a student organization, not the school itself. The College Republicans arguably were woefully juvenile in their choice of a speaker. It is unsurprising that politically engaged individuals of college age and of every political stripe make statements or undertake actions that are sophomoric, if not downright offensive. I do not think students need or ought to be protected from most of their colleagues' idiocies, nor ought academic institutions be held responsible for them.

USING THE CONFLICT AS A MOMENT FOR EDUCATION

None of this implies that institutions of higher education have no obligations to do a better job of overcoming the obvious, residual, and persistent consequences of numerous social and political evils, including racism and sexism. The solution lies not in pretending that such evils do not exist by enforcing superficial homogeneity on thought and speech. Rather, fulfilling this duty demands that college and university administrators demonstrate courage, something they often fail to do—as Veblen recognized a century ago. Administrators can and should defend the value of free speech aggressively *and* condemn bad speech forcibly.

Some have demonstrated how this can be done. The "Chicago principles" issued by the University of Chicago epitomize a thoughtful and historically grounded statement on the centrality of freedom of expression in higher education.[10] Similarly Dr. Lauren Robel, executive vice president and provost at Indiana University-Bloomington, exemplified the ability to affirm the university's commitment to and obligations under the First Amendment while forthrightly condemning a professor's social media posts as "vile and stupid."[11]

In finding courageous ways forward, it is important to acknowledge that all institutions operate with constraints, with incompatibilities—indeed, often impossibilities. Herein lies the teaching moment at Southwestern State. Bring the students into a university-wide committee, and allow them to participate in making the challenging decisions. Teach them about the history of the struggle of free speech in universities in the United States generally and at Southwestern State in particular. As part of the conversation, confront the hard questions of how to determine what is unacceptable speech and who gets to decide, as well as the possible consequences of any choice. Teach students about the legal limits that constrain the university's options, and have university counsel detail the costs of any litigation and the likelihood of losing in court. Allow students to be partners in deciding what new programs should be created and determining what should be cut or allowed to stagnate as monies are reallocated. These events present a wonderful opportunity for a valuable process of learning and engagement. It should be embraced, not ignored.

Southwestern State is an institution of higher education, so let it educate.

Edward L. Queen directs the D. Abbott Turner Program in Ethics and Servant Leadership at the Emory University Center for Ethics. He received his BA from Birmingham-Southern College, his MA and PhD from the Divinity School of the University of Chicago, and his JD from Indiana University School of Law-Indianapolis.

COMMENTARY

Hate Speech, Campus Climate, and the Relevance of History in Establishing First Amendment Limits in Schools

KRISTEN BURAS

The Faculty Senate chair at Southwestern State University said the "campus is fully committed to free speech in all its forms." Yet free speech is not anywhere acceptable in *all* its forms. First Amendment limits exist—defamation is one example. A calibrated approach to this case would explore how competing interests can be mediated when free speech is involved. We might ask: Should the value of free speech outweigh the value of racial equity? I argue that critical race theory (CRT) is instructive in answering this question.

CRT prioritizes analyses of race and racism and challenges ahistoricism.[12] Understanding racial formation—how constructions of race change over time due to struggles between racially dominant and subordinate groups—is central. Through resistance to white supremacy and social movements, racially oppressed groups have acquired more expansive rights, but not without retrenchment by whites.[13] The history of white supremacy must be considered as a force that gives meaning to language and shapes the way language is used by disparate groups as well as its effects.

First, I contextualize the conflict and account for why the College Republicans view themselves as a silenced minority. Second, I examine the role of history in mediating competing interests in educational contexts where free speech is involved. I agree with legal scholar Charles Lawrence that "the context of the power relationships within which speech takes place, and the connection to violence must be considered as we decide how best to foster the . . . fullest dialogue within our communities."[14]

POLITICS OF RETRENCHMENT

Carter G. Woodson established African American history as a discipline. He founded Negro History Week—now Black History Month—to infuse Black history into schools. Decades later, inspired by Civil Rights and Black Power movements, African American students demanded Black Studies programs on college campuses. A history of white supremacy necessitated similar demands by Latinx and Indigenous students.

The limited-to-modest gains that resulted from these efforts did not go unnoticed by whites. A neoconservative countermovement took shape in which all except the most benign forms of multiculturalism in schools were criticized as undermining national identity—that is, white domination.[15] A well-funded network of conservative think tanks and initiatives emerged to restore the Western tradition supposedly undermined by the identity politics and movements of the 1960s; this included conservative student organizations on college campuses.[16]

Increasingly, some whites have viewed themselves as the new oppressed, as though minoritized groups now exercise ruling power. Yet college access and retention for students of color has not reflected a gross shift in power. Tara Yosso's research reveals that out of one hundred Chicana/o elementary students, fifty-six will drop out; of the forty-four that graduate high school, only seven will obtain a college degree.[17] The Eurocentric curriculum has also remained despite establishment of Black, Chicano, and Native American Studies departments.

SOUTHWESTERN STATE

Enter Curt Lyle at Southwestern State. The College Republicans (part of a white majority) *feel* their views are marginalized through a "one-sided" education. When historically *your* side has been the prevailing one, the presence of another side may be experienced as an assault. Lyle's invitation, under the auspices of free speech, becomes an occasion to reassert power.

At the center of the controversy are two competing interests: free speech and racial equity. Which should be prioritized? How would such a determination be made? History—the "context of the power relationships" emphasized by Lawrence—is instructive. Ignoring the long view is what enables the College Republicans to construe themselves as victims of a biased campus climate, even as they represent the racial majority and reap the benefits.

Whom did Southwestern State police ask for identification at a campus event, while others were not carded? Whom did racial slurs target and who paid the price of removing them from the multicultural sorority's door? Who let the incident pass without apprehending the offender? Which groups have requested Ethnic Studies on campus, to no avail? White students may complain that they feel marginalized, but historically who was/is? Daily microaggressions, connected to a history of white supremacist violence, are a problem for students of color. Lyle is another instance.

Words do not exist in a vacuum. They acquire meaning from the context in which they are uttered, and this includes past as well as present context. Free speech is not free of history. Historical harm to identifiable groups continues each time an institution of higher education enables hate rather than protecting students from it. In a political climate where undocumented youth remain in detention centers, Lyle's anti-immigrant pronouncements targeting undocumented college students are not spoken on neutral ground.

Moreover, schools are not street corners. The right to free speech is context dependent. Colleges are places where students merit protection while they pursue (and pay for) their education. Anything that creates a hostile climate for historically oppressed groups and demonstrably undermines access to education should be prohibited. Put another way, when speech threatens to compound historic and contemporaneous harm, there are justifiable limits on campus. As Lawrence emphasizes, "If the university fails to protect them [students of color] in their right to pursue their education free from [racial and gender] degradation and humiliation, then surely there are constitutional considerations."[18]

There is nothing inherently superior about First Amendment interests when weighed against other interests, including civil rights concerns. Whites have historically enjoyed the right to speak disparagingly about people of color with impunity. Lawrence rightly asks "why [those] who oppose all regulation of racist speech do not feel that the burden is theirs to justify a reading of the first amendment that requires sacrificing rights guaranteed under the equal protection clause."[19]

In *Words That Wound*, Matsuda presents a test for limiting racist speech, with prohibitions on speech in which the message is one racial inferiority, is directed against a historically oppressed group, and is persecutory, hateful, and degrading.[20] Resolving such dilemmas may not always be easy, but university officials would do well to consult history as a guide, rather than relying on the notion that "free" speech should be unconditionally endorsed over other compelling interests.

Kristen Buras is an associate professor in educational policy studies at Georgia State University. She is the author of Rightist Multiculturalism: Core Lessons on Neoconservative School Reform, *coauthor of* Pedagogy, Policy, and the Privatized City: Stories of Dispossession and Defiance from New Orleans, *and co-editor of* The Subaltern Speak: Curriculum, Power, and Educational Struggles, *among other books.*

COMMENTARY

Inclusive of What? Fostering Ideologically Inclusive Classrooms Based on Neutral Academic Standards, Not Politics

LARA SCHWARTZ

Authors whose works no college professor would place on a syllabus—except as case studies in demagoguery or political messaging—are regularly invited to speak to campus groups. And as a public institution, Southwestern State University should not adopt a policy changing that (which would likely not survive a legal challenge anyway). But controversies about campus speakers—which garner national attention disproportionate to such speakers' roles in campus communities—often make it more challenging to talk about the very different, and far more critical, question of how to make classrooms spaces where robust inquiry thrives and all are respected. That is the most interesting question to me. Because the First Amendment, which provides an easy answer to the campus speaker policy issue, is an essential bulwark against government tyranny, but it is nothing more.

It isn't a teaching tool.

It isn't a blueprint for how to live.

It does not tell us how to connect with one another, to grow as people, to make ourselves heard.

And it cannot command us to listen.

Yet all these things are essential to an academic community. And the students, faculty, and administration of Southwestern State have all, in their way, demanded them.

What does it mean to have an "ideologically inclusive" classroom? Surely, it does not mean a space where all ideas are on equal footing. That isn't a college classroom at all; it's Twitter or *The View*. Both of these fora for expression—the free website and the popular show that models civic engagement by having its hosts play roles as members of ideological tribes—serve a worthwhile purpose in our democracy, and I do not wish to denigrate them. But a college classroom is, by definition, a place where the range of accepted contributions is much more narrowly defined. It is assumed that in a classroom, only relevant comments that meet the discipline's standards for evidence and rigor will be welcome. It is understood that students and professors may not plagiarize nor fabricate, and that the types of ad hominem attacks and trolling that are acceptable on social media or talk shows—and even by invited campus speakers—have no place in the classroom.

As educators, we *want* students to be careful what they say in class—not because they are self-censoring thoughts that defy institutional orthodoxy, but because that is learning. Productive, academically rigorous, respectful discourse is a college-level skill, just like writing a persuasive paper or managing one's workload. Educators need the tools to help our students see these learning objectives as opportunities to become their best selves—not limitations on liberty. And too much of the discourse about intellectual diversity, self-censorship, and campus politics makes that hard to do.

Southwestern State should take the following steps to ensure that students understand that their good-faith contributions, regardless of personal political ideology, will be treated fairly within classroom spaces.

CORRECT THE RECORD ABOUT PROFESSORS' ROLES AND POLITICS

The increasing partisan divide about higher education means that many students arrive at college believing that their professors want to indoctrinate them. In fact, studies have shown that professors do not penalize students for their political views. Indeed, engaging with their professors, regardless of ideology, tends to make students moderate their views. Administrators are best equipped to reassure students and the public that neutral academic standards—not partisan affiliation—guide decision-making in academic spaces.

Faculty can also build trust by being explicit about our expectations. For example, they can include syllabus language that explains that students will not be graded on their politics or other factors unrelated to merit and course work, and they can have a frank discussion of community standards at the beginning of the term.

THOUGHTFULLY ADDRESS THE TRANSITION FROM K–12 SPEECH RULES TO COLLEGE

Students spend the first thirteen years of their education in extremely speech-limited environments. Though students have recently won cases challenging punishment for off-campus speech (such as social media activity), K–12 schools wield a great deal of power to limit expression during the school day. Schools have the authority to limit speech and even dress they deem "disruptive" and to wield it punitively. Students are told that their bra straps and short-shorts—to say nothing of their Black Lives Matter T-shirts or Trump campaign hats—can disrupt the educational process. We should not be surprised when students educated in these restrictive environments either self-censor or call for limitations on speech—whether by professors or invited speakers. Schools should build conversations about the First Amendment, robust political engagement, and college speech communities into orientation.

Furthermore, those in higher education who care about student speech rights should consider working to protect student speech and expression at the K–12 level. Because conduct and dress codes are disproportionately used to penalize students of color, this will not only serve the interest of promoting open dialogue; it will be a step toward educational equity.

REJECT ALL CALLS FOR PARTISAN LITMUS TESTS FOR FACULTY

It is true that most professors are liberal, and it's understandable that some conclude that this affects students' access to quality education. But that conclusion—which isn't borne out by any study of higher education—misses the mark. First, although some partisan positions—notably opposition to abortion—have remained stable over time, others change. Until the 2016 Republican primary, relatively free trade was considered a conservative and Republican position, and protectionism more left wing. In the late 1960s, partisan alignments flipped entirely. Given that an academic career lasts decades, attempting to hire people based on their partisan affiliation might not even be an effective way of ensuring various viewpoints are represented.

But more fundamentally, a political litmus test would undermine faith in higher education by conceding the argument that professors teach based on their partisan ideology and that college is about indoctrination.

INVEST IN INCLUSIVE PEDAGOGY AND DIALOGUE ACROSS DIFFERENCE

Notably, in the Southwestern State case, students from across the political spectrum expressed concerns about their access to conversations where they could be heard and understood. The university should invest in resources to help faculty facilitate robust and inclusive classroom conversations. This includes helping faculty understand that they can take on controversial topics and require respectful discourse without running afoul of students' First Amendment rights.

Beyond the classroom, students should have opportunities to learn and practice the art of listening to understand and communicating to be understood. So much of campus life is performative, but many students want the chance to have real conversations beyond "owning" the other side.

BE FORTHRIGHT ABOUT THE INSTITUTION'S VALUES, EVEN WHEN THAT IS NOT POPULAR

Universities have an obligation to be fair. That is not the same as being neutral. There will come times when a university's mission of seeking and disseminating truth will put it at odds with some partisan position. And times, such as when controversial speakers come to campus, when a university's commitment to free speech disproportionately burdens its students with marginalized identities. Universities can, and should, make clear that honoring the First Amendment does not mean endorsing speakers who denigrate members of the campus community. Anti-racist or pro-inclusion statements will ring hollow, however, in a campus where people of color are grossly underrepresented.

Lara Schwartz teaches at American University School of Public Affairs, where she founded and directs the Project on Civil Discourse. She was a 2019–2020 fellow at the University of California National Center for Free Speech and Civic Engagement and has served as an inclusive pedagogy faculty fellow at American University's Center for Teaching, Research and Learning. She is coauthor of How to College: What to Know Before You Go (and When You're There), *a practical guide to the college transition.*

CHAPTER 3

Faculty Activism on Social Media

Implications for Professional Advancement

ASHLEY FLOYD KUNTZ, AARON M. KUNTZ, AND JACOB FAY

In this case, a dean considers whether to factor social media activism into the tenure and promotion case of a Black woman scientist who has leveraged Twitter to call out insufficient diversity in a prominent lab.

Dean Henry Harrison had been putting off this task for days, but with tenure and promotion letters due to the provost tomorrow, he had to make a decision. How should he handle the conflicting recommendations from the departmental and collegewide committees for Dr. Jaleesa Reese, an assistant professor of biology?[1] The Biology Tenure and Promotion (T&P) Committee had recommended her for promotion and tenure, but the college committee recommended only promotion, not tenure. Reading between the lines, Dean Harrison realized the issue was Dr. Reese's social media presence, especially recent comments she had posted against prominent scientists at other institutions. This was the first time in his five years as dean that a faculty member's social media had been a contributing factor in tenure and promotion, and he was torn. Dr. Reese's social media presence was inextricably linked to the conflicting viewpoints expressed in the letters on his desk. Were a faculty member's comments on social media fair game for decisions of tenure and promotion? How distinct were the lines of personal political activity and professional activism?

Dean Harrison thought back to Dr. Reese's track record at the institution. They had heavily recruited her seven years ago. Having been trained at Cornell and completed a postdoc at Vanderbilt, she had impressive academic qualifications. Their campus, a Midwestern flagship with a strong national reputation for research, had an ambitious plan to expand the faculty, especially in STEM fields, and Dr. Reese's research aligned well with National Science Foundation funding priorities. In her first two years at the institution, she had focused on building her lab and applying for grant funding and she had secured modest grants from NSF and begun publishing at a steady pace.

At the same time, Dr. Reese cultivated an active social media presence, especially on Twitter. Dean Harrison had sent a memo to all College of Arts and Sciences (A&S) faculty encouraging them to share publications on social media to generate buzz for their research. Dr. Reese began using her Twitter account to do so, and the A&S communications specialists retweeted these posts to promote innovative research happening at the university. She also used her Twitter account for personal reasons, whether to post cute photos of her dog or share professional development tips from her sorority.

In her fourth year, a teaching encounter prompted Dr. Reese to begin using her Twitter account for the purposes of advocacy and activism. The idea came to her after she mentioned pioneering scientist Percy Julian in class, and not a single student—including the three Black students—had heard of him. They were completely unaware of his research synthesizing plant sources to mass-produce steroids.[2] For Dr. Reese, who had minored in African American studies as an undergrad, this was yet another example of the failure of predominantly white institutions to educate students about the important contributions of Black scientists. She began a weekly Twitter series called #blackscience in which she posted about a prominent Black scientist each Monday morning.[3] The series caught the attention of other scholars, and multiple professional organizations began retweeting her posts. As her following grew, she also developed a teaching blog in which she shared ideas for other faculty to practice what she termed "actively inclusive teaching" in their courses. Her Twitter following grew to more than five thousand, and the *Chronicle of Higher Education* asked her to contribute an op-ed.

As her social media following increased, so did her citation count. Having often felt invisible as a Black woman in science, Dr. Reese was pleased that people were noticing her work, and she was thrilled when graduate students and other young scientists from underrepresented groups responded to her posts. She realized that other scientists felt the way she did—overlooked, undervalued, and discriminated against. As the Black Lives Matter movement grew, Dr. Reese started a new Twitter campaign—#BLMinSTEM—which she used to call out discrimination and prejudice within the field. She noticed that when her posts were more provocative or politically charged, more people engaged with them, and the #BLMinSTEM campaign quickly raised her follower count to ten thousand.

Dean Harrison was only nominally aware of Dr. Reese's activism on Twitter. He didn't make it a practice to monitor faculty social media accounts, but the departmental and university-wide committee letters both hinted at disapproval, and one external reviewer had commented directly on her Twitter usage. So, despite his discomfort in doing so, he scanned her Twitter feed:

> Google Black science and you get comic books. Nothing about Carver, Jemison, Johnson, or Daly until page 4. Sign me up for the #algrithm justiceleague. #BLMinSTEM #codingbias[4]
>
> TFW you try to comment at a conference and the panelists ignore you. #BLMinSTEM
>
> Raise your hand if you're the only Black scientist at your entire institution. #BLMinSTEM
>
> Hey, American Society of Biology, how come there isn't a single Black person on your board? We see you. Do you see us? #BLMinSTEM
>
> Let's talk tokenism. How many committees are you "invited" to serve on? I'm at 5 and counting. #BLMinSTEM

He suspected it was her latest campaign—#whitelabsmatter—that had raised some concerns among her peers. This new initiative was her most direct attempt to dismantle the pernicious racism in her field. Believing her colleagues were too savvy to express racist sentiments directly, Dr. Reese had still observed multiple talented students of color turned away from graduate funding and postdoc opportunities. There was always some other reason given, but she felt certain the issue was race. So she began researching the lab composition of senior scientists in the field and tweeting them to her large following:

> How can we expand the #blackscience pipeline when we can't even get a seat at the bench? #whitelabsmatter
>
> Something's missing in the chemistry department at WU—a single postdoc from an underrepresented background. #whitelabsmatter

What prompted the most controversy was a thread she developed focusing on Dr. Elden Kleine, a prominent biologist and president of the American Society for Biology:

> How can Elden Kleine lead our profession when he won't support scientists of color? #whitelabsmatter
>
> 15 years—that's how long it's been since a student of color was admitted to the Kleine lab. What's the word for that? #whitelabsmatter

To that post, one user replied:

> Racism. No other word for it. #whitelabsmatter #kkkleine

Dr. Reese had retweeted the user's comment, and the new hashtag #kkkleine soon took hold. Other faculty, many of whom were outside of the sciences, began retweeting the posts about Dr. Kleine, tagging him and his university and calling him a racist. Graduate students at his institution joined in targeted Twitter attacks and signed an online petition calling for his dismissal. Dr. Kleine ultimately closed his Twitter account. In an op-ed for *Science* magazine, he defended his record by pointing to the fund he established at the American Society for Biology to support conference travel for postdocs from underrepresented backgrounds. He also noted his strong record of supporting female scientists. But, he said, few students of color applied to work with him, and he made all decisions based on student readiness to excel in his very technically sophisticated lab. His op-ed only fanned the flame on Twitter, with Reese and many others saying his comments completely ignored serious questions of access and equity.

Dean Harrison took a deep breath as he closed his browser window and turned his attention to the committee letters at hand. The letter from the department's T&P committee focused largely on Dr. Reese's scholarly outputs, history of external funding, and mentorship of graduate students. More procedural in nature, the department's letter listed accomplishments with only vague statements on areas for improvements in the field, including one remark about "further developing political savvy within the field." Ultimately, the letter articulated unanimous support for her tenure and promotion. The collegewide committee, however, was differently critical. While still listing Dr. Reese's accomplishments in the areas of research and teaching, this letter contained a subsection devoted to "academic citizenship and colleagueship" that questioned her impact on the larger field. As evidence for their concerns, the collegewide committee pointed to a few lines in a letter from one external reviewer who took issue with Dr. Reese's social media engagement:

> Dr. Reese has proven to be savvy in her ability to use social media to amplify her accomplishments in research. Unfortunately, she has turned away from promoting her own accomplishments and towards attacking others for political reasons unrelated to the field of biology. As a result, I find Dr. Reese to be uncollegial at best, and, more likely, detrimental to the field. Because your university cites *colleagueship* as a contributing factor towards tenure and promotion, I cannot, at this time, recommend her for the rank of associate professor with tenure.

Referencing these statements, the collegewide letter recommended that Dr. Reese be promoted but without receiving tenure. They articulated their rationale that promotion was achieved through scholarly productivity, but tenure should be reserved for those who demonstrate a positive and productive impact on the candidate's field of study. The departmental letter made no mention of such concerns.

Dean Harrison knew the notion of "collegiality" was ambiguous at best and had never been used to deny tenure and promotion at the institution; however, it was listed in the handbook as something for the committees to consider as an element of teaching, research, or service. Because of its ambiguity, he wasn't sure the collegiality criterion carried much weight with the provost, Dr. Barbara Franks. As a former marketing professor, Dr. Franks would probably be more concerned with the image problem associated with having a junior scholar publicly shaming senior scientists at other institutions, which might hurt peer reviews in national rankings. And, of course, Dr. Reese's Twitter campaigns could have a negative impact on the institution's efforts to expand the number of tenure-track faculty, which was one of Dr. Franks's major priorities and also tied to the issue of national rankings.

Concerned about making a decision based on loosely defined criteria, Dean Harrison had contacted the university's legal counsel to ask for a specific definition of collegiality in relation to tenure and promotion. Their letter to him included a series of key points drawn from publications by the American Association of University Professors (AAUP) and recent cases at other institutions:

- The AAUP takes an expansive view on academic freedom, arguing that it protects faculty to research and teach what and where they please so long as they do not "introduce into their teaching controversial matter which has no relation to their subject." And—while they should exercise restraint given their "special position within the community"—they are free to say what they please as private citizens without fear of institutional sanction.[5]

- Some institutions have interpreted the 2006 Supreme Court ruling in *Garcetti v. Ceballos* to permit limitations on public college and university faculty members' use of social media. Notably, the Kansas Board of Regents now holds faculty accountable for social media use that interrupts harmony within close working relationships, impairs the faculty member's performance, or "otherwise adversely affects the employer's ability to efficiently provide services."[6]
- The case of Professor Steven Salaita's dismissal from the University of Illinois at Urbana-Champaign (UIUC) in response to his tweets about hostilities in Gaza raised questions regarding the intersection of free speech, academic freedom, and collegiality. The university's decision to dismiss Salaita resulted in years of litigation and, ultimately, a $600,000 settlement.
- The AAUP argues against academic policies that situate collegiality as a "fourth criterion" (in addition to the traditional triumvirate of teaching, research, and service) in relation to tenure and promotion decisions.[7]
- The AAUP advises that if collegiality is a stated consideration, it be folded into the established areas of teaching, research, and service.[8]

Dean Harrison recognized that his institutional policies followed the AAUP suggestions for a folded in approach whereby collegiality is established as a contributing factor to activities in teaching, research, and service, but not a stand-alone category. Yet it was the very ambiguity inherent in this folded in approach that seemed, at this time, so incredibly frustrating. Unlike the lists and categories of activities cited by the departmental letter, notions of collegiality could not be directly measured. Moreover, there was no stated guidance on how speech, especially within the new frontier of social media, contributed to the notion of collegiality.

How, then, to evaluate collegiality? The collegewide committee—and the external reviewer they referenced—obviously felt that faculty speech on social media was indicative of collegiality. Further, they judged that Dr. Reese's speech on social media was a serious affront to collegiality, enough to warrant a denial of tenure (but not promotion). Dean Harrison wasn't sure. Dr. Reese did not equate Dr. Kleine with the KKK, but she did retweet a post that did so, and that post sparked very real consequences for a leader in the field. Was her social media activity uncollegial or harmful, or was it an example of engaged academic citizenship or public activism?

Social media seemed to blur the boundaries between faculty members' personal, professional, and civic lives. Should it be fair game for questions of tenure and promotion? Dean Harrison didn't make it a habit to monitor faculty members' social media use. If he used it to inform this decision, how could he fairly incorporate it in future cases? What would such a process look like, and how might including speech made on social media impact academic freedom, not just for Dr. Reese but for other faculty at the institution? How would doing so impact institutional efforts to expand the faculty?

Finally, how did issues of equity and inclusion bear upon this case? To what extent did Dr. Reese's position as a member of an underrepresented racial group in the academy (particularly in the sciences) shape the way she—and the comments she shared on social media—was perceived by colleagues in her department, the college, and her field more broadly? Given these complexities, how should he respond?

COMMENTARY

Social Media Activism Is Valuable Service

CHANDA PRESCOD-WEINSTEIN

THE ROLE OF CIVIL RIGHTS LAW

Interestingly, the dean articulates the answers to his own questions. For example, in asking whether "collegiality" should be a factor in this tenure case, he notes it has never been before, even though it is included formally in his institution's tenure and promotion guidelines. The decision of the college committee to introduce collegiality—for the first time—means that Dr. Reese is being evaluated according to a different metric than colleagues previously up for tenure. As she is likely a barrier breaker in her field—since Black women faculty in STEM remain rare—differential treatment of her tenure case could be interpreted as motivated by race in violation of the Fourteenth Amendment's Equal Protection Clause and the equal employment provisions of Title VII of the Civil Rights Act of 1964.

Punishing Dr. Reese for her social media use is inextricably tied to her identity because her identity is a factor in why she shares ideas on social media. Dr. Reese's activity on social media has value because it has clearly reached populations that traditionally feel marginalized in academic spaces. On social media, Black women and other underrepresented-group scholars have the ability to discuss the state of their fields in ways that were previously closed off to them within these fields' institutions and associations.[9] This approach evades "old boys' networks" and provides a forum for free exchange of ideas between Black and other marginalized scholars, although a recent report indicates Black academics are disproportionately targeted for doing so.[10] Importantly, predominantly white and male academic spaces are rarely or never subjected to the same level of scrutiny in tenure and promotion decision processes because they function as the norm that is protected by shared beliefs, including sometimes discriminatory or biased practices. For example, in the cases of Lawrence Krauss and Geoff Marcy, white male astronomers accused of sexual harassment and assault, their abuse of power was long protected or ignored by their institutions and professional societies.[11] Accusations of harassment and assault had been made at former institutions prior to their most recent appointments. Yet the harassment complaints were not a barrier to tenure or promotion—a stark contrast to the proposal of the college committee to deny Dr. Reese tenure.

ETHICS VERSUS POPULARITY

The ethical and moral choice for the dean is clear—he should not punish Dr. Reese. The only real challenge he faces is the uncomfortable experience of overruling his colleagues who are unable or unwilling to acknowledge that her calls for justice are a matter of human rights (and associated laws) that transcend other institutional considerations. The collegewide committee is effectively enforcing a definition of "collegiality" to avoid upsetting established norms that are harmful, and not collegial, to Black women. Indeed, in the scenario as presented, the dean acknowledges that Dr. Reese is engaging in a "direct attempt to dismantle the pernicious racism in her field." He knows that she faces a playing field made uneven by racism. Punishing her for addressing morally reprehensible, illegal working conditions should be a non-starter.

This case also raises a basic question about whether her comments about a prominent scientist have anything to do with the quality of her research, teaching, and service to the community. While the departmental tenure and promotion committee chose largely to ignore these comments, arguably they should reward Dr. Reese for engaging in important service to her professional community. By drawing attention to structural racism and how well-known and powerful scientists contribute to it, Dr. Reese created an opportunity for the community to confront barriers to excellence and fairness. What academics who are hostile to change sometimes dismiss as "activism" must be recognized as work and service.

ANTI-RACISM IS ESSENTIAL LEADERSHIP

Engaging in critique of one's own academic field takes tremendous leadership, competence, emotional effort, and time, which scholars who choose silence may use to advance their technical work. Black women scholars who make these critiques are not seeking fame or promoting themselves, but rather working to make their chosen fields of study ones that they can live and work within, ones that are more equitable and fair for their colleagues, and ones that current and future Black students can pursue with fewer racist barriers than current junior faculty. In other words, Black women scholars who speak out about racism, sexism, and the unique ways they combine—*misogynoir*—are making significant and usually unheralded contributions to their scholarly communities by leveling the playing field not just for themselves but other Black scholars.[12]

The collegewide committee letter states that, "tenure should be reserved for those who demonstrate a positive and productive impact on the candidate's field of study." There is a contradiction inherent to criticizing Dr. Reese on these grounds. Her impact on the field is not only significant, but also positive. The focus on how Dr. Kleine has experienced the subsequent backlash to his lab management is a distraction—it centers the experience of a white male scholar while ignoring the reason that so many Black scholars, including students, responded strongly to his failure to train students of color. What meaning does an institutional commitment to "equity and inclusion" have if a Black scholar is punished for pointing out the institutional failures of her field to provide equitable opportunities to Black student scholars?

It is not enough to "tolerate" this work by junior Black women scholars. Consistent with the core higher education mission of learning, research, and study, institutions should explicitly credit and support service performed by junior scholars to improve their home institutions and larger academic communities by calling out racism and bigotry. Therefore, the framing of a "distinction" between personal political activity and professional activism is misleading. While such a distinction is important in defense of academic freedom (e.g., public support for or opposition to a political candidate should never be used in a tenure or promotion decision), critique of one's own institution, academic societies, or field is service work. It is intended to improve the quality of the academic field and the scholar's home institution, to strengthen its scholarly enterprises by making it more welcoming and equitable, and to recognize that there is no artificial barrier for Black women scholars between misogynoir, racism, sexism, or other bigotry faced within academe and without.

Although all of these considerations should outweigh concerns about reputational damage, it is worth noting that the dean is ignoring the risk of reputational damage among Black scholars and students—as well as members of other marginalized communities—if Dr. Reese is denied tenure. The case of Steven Salaita was not only costly for UIUC, but it also led to censure from AAUP and an academic boycott and, as is evidenced by his consideration of the case, continues to be associated with UIUC's reputation years after the episode concluded. Dr. Reese is unlikely to be quiet about her tenure denial and will be able to present extensive evidence of having satisfied the scholarly and pedagogical requirements for both promotion *and* tenure. Failing to tenure Dr. Reese puts the institution at risk of fiscal, reputational, and moral damage.

Chanda Prescod-Weinstein, PhD, is an assistant professor of physics and core faculty in women's and gender studies at the University of New Hampshire. Her scientific research focuses on dark matter and early universe cosmology, and she has a secondary expertise in Black feminist science, technology, and society studies.

COMMENTARY

The Boundaries of Calling Out

Sigal Ben-Porath and Dustin Webster

What is the role of activism and of public extramural speech in the assessment of scholarly merit? Can raising one's voice to advance a public agenda, whether related to one's domain of study as in this case or separate from it, be seen as relevant for the professional review of a scholar's work? Dr. Reese is engaging in a "callout"—a form of activism—in a quest to advance justice. Agreeing that her goal—better representation of people of color in positions of power within the discipline—is laudable, at issue are her means and whether they merit punitive professional review. Is calling specific people out permissible? Is it appropriate for advancing Dr. Reese's goal? Should callout activism be an aspect of her professional review? We argue that calling out is sometimes an acceptable professional tool and that even when it crosses the lines of professionalism, it generally remains protected from penalty, though can still be a relevant matter for professional feedback.

Callouts are frequently used on social media to accuse others of wrongdoing, utilizing the medium's availability to all users independent of power, permission, or proximity. As in this case, callouts may be based on the author's appraisal of another person's actions and require no evidence or debate. While callouts can serve as a remedy for the silencing or voicelessness of marginalized individuals and communities, they can also cause significant harm to their targets, and swiftly mobilize others to amplify accusations.

IS THE CALLOUT PRODUCTIVE AND JUSTIFIED?

Dr. Reese's callout tweets are driven by concerns that people of color are underrepresented in the sciences and that Dr. Kleine "won't support scientists of color" and is biased in his lab hiring. It is important to differentiate these concerns, as the letters in Dr. Reese's file seem to do. These facts also do not easily lend themselves to the suggestion that Dr. Kleine is consciously and overtly racist, which would make targeting and exposing him reasonable. Is it possible that he could be blameless? We might imagine that he cares deeply about social inequities and considers the lack of diversity in his field to be a serious problem. He recognizes his own privilege. He is continually frustrated by the fact that he receives so few non-white applicants to his lab, which he sees as a consequence of broader problems that he is trying to address. If this were the case, then personally calling him out as biased would be unjust. Such a callout would not advance racial equity in biology, and the callout would be unjustified and unproductive. Still, the facts of the case, including Dr. Kleine's leadership position in a professional organization, make it hard to assume that he is powerless to do more.

What seems more likely is that, while not explicitly biased, Dr. Kleine has contributed to the perpetuation of structural injustices through negligence. In this case, targeting Dr. Kleine might make sense because he could do more than he does. In this scenario, we might assume that he acknowledges no benefits accrued through his own racial identity, nor is he concerned with solving racial inequity problems. He believes that the homogenous racial makeup of his lab is a result of who chooses to enter the field and that there is more or less an equal opportunity for anyone, regardless of race, to do so. It is conceivable, though not verifiable, that some of his decisions in hiring are a result of unconscious biases. Thus, Dr. Kleine may have some responsibility for racial inequality in the field.

While Dr. Reese's callout in this case would be justified, there would still be reason for Dean Harrison to mention to her that some of her colleagues have raised concerns. He could suggest that it would be more expeditious to draw attention to the structural problems in the field and their manifestation in Dr. Kleine's lab, rather than to denounce him publicly in stark terms. The dean could raise all this with Dr. Reese in light of the committee's notes, and the committee might reasonably expect him to do so. He might note that if Dr. Reese hopes to force an intervention into Dr. Kleine's hiring practices, a best-case scenario might result in diversifying Dr. Kleine's own lab over time, but little impact would be made on addressing the larger racial inequities in the field and beyond. Dr. Reese may or may not be justified in her personal accusations against Dr. Kleine, and her virtual activism may not always be justified or appropriate, but the dean's decision must also take into account her freedom of expression, the protection of extramural speech, and the importance of fair measures of professional assessment.

IS THE CALLOUT PROTECTED?

Dr. Reese has the right to engage in extramural political speech, even if her superiors may question the justifiability as well as the form of her claims. One suggestion they raised was to promote her, but not to give her tenure. Such a decision would be unreasonable on the part of the university. It would keep her in a tenuous position and signify a lack of trust, a longer phase of supervision, and possible loss of status. All this would be based on her engagement in political and professional expression, which, while controversial, should still be protected. That the speech is protected means, in this case, that it should not be used as grounds for terminating Dr. Reese nor for denying her a promotion, which the other letters in her file indicate would be merited. However, although engaging in activism on social media is a legitimate choice, it should not be beyond the realm of workplace discussion and mentorship by the dean, especially in a junction such as that provided during consideration for tenure and promotion.

Had Dr. Reese called out problems in the field of biology at large, she might be more justified and at the same time raise fewer concerns while bringing attention to the problem. Targeting an individual colleague complicates the matter. Dr. Reese's goals of working toward racial equity in the sciences are noble and sorely needed, though the dean may reasonably inform her of the concern that this ad hominem approach has raised among some of her colleagues during her tenure assessment. Such conversation would be warranted as a way of facilitating an exchange between colleagues about tough issues. At the same time, extramural speech should remain in this, and most other cases, outside the purview of tenure and promotion assessment and should not affect the dean's decision on Dr. Reese's professional path.

Sigal Ben-Porath is professor of education, with secondary appointments in philosophy and political science, at the University of Pennsylvania. Her work focuses on normative analysis of education policy and practice. Among her recent books is Free Speech on Campus *(Penn Press, 2017).*

Dustin Webster is a former teacher and a PhD student at the University of Pennsylvania Graduate School of Education, where he studies philosophy of education. His interests include character and virtue education and philosophy in K–12 schools.

COMMENTARY

Collegiality or Civility? The Unjust Consequence of Eloquent Rage

TERAH J. STEWART

For me, this case is centrally about civility. In an effort to advocate for a more equitable and just discipline, field, academy, and world, Dr. Reese boldly called attention to *symptoms* of an unjust system. Viral critiques of individuals, institutions, and social/cultural systems sometimes *seem* harsh or unfair, but these sentiments are rooted in the desire to police minoritized individuals' reactions to oppression. In doing so, the focus shifts to how a critique or callout is expressed—even when the critique is legitimate.

HARM, INJUSTICE, AND WHITENESS

I do not believe that Dr. Reese wronged Dr. Kleine through her callout. While Dr. Kleine's humanity cannot be denied, centering his experience as a white man in a broader conversation about equity and justice is a manifestation of white supremacy and the reproduction of dominance. For the sake of analysis, even if one were to believe that Dr. Reese harmed or wronged Dr. Kleine with her callout, it would be an individual-level harm. Contrary and more important than individual harm is institutional, systemic, and sociocultural harm (which *also* individually harms). Minoritized people experience such harms every day in the academy and the world. Said differently, that one is suggested (or assumed) to be a racist—and the potential corresponding consequences—are not worse than the violence of experiencing and trying to survive systemic racism. To maintain that it is reinforces dominance and centers the needs of the powerful and systemically privileged over the histories and legacies of minoritized people, which has often been the case when civility is a/the standard.

The issue of Dr. Reese's lack of perceived civility or collegiality is troublesome because civility as a concept is inherently rooted in power. For example, the case itself mentions that Dr. Kleine experienced "very real consequences" as a result of Dr. Reese's post—consequences that seemingly amounted to deactivating his Twitter account and feeling compelled to write an op-ed in his own defense. In a real-world case, he may have even experienced more severe consequences, and it likely caused him a great deal of discomfort to be viewed as a racist. Yet that discomfort does not supersede *experiencing* racism, being limited by racism, and suffering the deathly consequences of racism; to believe so is a form of white fragility that often "distorts and perverts reality."[13] To position a callout by Dr. Reese and subsequent dogpile by the masses of social media users—over whom she has relatively little control—as an "attack for political reasons" *is* a distortion. To potentially deny her contributions in teaching, research, and service at the behest of reviewers who disliked the way she vocalized her concerns in a public forum *is* a perversion. It is not on Dr. Reese to prove that Dr. Kleine is a racist; it is on him to prove he is not.

The mere fact that so much of my commentary—and common responses to real-life examples that resemble this case—is focused on whether *Dr. Kleine* was actually harmed or not, wronged or not, is a classic manifestation of white supremacy and a distraction from the people who are harmed by oppression *every day*. I focus on Dr. Kleine because I know how white supremacy/fragility works; it will distract, it will derail, it will redirect. It is in anticipation of those logics that I address him. How is it that this case, despite its complexities with identity, social media, academic culture, and broader public opinion on equity, social justice, and "social justice warriors," boils down to Dr. Kleine's misfortune? Do his experiences, feelings, and reputation matter? Absolutely. Do they matter more than speaking truth to power and advocating for equity and justice? Absolutely not. And it goes without saying that Dr. Reese's point still stands: it has been fifteen years (and counting) since a student of color was admitted to Dr. Kleine's lab. Why is *that* not our focus? Why should not Dr. Kleine be expected to answer and explain it?

RETHINKING COLLEGIALITY AND CIVILITY

What if we thought about collegiality differently? What if it was collegial to point out when #YourSlipIsShowing?[14] I argue that highlighting a critical issue—such as lack of equitable or justice-oriented lab outreach/hiring—*is* being collegial even if it still is not civil, especially if equity and justice are shared values. Further, it would be an opportunity for those who care about inequity and injustice and their symptoms to rectify their praxis. That is to say, any potential harm Dr. Reese might have caused is in essence an opportunity to redress more severe and systemic violence against minoritized people, which should, after all, be our focus. A moral and ethical norm *should* be disrupting power and oppression deliberately. What would the possibilities for freedom be if we all agreed?

Toni Morrison wrote "definitions belong to the definers and not the defined," a sentiment that applies in this particular case.[15] The *1940 Statement of Principles on Academic Freedom and Tenure* currently outlines the most recognized academic freedom statement, endorsed by approximately 250 scholarly and professional associations.[16] The statement frames three principles for academic freedom, the third of which relates to the special obligations of faculty, including exercising appropriate restraint and respecting the opinions of others. Today, as I am writing, Black women make up roughly 3 percent of full-time faculty at degree-granting postsecondary institutions.[17] In 1940, the professoriate was even less diverse. The principles written then, which guide academia to this day, did not reflect the potential hazards that lay waiting as minoritized persons began to enter the academy and advocate about social issues. Recent attempts by the AAUP to account for "extramural utterances" on social media have also neglected to address the hazards minoritized persons face.[18]

Who gets to decide who or what is collegial? Civil? Who gains from these definitions? Who suffers? I hesitate to name Dr. Reese's actions as anger for fear of invoking the "angry Black woman" stereotype, but I end on the words of Brittney Cooper, who has written extensively in the defense of Black rage. She offers, "Rage is costly. And its costs are directly proportional to the amount of power any given woman or girl has when she chooses to wield it."[19] Indeed, there are always costs to our decisions, seemingly more so when we hold multiple minoritized identities.

However, when these instances arise, the real indictment is on the shoulders of those who deem this action uncivil or who focus on how the hyperprivileged were "harmed/wronged," not on the person calling attention to white supremacy, oppression, and injustice.

Terah J. Stewart (he/him) is an assistant professor of student affairs and higher education at Iowa State University. His research is focused on people and populations in the margins of the margins—students with multiple minoritized identities, hypermarginalized identities, and stigmatized identities.

COMMENTARY

From Tweeting to Thwacking

JENNIFER WEMIGWANS

THE MEDIUM IS THE MESSAGE

It is evident that striving for recognition at her university and in her field led Dr. Reese to succumb to a social media platform that is not so much designed for thoughtful interactions as hostile encounters. As an underrepresented minority in the academy and the field of biology, her exchanges on Twitter went from sharing resources and information to intentional posts that were politically charged.

Social media is not an altruistic forum. Free speech is not necessarily predicated on the cheerful, gentle, and soothing sounds of *tweeting*, but on the aggressive attacks of *thwacking*, which aim to galvanize and alienate groups of people. Choosing to use incendiary communication platforms like Twitter comes with costs.

In-depth commentary is impossible on Twitter, where the 280-character limit per tweet lends itself to advertising slogans, which are generally short, memorable, and evocative. It is precisely for this reason that users tend to post messages that arouse anger, hostility, or passion. Users feel pressured to escalate comments, or as Dr. Reese observed, to be more *provocative or politically charged*, in order to stand out among the 145 million daily Twitter users.

This pressure is evident when the controversial thread on Dr. Kleine escalated from the hashtag #whitelabsmatter to #kkkleine. By connecting him with the American white supremacist Ku Klux Klan, this hashtag moved away from tweeting to thwacking. As a result of the escalation of posts on Twitter, Dr. Kleine received many blows both online and offline. It is this thwacking that an external reviewer of Dr. Reese's tenure case called out, putting her tenure at risk.

The academy is a structure that reproduces and creates hierarchies of faculty ascension—a "survival of the fittest" ladder where only the strongest continue to climb and gain prominence. Calling out, attacking, and taking others down is fair game—until it's not. In this case, multiple political discourses are intersecting that involve circulations of power and capital, histories of dispossession and race, and notions of governance and inclusion.

This context makes it difficult to condemn Dr. Reese for her actions on Twitter. She did what the university expects and even demands of tenure-track faculty, which is to brand her research and academic work in order to make herself visible in her field and thereby create worth and value for the university.

INDIGENOUS WORLDVIEWS: A RADICAL INTERPRETATION

With this framing of the case in mind, I will now employ a radically different perspective rooted in Indigenous worldviews and values to identify ethical dimensions of this case. From an Indigenous perspective, the academy is "an arm of the settler state—a site where the logics of elimination, capital accumulation, and dispossession are reconstituted—which is distinct from other frameworks that critique the academy as fundamentally neoliberal, Eurocentric, and/ or patriarchal."[20] In "Refusing the University," Sandy Grande questions whether we should "hospice" the university in order to move toward "solidarities (that) can be developed among marginalized groups with a shared commitment to working beyond the imperatives of capital and the settler state."[21] It is notable that the ethical questions posed in this case study locate the university uncritically as an arm of the settler state. Challenging this premise and applying the notion of refusing the university raises substantial implications for the ethics of Dr. Reese's actions and the dean's decision about how to handle her tenure case.

These implications include the hypocrisy of the university's punishing Dr. Reese for her presence on Twitter when the dean himself actively solicited social media use by faculty to raise their public profiles. Encouraging faculty to establish public profiles is a key marketing strategy for universities and speaks to the fact that Dr. Reese's worth is measured by the quantity of potential students and research dollars that she generates. In a modern capitalist system, faculty are equated with their reproduction value and extraction of profit.

Inclusion in the university, as the external reviewer implies, is offered within *certain* parameters of respectability and collegiality *as defined* by the university—in this case, colleagueship. Dr. Reese's transgression of the norm of *colleagueship* on social media threatens her future inclusion in the university because she is now seen as unable to participate within the parameters of *respectability* that characterize the university's governance.

Academics engaged in issues of dispossession involving race threaten power structures in the academy. In this particular case, the bottom line is capital accumulation, not deep learning or dialogue on complex issues of dispossession, race, and alienation. As a result, the colleagueship that Dr. Reese engendered with other black scholars and people of color in choosing to disrupt hierarchies of white scientists was denied and denigrated because it challenged the very foundations of the university as an arm of the settler state. To know the university in this way is to understand that notions of academic freedom and shared governance are limited.

What does it mean to have *real* academic freedom—the kind of freedom that is not determined by the university's parameters of respectability and collegiality, which are mired in protecting the structures of the settler state? What kind of academic community could emerge if faculty weren't pressured to submit to the self-serving enterprise of branding for the purposes of ascension within the university? What kind of academic could Dr. Reese become if she were not putting her energies into constant self-promotion for the purposes of branding her work and herself?

Refusing to comply with the existing structures of the university requires a radical shift in thinking. My understanding of academic freedom and shared governance is based on Indigenous worldviews and values aligned with dismantling and challenging settler state institutions that create competitive hierarchies of individual worth and labor. Indigenous governance and freedom recognize that all individuals have intrinsic values and gifts to share with their communities. Knowledge is a shared construction that is not owned or created by any one individual. Rather, knowledge is community-centered and is rooted in values of reciprocity, humility, and mutuality. Knowledge sharing extends to being in good relations with all life, including plants, wildlife, water, and lands, which entails responsibility and working collectively to uphold Indigenous governance and freedom. These strategies embrace a value system and structure that is radically different from the settler state. Indigenous values shun constant self-promotion and are incompatible with the rise-to-the-top settler-selfism promoted by universities to prop up academic stars for the purposes of marketing.

In reflecting on this case, I propose that we move away from tweeting and thwacking and join Dr. Grande in *refusing*. It is important to think critically about the ways in which the university is an arm of the settler state and is deeply invested in modern capitalist extraction for the purposes of ongoing accumulation of wealth. As academics, we must assert ourselves as more than commodities to be sold at academic auction to the highest student bidder or funder. Instead, we can serve as beacons for alternative ways of thinking and living—investing in knowledge sharing, engaging in difficult dialogue and ideas with respect and grace, and challenging existing structures by learning about alternative knowledge systems and values.

Jennifer Wemigwans, PhD, Ontario Institute for Studies in Education, University of Toronto, is a producer, writer, and scholar specializing in the convergence between education, Indigenous knowledge, and new media technologies. Her book A Digital Bundle: Protecting and Promoting Indigenous Knowledge Online *(University of Regina Press, 2018) explores the prospects of education and digital projects in a networked world.*

COMMENTARY

Professional Norms and Academic Social Media Use

HARRY BRIGHOUSE

Dean Harrison doesn't have much of a choice; his letter is not difficult to write.

WHY TENURE DR. REESE?

This conclusion has almost nothing to do with the plausibility of Dr. Reese's judgment about Dr. Kleine nor with how civil or otherwise Dr. Reese has been on social media.

Dr. Reese's judgment about Dr. Kleine—that his lab discriminates against racially minoritized researchers—seems quite plausible. Suppose, counterfactually, that she was accusing a small academic department for having an all-white faculty. Many such departments make affirmative efforts to hire racially minoritized professors but remain all white. Hiring in such departments can be rare, and hires are almost always done one at a time. Additionally, some disciplines have serious pipeline problems, and anti-discrimination law, rightly or wrongly (I think wrongly), prohibits discrimination in favor of racialized minorities at the point of hiring. In such a case, Dr. Reese's campaign would be naive and groundless. However, a successful lab hires several postdocs a year who come and go, and the biological sciences do not have the kind of pipeline issues that some smaller disciplines have. It might be possible that the racial composition of the Dr. Kleine's lab is innocent, but it is much more likely that serious discrimination is occurring, probably with the collusion of the HR department.

A WORSE CASE

Since the dean's decision in this context is fairly straightforward, let's take the counterfactual case—that Dr. Reese's activism targeted a small, all-white department of a discipline such as linguistics. In that context, her accusations would be unfair, and her tweeting uncollegial. Still, even if this were so, Dean Harrison should endorse her tenure application for several reasons.

First, he should be making the decision about the whole case. There seems to be no other negative to Dr. Reese's file and, in particular, no other suggestion of uncollegiality. Few colleagues are collegial in every single respect. Some are bad departmental citizens or selfish in their choices about teaching. Others frequently decline or make themselves unsuited to service opportunities for the campus. If she is indeed uncollegial in this one respect, the dean and/or her departmental colleagues should discuss that with her. This would merely constitute one defect in an otherwise worthy file.

Second, only in extreme cases should the dean look beyond the file itself. What would constitute an extreme case? I can't articulate a principle, but here are a couple of obvious examples. Suppose that a pattern of self-consciously and unambiguously racist or misogynistic expression on social media, or a proven accusation of sexual harassment of a staff member or students, came to light after the tenure file was put together. Then, the dean should consider denying the case. Otherwise, the file should be the sole basis for his judgment.

The third reason, which will frame the rest of my commentary, is that academic culture has not yet established, nor is there even much of a discussion about, what norms we should abide by when approaching our publicly visible social media use. Without a policy, or at least a set of conventions, about those norms, denying tenure on the basis of Dr. Reese's Twitter posts would be arbitrary.

NORMS FOR ACADEMIC USE OF SOCIAL MEDIA

What should a set of norms around academic use of social media look like? I am not asking what should be protected by academic freedom or freedom of expression but, rather, what norms scholars should abide by within those protections. I cannot give a full answer to the question, both because space is limited and because I don't have one.

Two considerations, though, will be important components of an adequate answer. Academics have special responsibilities to actual and potential students and to the public good. Norms concerning publicly visible social media conduct should adequately reflect those responsibilities.

Here's one responsibility to actual and potential students: they must be able to enter our classrooms trusting that we respect them and are eager to ensure their learning. Among the problems with the Steven Salaita tweets referred to in the case were his assertion that anyone supporting Israel is "hopelessly brainwashed" and another saying "Zionists: transforming 'antisemitism' from something horrible into something honorable since 1948." Seeing those tweets, many Jewish students—and even many non-Jewish students who simply affirm the right of the state of Israel to exist—might reasonably have difficulty assuming that he would respect them in the classroom.

Or, consider the case of Damon Sajnani, a UW-Madison professor whose tweets about the murder of several police officers in Texas during the summer of 2016 were most naturally interpreted as celebrating those murders. Students aspiring to police work, or whose family members work as police officers, might reasonably be anxious about taking his classes.

In defense of both Salaita and Sajnani, one might argue that, in context, their tweets are ambiguous, sarcastic, and/or ironic. Perhaps they did not mean what they said. But both should know that they are expressing themselves on a platform that does not, except in very niche corners, support the communication of sarcasm or irony. Misunderstandings abound in social media posts in the absence of the usual pragmatic indicators with an audience that does not share one's assumptions. Actual and potential students will *reasonably* feel unwelcome, disrespected, and alienated.

Perhaps this consideration is, in some circumstances, overridden by others. For example, a Twitter thread might reasonably be misunderstood by potential students, but it might also reach and influence a broad academic audience in one's area of specialty. I am not claiming that the interests of actual and potential students should *trump* other considerations, just that they should *inform* the norms we adopt.

Academics can contribute to the public good in numerous ways, including through their teaching, their research, and its effective dissemination. But on social media, academics are especially well placed to provide otherwise rare modeling of reasoned and reasonable discourse. Academics can be independent of corporate interests, and unlike journalists, religious leaders, politicians, and activists, they do not depend for their living on attracting a mass audience, maintaining a congregation, or catering to the opinions of constituents. Thus, they have an unusual freedom from the material incentives that lead others to distort the arguments and positions of others and, in some cases (think of Rush Limbaugh or Anne Coulter), deliberately to toxify discourse.

Again, this consideration might be overridden by others. Sometimes the value of the norm of straightforward, reasonable contribution to public discourse can be trumped: harshness and rudeness can be apt. In fact, Dr. Reese's retweet of #kkkleine may, in the context of this case, fall within that category (whereas, in the alternative scenario described earlier, it would not).

I have merely proposed two considerations that I hope a broad, reasoned, and inclusive academic conversation aimed at arriving at a workable and productive set of norms for social media engagement would take into account. Even if we had such a code, one-off or rare violations of it might be occasions for conversations or perhaps disciplinary action, but rarely would they be a cause for denying tenure or firing a violator. In their absence, though, Dean Harrison—like me and everyone else—lacks the legitimacy to determine a decision as significant as tenure by reference to his idiosyncratic norms.

Harry Brighouse is Mildred Fish-Harnack Professor of Philosophy and Carol Dickson-Bascom Professor of the Humanities at UW-Madison, where he directs the Center for Ethics and Education. He is author, with Helen Ladd, Susanna Loeb, and Adam Swift, of Educational Goods: Values and Evidence in Decision-Making *(University of Chicago Press, 2018).*

COMMENTARY

Old Racism in a New Form: *Uplift Suasion* in Appeals for Collegiality

Ed Lee III

The idea that Black people should adjust their behavior to conform to White expectations of civility is not a new social development. In this case, we see an academic institution appealing to collegiality to regulate the conduct of a Black faculty member. It is the latest version of what Ibram X. Kendi describes as *uplift suasion*, the idea that changing Black behavior to conform to White expectations is the linchpin to resolving social and political inequities. Kendi argues that the end of the Civil War birthed a new form of racism that conditioned the acknowledgment of Black people's humanity on their behaving admirably and in a manner that supported the established moral and social order.[22] Abolitionists recommended that former slaves abstain from loud, overly opinionated, and disruptive behavior to prove that they were worthy of their new freedoms and opportunities to inhabit White spaces. Additionally, they encouraged Blacks to publicly comport themselves with dutiful civility and pursue a cheerful camaraderie with Whites. The case study reveals how uplift suasion can easily creep into discussions about the inclusion of Black people in predominantly White teaching and learning spaces.

While the strategy of uplift suasion lacks the historical and analytical support to be considered an effective tool for challenging racism or creating structures of belonging, it remains a mainstay in discussions about barriers to Black advancement. Kendi argues that many institutions continue to hold compliant and docile behavior as the cost of Black inclusion and equitable treatment. Unfortunately, this Faustian bargain leaves racist policies, practices, and norms unchallenged.

THE DOWNSIDE OF EMPHASIZING COLLEGIALITY

Ambiguous standards like "collegiality" and "academic citizenship" are the latest versions of uplift suasion. They implicitly blame the nonconformist behavior of Black professors and students for their inability to excel in predominantly White academic spaces instead of focusing on discriminatory practices. When it comes to exploring how and when we should regulate faculty's social media participation, we may find that many of the critiques of Dr. Jaleesa Reese's Twitter posts are old wine in a new bottle.

The criticism of Dr. Reese's social media activity reveals how standards of professionalism can serve to normalize whiteness and threaten the academic freedom of faculty members advocating for historically marginalized communities. Even as our professoriate and student bodies slowly diversify, far too often inclusion requires cultural and communicative conformity by those integrating academic departments. For many in situations resembling that of Dr. Reese, the choice is between silence or becoming an organizational outcast. When they are unwilling to capitulate to subtle demands to act in ways that are more comfortable for the more powerful members of the organization, vague and opaque standards are used to assess their long-term viability. Unfortunately, ambiguous standards like "academic citizenship" and "colleagueship"—those used to argue against tenure for Dr. Reese—are rarely renegotiated and clarified to accommodate cultural differences. These loosely defined expectations are used to silence or punish academics who are perceived to lack "political savvy" or are deemed "uncollegial." For the college-wide committee evaluating Dr. Reese's tenure application, political savvy means accepting the underrepresentation of Blacks in the STEM fields. Additionally, uncollegiality is having the audacity to challenge her colleagues to account for decisions that result in them exclusively working with White students in their labs.

THE UPSIDE OF EMPHASIZING STUDENT SUPPORT

As higher education administrators debate whether to regulate faculty's use of social media, they should acknowledge the benefit of tweets like those written by Dr. Reese for creating welcoming learning communities for students from historically underrepresented communities.

Lack of belonging has far-reaching consequences for academic performance and persistence. Research on belonging using data from graduate students studying mathematics, physical sciences, engineering, and computer sciences at Berkeley, Caltech, Stanford, and UCLA found that participation in threatening academic environments "drains attentional resources away from academic tasks" and "can lead to avoidance, disengagement, and disidentification."[23] These researchers concluded that one factor contributing to lack of belonging in STEM doctoral programs is the opaque standards and expectations guiding student evaluations.

Social media presents an opportunity for educators to cultivate "actively inclusive teaching" practices that emotionally support underrepresented students by publicizing Black scientific excellence and challenging standards that hinder Black persistence. Twitter posts like those created by Dr. Reese serve as a countervailing force to the exclusion many Black students experience in math, science, and engineering departments. Dr. Reese's deployment of "#blackscience" and "#BLMinSTEM" sparked much-needed conversations about the underrepresentation of minorities in STEM education. They can serve as springboards for developing supportive and affirming coalitions. At a minimum, her messages signal to Black students that their concerns are not personal; they are institutional and systemwide.

CUES OF BELONGING MATTER

We should not underestimate the importance of Dr. Reese's social media presence for students who interpret the dominant cues as indicating that their race limits their ability to become rigorous and highly acclaimed scientists. Claude Steele revealed how perceived threats to students' identities can negatively impact academic performance by breeding mistrust and a need to disassociate from harmful environments.[24] Steele concluded that administrators and professors can reverse the damage: "[I]f enough cues in a setting can lead members of a group to feel 'identity safe,' it might neutralize the impact of other cues in the setting that could otherwise threaten them."[25] Dr. Reese's Twitter messages are examples of identity safe cues. Just as important, one wonders why her posts are not readily interpreted as a form of academic citizenship that strives to privilege the needs of some of the more vulnerable students pursuing a STEM education?

Finally, the prevalence of cues of nonbelonging that permeate Dr. Kleine's lab may explain his inability to entice students of color to apply to work with him. His nonresponsive reference to a "strong record of supporting female scientists" presents support for White women as a sufficient response to the lack of racial diversity. It is not. Additionally, his argument that all his decisions are "based on student readiness to excel" ignores the unique ways that racism informs who is perceived as ready. Unfortunately, Dr. Kleine's statements reveal that he is uninterested in addressing the assumptions and norms that make his lab a hostile space for students of color. Unlike Dr. Reese's Twitter messages, his explanation of the lab's inability to attract students of color is devoid of the identity safe cues that are needed for Black students to thrive.

With this in mind, Dean Harrison should write a letter to the provost recommending Dr. Jaleesa Reese for promotion *and* tenure. Failure to do so legitimizes appeals to uplift suasion used to control Dr. Reese's speech and shield inequitable and exclusive policies from critique. A denial letter based on vague behavioral standards punishes Dr. Reese for challenging discriminatory practices in a manner that failed to conform to the dictates of the most privileged members of her community.

Ed Lee III, EdD, is senior director of Emory University's Alben W. Barkley Forum for Debate, Deliberation, and Dialogue. His work explores the interplay between communication, culture, and diversity in creating more innovative and responsive policies and practices. Ed is national media commentator for US presidential debates and the use of arguments in public discourse.

CHAPTER 4

Institutional Responses to Sexual Misconduct and Assault on College Campuses

MEG EVANS, JOY ELIZABETH MOSLEY, AND JACOB FAY

This case presents administrators at a small liberal arts college determining how to balance legal compliance with shifting Title IX regulations alongside ethical obligations to their students.

Tamika Wells, the Title IX coordinator for Rustin College, smiled at the eight faces in the Zoom window on her computer monitor[1]: "As you know, the secretary of education has finalized the new 2020 regulations addressing sexual violence on campus under Title IX.[2] We must be in compliance by this fall. Many components of the final regulations may be at odds with steps we took to comply with the 2011 'Dear Colleague Letter' (DCL).[3] President Clark has asked us to prepare a statement outlining how we will fulfill our priority of caring for students while establishing a Title IX process that abides by the regulations and provides a safe learning environment for students."

Tamika knew this would be a difficult conversation. Rustin—a small liberal arts college nestled in the hills of a rural Appalachian community—had already witnessed deep divisions about how sexual violence should be handled. Like many colleges around the United States, Rustin had seen a disturbing rise in the number of reported incidences of sexual misconduct on campus over the past decade. Many members of the college community understood the 2011 DCL guidance as a needed response to an emerging crisis, but not everyone agreed with the policy changes Rustin had implemented. The new regulations marked the latest shift, increasing uncertainty among students, faculty, and staff alike as Rustin prepared to return to on-campus classes in the fall of 2020.

Amid the complex changes included in the new regulations, one central point of contention was the extent to which colleges should use court-like processes in responding to claims of sexual harassment and assault. Some saw formalization of these processes as a positive—as the best way to ensure that all members of the campus community would be treated equitably. But others worried that a reliance on "college courts" was not the best way to care for students.

Over the years, the use of court-like procedures on college campuses had led to national debates about what burden of proof should be required to hold someone responsible for sexual assault in the college context. Before the 2011 DCL, Rustin and many other colleges employed the *clear and convincing* standard—requiring that the evidence show a claim is *substantially* more likely than not to be true.[4] The 2011 DCL made a significant shift, instructing campuses to use the less stringent *preponderance of evidence* standard. With this standard, the evidence must show only that a claim is more likely than not to be true.[5]

This shift had sparked a contentious debate at Rustin in recent years. Tensions escalated in 2017 when a white female sophomore accused a Black male senior, who was a star athlete, of sexually assaulting her. The incident tore at the bonds of a campus already struggling to navigate race, power, and privilege. Some students, mostly but not entirely male, voiced concerns that the lower preponderance of evidence standard encouraged false claims of sexual assault. Other students, including many of the small number of Students of Color who attended Rustin, worried that the shift to the lower standard was having unintended effects that perpetuated the long history of race-based injustice in the handling of sexual assault and misconduct both on campus and in society more broadly. However, other students defended the shift, noting that the preponderance of evidence standard leveled the playing field for victims of sexual assault and their alleged perpetrators in resolving encounters that often occur behind closed doors and are notoriously difficult to adjudicate. Emotions flared again when the female student abruptly withdrew from Rustin the next fall. The controversy eventually died down, but tensions continued to bubble beneath the perceived calm. The 2020 changes to the Title IX regulations promised to resurface these debates and raise new ones.

As the meeting got under way, Tamika opened the floor for discussion, bracing for impact. David Barnes, assistant to President Clark, jumped in. He was anxious to steer Rustin away from messy controversies like the debates that had consumed the campus not long before: "Should Rustin even be involved in adjudicating sexual assault cases? Shouldn't the police handle that? Our small college is not equipped to be a mini police force that is also judge, jury, and executioner all in one."

A few others nodded their heads in agreement. No one was particularly happy with how the events in 2017 had played out.

"Come on, David," said Chris Holcomb. A highly respected professor in the sociology department, Chris had been instrumental in bringing students together to talk about the controversy in 2017. "If we just left it up to the police, it would inevitably take all power and agency from the victim. It is well known that our criminal justice system discourages victims from coming forward. Now, I admit that determining what processes we should use is not simple, but we can't just leave it up to the police."

Tamika reminded the group that David's hope was simply not possible, "Let's keep in mind that our focus today is not whether Rustin should be handling Title IX complaints internally, but how to create the most equitable and safe campus for our students. Jordan, could you brief us on the new regulations?"

Jordan Lovett, Rustin's general counsel, smiled: "I'm sure you all had plenty of time to read my email last week, but let me highlight a few points. The regulations do provide some leeway in the processes we use to address sexual misconduct and assault. One big issue is the appropriate standard of evidence. We have been using the preponderance of evidence standard in keeping with the 2011 DCL guidance, but the new rules provide more flexibility. The regulations also change the definition of sexual harassment and require that we provide live hearings with cross-examination, while also giving us permission to use alternative informal methods."

"So, we can choose which standards we want to employ?" asked Taylor Saunders, the student representative on the committee.

"Yes, but there's a catch," said Jordan, "the new regulations require schools to use the same standard of evidence for student complaints as employee complaints, including faculty. Schools must also apply the same standard to all formal complaints of sexual harassment. So we have some flexibility to choose our standard, within certain boundaries."

"I question the reasoning behind letting schools choose. Isn't there a reason to prefer one standard to the other for everyone?" asked Chris.

"I think so," said Jing Wu, the dean of students. "Colleges need to balance power appropriately when it comes to these sorts of claims. Remember, the school is the one that brings the charges, not the student. The school investigates and charges students with violations of the school's conduct code, and the school needs to prove its case. Imagine an individual student going up against all the resources Rustin can deploy. The balance is not equal between an individual—even our most well-resourced students—and the school, so the school should have the higher burden."

Jennifer Yeats, one of Rustin's survivor advocates, shook her head: "Yes, but students still need to report complaints for the college to act. If they don't feel like the college will do anything or they are frustrated that the college can never meet the burden of proof, victims will be deterred from reporting. There is a reason that preponderance of evidence is the standard used in most other civil rights contexts. Not to mention that we've all seen and heard how the criminal justice system has failed to do right by victims of sexual assault. Colleges and universities have a chance to do better. Continuing to use the preponderance of evidence standard is the best way to do that."

Joan Martin, the vice president of student affairs and the deputy Title IX coordinator, shrugged: "I'm not sure. We've seen some really egregious cases at other institutions of accused students not even being apprised of the details of the complaints against them. The American Association of University Professors advocates for the clear and convincing standard, as does the American College of Trial Lawyers. Both suggest that it is much more likely to protect due process rights."

Chris added, "Well, if we've learned anything in recent years from all the wrongful convictions and exonerations of Black men, it's that even our court systems using higher standards of evidence regularly get things wrong. I think we need to move away from court-like proceedings, not toward them."

"What about false accusations?" David interjected. "I hate to be the one to bring this up, but part of my role is to be concerned about our public image. We aren't serving our students if some of them are living in fear that their college career may be ruined due to an unfair school complaint process. I think the 2011 DCL went too far and we have an opportunity to rectify that now."

"Well, we do know that false accusations of sexual assault are very rare," Tamika said.[6] "Some researchers have estimated that the number could go up under a lower burden of proof, but that is not a certain outcome by any means."[7]

"Not to mention," Jennifer said, "that—again—it takes a whole lot to bring a claim in the first place. Simply sticking with the lower burden of proof does not turn off other social pressures. I don't think it's fair to assume simply changing the standard of evidence will result in more or fewer false claims."

Alex Austyn, the director of Rustin's Gender, Sexuality, and Women's Center, was visibly frustrated: "We aren't looking at the whole picture here. Choosing a standard of evidence is not all that is on the table. The new changes are wide-ranging. The definition of sexual misconduct in the 2011 DCL guidance is 'unwelcome conduct of a sexual nature,' but the 2020 regulations change this to actions that are 'severe, pervasive, and objectively offensive.' They require live hearings with cross-examination. And they also allow for institutions to use 'informal' processes to address sexual misconduct. I mean, what is the bar for sexual misconduct with the new definition? These are really weighty changes."

"Requiring cross-examinations is ludicrous," responded Jennifer. "I have enough difficulty encouraging survivors to talk to each other and me about their experiences. If they have to face the retraumatizing effects of a live cross-examination, students will be even more reluctant to report. I know that the new regulations allow for technological assists and require the party's advisor to conduct the cross-examination. But if students know that they will be cross-examined as a part of the process, it is going to make it even harder for them to come forward. This requirement could bury claims before we hear them and make it impossible for us to care for all our students, to say nothing of the additional resources we would have to pour into having an appropriate number of advisors."

Joan interjected, "I agree that some of the other aspects of the new regulations are troubling. But isn't there an opportunity in some of them as well? In my role working with Title IX cases, I've seen the outcome be a lose-lose situation for both parties. Too often neither party walks away believing justice was achieved. Couldn't we use the space for informal processes to try some of the restorative justice approaches our students have been talking about?"

Chris took up Joan's lead, "We have been clamoring for restorative justice practices for a while now, and many students are behind it. But I am worried about treating it as an informal practice. Restorative justice is an alternative framework for thinking about discipline, and formal consequences can and do emerge from restorative practices. In fact, questions of burden of proof are largely beside the point if we work from a restorative rather than retributive framework. But, if we treat restorative practices simply as an informal process, students who are victims of assault may feel pressured to use them rather than take formal steps against a perpetrator. And that isn't what we want."

"And we need to remember that sexual misconduct and assault are not experienced equally by all our students," Alex observed. "Women—particularly Black women—and LGBTQ students experience sexual violence at much higher rates than do cisgender, heterosexual males. Whatever we choose to do, we need to be aware of that fact. I think there is a serious question about how to adapt to the new regulations in a way that is responsive to these disparities."

Jing jumped back in, "Isn't this why we need clear and stable procedures? Changing how we handle cases every few years is a problem."

"Agreed, clarity is crucial," Tamika responded, "The standard of evidence is part of it, but not all. We learned the hard way in 2017 that transparency is important. My goal for us now is to identify how Rustin will respond to the new regulations with as much clarity and fairness for all of our students as possible."

There was a pause. Tamika could read in the faces on her screen that the conversation felt stuck.

"What's best for students?" asked Taylor, who had been listening attentively to these exchanges. "I think the question should be: What do we need to do to make our campus a safer, more welcoming space for all students? We don't need campus to be a bubble, but we do need it to be a place that is safe and welcoming, so that all of us can learn. How do we accomplish that within these new regulations?"

"You're right, Taylor," said Tamika. "It is easy to get lost in the minutiae, but we should remember our fundamental task."

Identifying a path forward in light of the new regulations would be challenging. How should Rustin, and other colleges and universities, fairly weigh the competing interests of all their members in their processes for handling claims of sexual misconduct and assault? What ethical and practical considerations matter, and how should they shape the processes institutions of higher education put in place?

COMMENTARY

Shifting the Conversation Beyond Rules and Compliance to Education and Power

Michele S. Moses

While Rustin College staff members deliberate, they must consider how to handle several shifting guidelines within the Title IX rules. Under the Trump administration, the definition of sexual misconduct changed, and institutions faced a choice of whether the claimant's case hinges on a *preponderance of the evidence* or the much more stringent *clear and convincing* standard. In light of the difficulties described in the case, Rustin administrators are understandably focusing on this choice and its implications. A related concern is the shift from the Obama administration rules against cross-examination or direct mediation to the Trump administration's requirement for live hearings with cross-examination of each of the parties by a representative. Such complexities could make the reporting process more difficult for sexual assault survivors and result in public scrutiny for the institution. For example, students at the University of Denver (DU) posted painful stories of sexual assault on Instagram to push the institution to reform its practices. As one DU student posted: "I thought I was going to die that day . . . All I wanted to do was report it, however, he had told me that nobody would believe me . . ."[8] Examples like this underscore the importance of the decisions facing Rustin educators for both the students involved and the institution.

POLITICS AND POWER

Such decisions are especially difficult because partisan politics have distorted the problem of sexual assault on campus. Instead of framing this issue as a grave matter of violence primarily against women or as a critical problem for both higher education and society, sexual misconduct cases have become a battle between conservative and liberal worldviews. The Obama administration and its supporters prioritized survivors' rights and experiences, calling attention to historical power arrangements, social structures, and legal systems favoring alleged perpetrators. By contrast, the Trump administration and its supporters emphasized concerns that people (that is, men) might be unjustly accused of rape or sexual assault or denied due process. Although complicated to measure, research is clear that people only rarely make false accusations.[9] But even this clarity regarding false accusations becomes complex when race is taken into consideration; research also shows that Black men are more likely to be treated unjustly when accused of sexual assault.[10] The interaction of race and gender with campus rules and compliance requires educators to understand the relevant history and research.

As the Rustin case demonstrates, choosing a standard of proof and developing a process for sexual misconduct cases is not straightforward, especially in the present political context. However, as one character noted, "[S]exual misconduct and assault are not experienced equally by all our students. Women—particularly Black women—and LGBTQ students experience sexual violence at much higher rates than do cisgender, heterosexual males. Whatever we choose to do, we need to be aware of that fact." I understand this to be a central point and believe campus leaders must be prepared to take a stand for what is right even if the issues are politically controversial.

EDUCATION

What I want to point out here is that colleges and universities would be acting irresponsibly if they were to treat concerns about false accusations as if they had the same moral and epistemic stature as concerns for survivors and victims of rape or sexual assault. Among other serious injustices and harms, this can lead to—in Deweyan terms—deeply *miseducative* experiences for students; that is, experiences that have the "effect of arresting or distorting the growth of further experience."[11] What do students learn when colleges and universities legitimize the unlikely scenario of a false accusation? They learn that often those with more social power are more likely to be given the benefit of the doubt. What do accusers learn when their college seems more concerned with the rights of the accused? They learn that their college is less concerned about victims of sexual assault.

How sexual misconduct is defined, what standard of proof is used, and how victims and survivors are treated in college hearings will teach students about the college's values and priorities. In my view, if Rustin educators decide to adopt a more stringent definition of sexual misconduct or settle on the "clear and convincing" standard of proof, they will not only make painful situations worse for survivors but will also foster experiences for students that are either of dubious educational worth or profoundly miseducative. Dewey maintained, "The quality of any experience has two aspects. There is an immediate aspect of agreeableness or disagreeableness, and there is its influence upon later experiences."[12] Rustin's decisions around Title IX policy matter for students now, but also into the future.

What is at issue in the case is not just about rules and regulations; it is a live issue for Rustin students, as it is for students on other campuses, and especially minoritized and marginalized students. Notably, 23.1 percent of college women and 5.4 percent of college men are raped or sexually assaulted during their undergraduate years.[13] Even the college's stated commitments will have an impact (symbolic and practical) on Rustin students and other members of the college community. Just decision-making on issues related to sexual misconduct requires those in leadership roles to privilege the social contexts and perspectives of those involved who are in the least dominant social positions.

CONCLUSION

In 2018, then–Secretary of Education Betsy DeVos claimed a commitment to safe campus environments: "This starts," she said, "with having clear policies and fair processes that every student can rely on. Every survivor of sexual violence must be taken seriously, and every student accused of sexual misconduct must know that guilt is not predetermined."[14] The problem I see here—one that Alex was getting at in the case—is that there is not an equivalent level of risk or harm associated with *being a victim* of sexual assault and *being accused* of perpetrating that sexual assault. Secretary DeVos seemed to be putting forward Title IX rules in a vacuum, separate from and without considering how systemic sexism, racism, and misogyny as well as power disparities by race, gender, and sexuality shape the social contexts in which sexual misconduct and violence occur and ultimately are adjudicated.

Educational institutions like Rustin have a responsibility to educate students and other members of the community around issues of sexual violence. Culture has to change, particularly that of toxic masculinity. However, a strong focus on regulations and compliance detracts from the moral and institutional imperatives to help students understand consent, develop empathy, and respect others' agency and humanity.

Michele S. Moses is professor of education at University of Colorado Boulder. She is a philosopher of education centrally concerned with education policy and social justice. Her research has examined political strategies to dismantle affirmative action, what it means to opt out of public education, and disagreements over viewpoint diversity and academic freedom on campus. Her most recent book is Living with Moral Disagreement: The Enduring Controversy about Affirmative Action.

COMMENTARY

Moving Beyond Compliance in Support of Healing

LAMEA "ELLE" SHAABAN-MAGAÑA

This case reflects sensitive Title IX issues within a context of diverging interests, voices, and action paths. My reflections on this case are informed by my leadership of a center that provides free, voluntary, and confidential advocacy and counseling services. I understand myself as accountable to the hundreds of survivors with whom our center has worked, as well as the scores of victims across our nation's campuses. I proceed also cognizant that most of us, whether aware or not, know someone who has experienced sexual violence.

HEARING THE SUBJECT AMONG THE "EXPERTS"

Reflecting hierarchical bureaucracies and multivalent agendas, the case presents a realistically dizzying array of characters. The scenario includes a Title IX coordinator, university president appointee, dean of students, university counsel, professor, student representative, survivor advocate, and VP of student affairs. Others could include: office of student conduct, campus and community law enforcement and health services, district attorney's office, residential communities, Greek affairs, faculty senate, student government association, parent support office, activist student organizations, and more.

Fueling this disorientation, the May 2020 Department of Education "Final Rule" guidance was over twenty-three hundred pages long, and despite concerns shared from survivors and practitioners in the rule's preview period, significant alterations were not made in the final document.[15] So complicated are these procedures that flowcharts are now commonly made available to administrators and published on campus websites to help students to decipher Title IX basics. Utilizing "administrative rationalism" for problem-solving, experts talking behind closed doors is the norm guided by a top-down tradition.[16] As a result, victims must often call on a victim advocate or case manager to navigate among campus actors and gain an understanding of the institutional priorities entangled within "campus safety" rhetoric.

Through our practices, we decide who is afforded options to speak and be heard, and under what conditions. Victims will likely be retraumatized in live, court-like hearings, vulnerable to questions posed by a representative appointed by their violator, or via "informal" procedures that still integrate institutional oversight and existing campus power differentials. Importantly, these Title IX protocols are enacted simultaneously with the affective, bodily, and spiritual experiences of victims, whose losses of emotional safety and bodily autonomy, among other casualties, have far-reaching implications of suffering from the trauma. Absent from the Rustin case is a victim speaking in their own interests. Subsequently, we construct human objects talked about, over, through, or for within these educational practices.

Amid these dense Title IX entanglements, the guidance postures as neutral under the veil of "due process," yet prioritizes perpetrator and institution protections over those of victims. The proceedings are dependent on a survivor coming forward, then participating in proving that the wrongdoing occurred, and finally establishing that the violations meet the multipronged definition. Exactly how and to whom the victim must disclose (via formalized, credentialed, and classified mechanisms) is codified and must be completed before the institution has "actual knowledge" of (and responsibility for under Title IX) the violence. The "truth" of the victimization is vetted via this system after rigorous reporting, investigative, and adjudicatory processes.

However, for the survivor, this knowing is at the site of bodily and emotionally lived experiences of which they are already acutely aware. Reflecting this, many advocacy campaigns adopt the phrase "start by believing" as a philosophical and practical imperative, challenging presumptions that what signifies truth is evident and an agreed-upon common sense and rejecting the existence of unity regarding whose truth matters. Title IX practices overburden survivors to push beyond the collective myth of false reporting and weigh decisions to publicly hold their abusers and institutions accountable despite rational fears of being disbelieved or having no meaningful affirming outcomes.

MATERIAL BODIES AND THE BODY POLITIC: INSTITUTIONAL BETRAYAL AND COURAGE

In determining "the most equitable process," we must account for variability in the costs and vulnerabilities experienced by individuals, recognizing the everydayness of implicit bias and structural inequities, which are felt routinely by victims and other marginalized populations (and made known via the multitude of voices from #MeToo, Black Lives Matter, and others, as well as empirical scholarship). Title IX—exposed to ongoing clarifications and sociocultural, historical, and political currents—was written as a remedy *against* sex discrimination but with intent *for* equity and gender parity. The reductive discursive practices surrounding Title IX have been, and continue to be, ones of legal regulation and compliance, normalizing certain responses that shape how survivors understand themselves and their agency in these processes.

Discursive practice, or "language in use," is a semiotics socially constitutive and conditioned, serving as an organizing and framing tool, power-implicit and value laden.[17] This case represents a familiar lexicon: standards, burdens of proof, reporting, due process, evidence, regulations, jurisdictions, adjudication, interim guidance, new rules. These words characterize compliance—and by extension, criminality discourses—in curious overlap of education with regulation and policing, enacting pessimistic orientations to uphold utopian missions for the common good. As the primary tool of campus sexual assault management, Title IX discursive practices impact material bodies and human histories and must be scrutinized for their capacities to shape survivor understandings of their education, worldviews, and themselves.

Compliance frameworks are starkly disconnected from the language and experiences of survivors, whose embodiment discourses describe, organize, and make meaning of their experiences, reflecting emotionality and viscerality along a continuum: rape, pain, fear, shame, hurt, injury, intervention, resistance, healing, and resilience. This divide between the institutions' responses and the victim/survivor agendas is a site of extended trauma and violence. As the case depicts, it is common to see survivors leave their institutions completely. Reliance on compliance discourses and hollow regulatory practices at the expense of transparency and survivor healing are examples of "institutional betrayal," referring to "wrongdoings perpetrated by an institution upon individuals dependent on that institution."[18]

Conversely, "institutional courage," defined as an institution's "commitment to seek the truth and engage in moral action, despite unpleasantness, risk, and short-term cost" calls for bridging this chasm between the victim/survivor orientation and the compliant regulatory institution.[19] In doing so, we invoke evolving discursive vocabulary upholding survivor-centric holistic practices such as: layering prevention efforts; connecting acts of sexual violence to macro systems of oppression; publishing campus-specific climate data and Title IX reporting and adjudication statistics; and maintaining structures of support for survivor healing, and harm grievance and protest, among others. Within this nexus, both freedom *to* and *from* are engaged, as are *personal* and *social* responsibility models, and *social justice* as well as oppression and violence. Prioritizing victim/survivor experiences undertakes moving not just *away from* sexual violence (exclusion, denial, and discrimination), but *to* a language and action of support, access, and positive social transformation.

Lamea "Elle" Shaaban-Magaña, PhD, leads a campus violence counseling and advocacy center. Honoring survivors' healing capacities, she remains mindful of a note left by a student: "I was here, and I survived. I believe that you can too. You are strong. You are resilient. You are beautiful. You are loved."

COMMENTARY

A Safer Campus Environment

JESSICA HARLESS

By focusing primarily on campus processes, standards of evidence, and due process, Rustin's committee finds itself deadlocked in weighing the competing rights involved in adjudicating sexual misconduct. That is, its members engage the issue primarily in terms of the individuals directly involved in cases. But like Taylor, the student representative, I wonder what happens when we look at issues of misconduct with *all* students' experiences in mind. What must the committee do to make "campus a safer, more welcoming space for all students?" I suggest that the committee go beyond the minimums within the federal mandates and consider the broader environment—Rustin's wider community and climate, as well as issues of harassment and hostility—in determining their particular institutional commitments. Even though new federal regulations omit it, Rustin can still elect to prevent hostile environments as part of its priority to "care for all students." There are two good reasons to do so: combatting further misconduct and ensuring effective learning.

ENVIRONMENT MATTERS

As Title IX was interpreted throughout the 1970s and 1980s, definitions of sexual misconduct broadened. The creation of a hostile environment became an equally important clause in the definition of harassment, and hostile environment claims were filed alongside those of assault, stalking, and abuse. The DOE's 2020 rules re-narrow the definition and release colleges from addressing "less severe" harassment, which is admittedly harmful but not actionable.[20] They free institutions from managing their environments and communities.

Yet a study by the National Academy of Sciences found that the top predictor of harassing and predatory behaviors *is* climate, explaining that "potential harassers will act out more in climates they see as permissive."[21] In short, rotten environments breed rotten behavior. If Rustin seeks to fight misconduct more permanently, it must get into the business of dealing with environments. Ultimately it must ensure they are safe—not only laden with physical safety and protection from sexual violence, but also a kind of psychosocial safety that quashes harassing hostility.

Both Taylor and Jennifer, the committee's survivor advocate, raise environmental questions about Rustin's campus community and climate. Jennifer notes that if college processes are seen as difficult and stringent, survivors will be deterred from reporting misconduct. Hers is a concern about how, even in the background, climate will affect the number and quality of incidents addressed. Misconduct will continue, uncited and untreated. Taylor's concern goes beyond formal incidents, to all students in general. It's noted that tensions from long-closed cases still "bubble beneath the perceived calm" across campus. Rustin should address even this type of broad, diffuse environmental concern because, left unchecked, hostility can affect students' learning.

THE LEARNING ENVIRONMENT

Hostile environments take a real educational toll. Retention research shows that hostile, isolating, or distressing environments lower student performance and even drive some students out of college entirely. We know that those experiencing hostility and harassment often self-select out of courses, opportunities, and events to avoid harm.[22] This is true not only for gendered harassment but also for hostility around race, ethnicity, religion, and sexuality. Of course, "safety" in a place sometimes means participants are insulated; they gather with like-minded people, retreat and find respite, and keep challenge or offense at bay. This is an important sense of safety in some social contexts. But as Taylor mentions, total protection ("a bubble") is not appropriate or desirable in educational spaces. These are places where a variety of participants engage with each other and with ideas; they interact, they exchange, and they are challenged. Another sense of safety is at work here, one that offers enough security for all to learn. Challenging and provocative experiences might be educationally productive (even necessary), but there is also a pedagogical need for safety.

Often in educational contexts, safety simply gets framed as a negative sense of safety when instead a positive sense of safety is meant.[23] Participants do not need safety *from* challenge, threats, danger, or discomfort, rather they need enough safety/support *to be able to* make and sustain contact with each other, to engage, and to face challenges. Central to Taylor's plea is a call for safety that generates engagement and real, sustained contact—not protection or coddling. The college has an educational interest in ensuring that enough positive safety, rather than hostility, obtains in its environment.

FOSTERING ENVIRONMENTS

Unfortunately for Rustin, assessing environments is difficult. What is challenging for some students feels hostile to others; what seems safe *enough* for some may make others grossly unsafe. And as is noted in the case, folks do not experience hostility and harassment equally, in either amount or kind, especially students of color, queer students, and other marginalized students. There isn't a common, monolithic experience for all participants in any environment. The committee, the college—no one—can fully, definitively, unilaterally declare a space safe. Besides, environments are always in flux and becoming, never settled. To sustain a learning environment is to constantly create and re-create it, attempt and re-attempt.

Despite this, Rustin College can take steps that target hostility and assert an institutional position against it. President Clark can publicly, repeatedly, state as much and underscore Rustin's priorities of "caring for students" and providing "a safe learning environment." The committee can declare its intention to go beyond the Department of Education's new minimums and aim for further-reaching commitments. While the DOE may not concern itself with "negative outcomes for those who experience" what it calls "less severe" forms of harassment, Rustin can declare its care for these experiences and these students.[24] Updates/revisions to the student code could be suggested in order to establish zero tolerance for harassment or hostility.

Other steps can foster positive safety and offer ways for the campus to practice engagement and sustained contact with each other, which Rustin students have attempted, especially regarding sexual misconduct, race, and power, since 2017. Rustin can sanction programming for students to keep working through the tensions and crises on campus, for voices to be heard, and for perspectives to be shared and tested. Professor Holcomb's efforts to convene students in productive discussion could be widened and provided with increased resources. The committee's role is not to recommend an exhaustive set of campus initiatives, but it can urge continued consideration of the wider environment. Doing so would cement Rustin's commitment to responsibilities beyond mere compliance and its commitment to caring for its students.

Jessica Harless is a PhD student in philosophy of education at the University of Illinois at Urbana-Champaign. Her research interests include higher education, college students, the public sphere, and educational ethics.

COMMENTARY

Feminist Governance, Transformative Peace

TROY A. RICHARDSON

Decisions at institutions of higher education are typically conveyed to faculty, students, and staff through formal letters from relevant administrators. In this commentary, I situate myself as an associate vice provost of feminist governance at the fictional Rustin College and craft such a letter to the Rustin community. In the letter, I aim to convey and clarify the difficult policy decisions presented in the case. I ground the letter in a perspective that is absent in the case itself—the feminist governance principles of Betty Reardon, Fiona Robinson, and Virginia Held—with the goal of reimagining what college leadership would look like if this approach were taken to be central to administering an institution.[25]

Dear Rustin Community,

I am writing to convey how we as an institution will continue to chart our path forward regarding the recent Title IX guidelines issued by the Department of Education (May 2020). Confronting sexual assault or harassment in any of its manifest forms requires unwavering commitments by our entire community.

Yet as administrators, we have responsibility to learn from community dialogue and are answerable for the policies we implement. I am writing to explain the decisions that are being implemented in response to the new Title IX regulations. Following an overview of our policy response, I will revisit in brief our ongoing commitments to implement feminist governance concepts of peacemaking and peacekeeping. The making of peace in feminist governance is not defined simply as the absence of violence, but rather a relationality-focused practice; peace is a continual, foundational practice of relational interdependence.

In partial accordance to the new regulations, we are making public here our investment in a complimentary two-step process led by alternative mediating practices. The new regulations allow us to "offer and facilitate informal resolution options, such as mediation or restorative justice." Thus, we have identified a group of mediators who have committed themselves to working alongside the relevant support services to the extent welcomed by the involved parties. Our mediative process provides appropriate and attenuated college-led inquiries of relevant information to address the nature of the harms and injuries to be attended to. As a matter of policy, we will continue to apply the "preponderance of evidence" standard. We commit to this standard insofar as a harm or series of harms becomes recognizable without necessarily requiring aggressive or invasive revisitations of traumatic events among the parties involved. At the same time, we recognize that successful mediation and restoration of physical, mental, and social peace to those involved requires standards of integrity and ethical commitments throughout these processes. Insofar as one or both parties may feel it necessary to pursue formal, live hearings to adjudicate the circumstances, Rustin College will meet our obligations as outlined by the new regulations. In either live hearing or mediation, the preponderance of evidence will be applied.

Rustin's policy decisions regarding the new regulations emanate from our ongoing commitments to feminist governance, wherein peace, peacemaking, and peacekeeping are guiding concepts and practices. This begins with a recognition of the acts of violence and dispossession that facilitated the creation of Rustin College.[26] Acknowledging Rustin College within the territories of the Indigenous Monacan peoples has symbolic and material importance. We uphold obligations of coexistence between Monacan, settler, and arrivant peoples to interrupt historical and ongoing contexts of paternalistic dispossession of Monacan peoples by the state. We at Rustin must learn the meaning of obligations to peace from within those Indigenous contexts, while also placing them in conversation with critical assessments of democratic traditions through the lens of relationality in feminist governance.

When we acknowledge the character of human sociality as emanating from relational dependencies within a natural/social world, we become attentive to those responsibilities needed for "holding space" for peace. "Relationality," writes Robinson, "is thus a claim about the most basic nature of human social existence. Beyond the claim that humans are 'social beings,' the relational ontology of care ethics claims that relations of interdependence and dependence are a fundamental feature of our existence."[27]

Employing feminist governance, Rustin College understands sexual assault and harassment in any form as an egregious tear in the fabric of interpersonal and social peace. Such aggressive behavior emanates from a patriarchy whose historical weight and continued exercises regularly inhere in the social lives of individuals whether men, women, queer, or straight. Where such assertions of a "power over" deny "relationships with," Rustin College witnesses the challenges for realizing a form of public safety that arises from peacemaking. Yet with Reardon, we think, "Only by directly confronting [patriarchy] and systematically working to replace it with new thinking, restructuring institutions, and more humanly enhancing relationships will we overcome it. To do so, we need a vision of a transformed global order and a framework of action to achieve it."[28]

Our policies must then employ a transformative vision of those moments of profound crises and trauma, situating violence and aggression in wider global contexts of masculinist exercises of power. To commit to peacemaking through mediation is a transformation of the normative meting out of punishment, as the latter reinvests in forms of "power over" and violence. Rustin College agrees with Betty Reardon and Tony Jenkins when they write, "The patriarchal system is not only a source of gender violence and inequality but of many egregious human rights violations, oppressive to both men and women. We would add to that argument that it also constitutes the most fundamental impediment to peace at all levels of the social order."[29]

A restoration of peace to individuals who have suffered forms of objectification through physical or verbal assaults may not always be realized. By actualizing the social, physical, mental, and material support, however, contexts for transformative practice for individual and collective healing and well-being do occur. Making peace requires making the material contexts conducive to such a goal. We conceive our approach in the broad terms of restorative philosophies that emphasize relational care at the center of the interdependencies of sociality. Such shifts can move individuals and society from patterns and practices of domination. For us, these are not gradualist projects, but imminent within the pedagogical relation itself; one of the premises of learning entails an exploration of the conditions for peaceful well-being within and among individuals.

We have briefly revisited here our feminist governance principles of relational interdependencies, peacemaking, and peacekeeping as the transformative philosophical grounding for our formal mediative protocols for Title IX "Final Rule." We believe our decisions to emphasize mediating restorative protocols with qualified staff applying a preponderance of the evidence standard enact these principles. We look forward to sharing more with you on our protocols for active peacemaking to end masculinist aggression—whoever enacts it—as it too often organizes most forms of power over and against women, arrivant, queer, and Indigenous peoples.

—Associate Vice Provost
Office Feminist Governance
Rustin College
tr@rustin.edu

Troy A. Richardson is associate professor of philosophy of education and American Indian and Indigenous studies at Cornell University. He writes and teaches courses on Indigenous peoples and decolonial philosophies, Locke and dispossession, philosophy of education, and Indigenous theory and autonomy.

COMMENTARY

The Promise and Challenge of Restorative Implementation

DESIRÉE ANDERSON

The Rustin case made me think about this question posed by Barbara Hudson: How does one "mov[e] away from punitive reactions which—even when enforced—further brutalize perpetrators, without, by leniency of reaction, giving the impression that sexualized . . . violence is acceptable behaviour?"[30] In trying to answer this question, I find myself responding with restorative justice. Personally, I'd like to see less of live hearings, direct cross-examination, and other adversarial, court-like procedures. On the other hand, I caution that if institutions of higher education are unwilling to truly reform our ideals of community, justice, and accountability, then the benefits of restorative justice will be lost.

A RESTORATIVE FRAMEWORK

Restorative justice is a framework "that embraces the reparation of harm, healing of trauma, reconciliation of interpersonal conflict, reduction of social inequality, and reintegration of people who have been marginalized and outcast for community transgressions"; it gives institutions another option to respond to and repair harm regardless of the standard of evidence set in place.[31] When applying restorative values and principles to the informal resolution process, the competing interests and needs of the community can be addressed. Restorative processes are led by the harmed party, voluntary, hyperfocused on accountability for all harms done, concentrated on safety for all, and centered on system accountability, which benefits the image of the institution.[32] Traditional conduct processes seek to find responsibility for the act of sexual harm, sometimes resulting in passive accountability that leaves the harmed party with questions unanswered and the person who has caused harm feeling alienated and aggrieved.[33] Restorative processes can dig deeper into the emotional, physical, communal, and structural harms and seek to create environments of care and compassion that deter hateful and destructive behaviors via a commitment to the community.

PROCEED WITH CAUTION

Restorative justice has the potential to be a truly powerful form of accountability and is often described in an "unequivocally positive—even idealized—light; as an exclusively benign and unquestionably progressive mechanism for facilitating inclusivity, reparation, resolution and, ultimately, healing and satisfactory closure."[34] I warn, though, that it is only as powerful as the strength of the communities for which it is practiced. I do not want to discourage the use of a restorative lens for sexual harm, but I do want to encourage individuals to consider how the application can, first, vindicate the harms suffered by the complainant and, second, rehabilitate respondents.

While institutions of higher education in the US may be seen as well-defined communities that fit the flexibility that restorative justice offers, they are also situated in contemporary Western culture that is grounded in a liberal individualistic paradigm, which is hierarchical and places a special emphasis on consequences[35]—quite the opposite of the roots of restorative justice. This means that institutions must invest extensively in both building community and realigning the community's ideals of justice. Otherwise, those who are without a community or without the right community may be deemed as undeserving of restorative justice.[36] And those who are disproportionately impacted may not have enough trust in the process, seeing it as too lenient or as an opportunity to let those with the most privilege "get away with it."

STRATEGIES FOR IMPLEMENTATION

First, institutions have to champion the idea that justice does not always mean severe punishment or dismissal. Institutions must engage in a conscious effort to get stakeholder buy-in while championing the notion of active accountability by means of listening, making amends with support, and consensus building. Reconceptualizing justice helps to diminish the idea that restorative processes are too soft or that they mean an absence of consequences. It helps the community understand that, while accountability may look different, obligations are met based on the needs of everyone involved.

Second, during the preparation stage, it is essential that both risk assessment and power imbalances are carefully considered. Restorative processes should be led by the harmed party, but facilitators should consider complainant safety and respondent accountability, as well as the psychological and emotional readiness of both parties to meet, and monitor for power imbalances between the participants.[37] Not every case should go forward using restorative processes, even if everyone says they agree to participate.

Third, and finally, institutions must invest in a whole-campus approach that centers the majority of its restorative processes on community building. An individual might not do the work to return to a community if they do not have one. Others might be unwilling to support and help that person make amends if that person is not a part of their community. Beyond building community for relationships' sake, it can also be used to address "precursor misconduct, such as binge drinking, hazing, or other behaviors that create the conditions in which sexual assault is most likely to occur."[38] Community-building processes should work in tandem with stakeholder buy-in and should engage the campus in getting on one accord about what consequences might look like in a restorative model of justice.

CONCLUSION

Restorative processes, when developed well, provide an ethic of care for not just the complainant but the respondent as well. In well-defined communities, people are more willing to see others as worthy of redemption and healing. More students may be inclined to engage with campus processes if restorative justice is seen as a viable option. Both respondents and harmed parties may find restorative processes beneficial as they allow for everyone to have an equitable voice, their outcome is dependent on the different parties' needs, and accountability can be met without (in some cases) the removal of individuals from the community. Restorative processes can right what are perceived to be the shortcomings of the traditional processes but only if institutions are intentional with their implementation.

Desirée Anderson, PhD, currently serves as associate dean of diversity and student affairs at University of New Orleans. Having worked in higher education for over thirteen years, she has committed her energy to address issues of bias and hate on college and university campuses. She also serves as a restorative justice national team trainer for the Center for Restorative Justice at the University of San Diego.

COMMENTARY

Title IX Compliance and the New "College Court"

PETER LAKE

There is more to legal compliance than navigating competing complainant and respondent interests. As someone who has worked in higher education law and policy for thirty years—professor, practicing lawyer, and former Title IX coordinator—I stress the importance of framing Title IX legal compliance issues. Once a law that mostly focused on college sports equity, Title IX has evolved to be more prominent in the fight to end campus sexual harassment and sexual violence. The 2020 regulations—the first in many years—represent a seismic shift in Title IX enforcement. The Department of Education (DOE) asserted it was merely creating a detailed and fair grievance process; but it established one akin to a court system, albeit a primitive one.

Tamika Wells, as Title IX coordinator, has been provided some "flexibility" by the DOE; but this flexibility places her squarely in the middle of attempting to resolve conflict between competing, perhaps irresolvable, interests on campus. The DOE has framed Title IX compliance around a complainant versus respondent dialectic. It is unclear whether students will actually benefit from the new "college court," or the DOE's way of framing the legal compliance issues under the new regulations.

Federal regulations command a compliance leadership role for Wells. But as a legal *coordinator*—not *manager* or *director*—Wells has the unenviable leadership task of "coordinating" compliance efforts around potentially irresolvable conflict(s). Many of the issues presented in the case admit of only zero-sum outcomes—for instance, complainants or respondents gain or lose advantage depending on the standard of proof. Does Wells have an impossible task in this case?

STUDENTS ARE FRAMING TITLE IX ISSUES EFFECTIVELY—LISTEN TO THEM CAREFULLY

Pondering this case, I was drawn to some of Taylor Saunders's comments. Wells should listen carefully to student voices. Federal regulation under Title IX focuses on *students and others* who have experienced impacts of sex discrimination in educational opportunities. Saunders's comments raise the possibility that Title IX response systems will be *distracted* by focusing on very specific *legal* issues related to the formation and delivery of a college court system. There are *other* ways to improve overall Title IX compliance. Ironing out the details of a college court (standard of proof, cross-examination, advisor roles, etc.) takes enormous time and energy—and leads to unstable legal resolutions that will be perpetually tested by courts and regulators. Campus stakeholders can ask legitimately: Is all this focus on legal issues related to college court working to achieve the ultimate goals of Title IX?

QUESTIONING CREATING A "COLLEGE COURT"

First, most students do not seek highly formal adjudicative processes to deal with sex discrimination. Many students actively seek to avoid such systems—by not reporting at all, by refusing to participate, and by asking for (and even demanding) less formal processes. In many other instances, there is nothing or no one to adjudicate. Students may bring situations forward from their distant past; colleges may have little to no power to punish or even identify a wrongdoer. Students often seek no-contact orders or arrangements, mediation, counseling, trauma-sensitivity in the classroom, contrition, transparency, authenticity, good prevention work, removal of people who present ongoing risk, consequences for bad choices—and, yes, sometimes, formal punishment of wrongdoers. Most of all, students typically desire an educational culture that *promotes* healthy and safe human interaction free from persistent sexual harassment and violence.

Second, there is the risk of creating complex systems of procedural fairness for a handful of very complex and contested matters—with no guarantee of social, or individual, justice. Perfect courtroom justice is an elusive goal. The innocent are still convicted from time to time; the guilty sometimes escape accountability; bias and unfairness of all types are difficult, if not impossible, to root out. Justice may be more likely in a court, but it is hardly inevitable. Crucially, the new regulations are untested; we simply do not know if they will work to reduce or eliminate sex discrimination. There are concerns that the new regulations may be counterproductive to those goals and enhance the risks of sex discrimination.

Third, the fight over college courts will go on indefinitely. When the 2020 Title IX regulations were "finalized," they were met instantly with legal actions challenging their validity. Meanwhile *other, potentially inconsistent,* legal mandates likely will proliferate, including cases from state and federal courts and state legislative requirements. Students like Saunders might see very different versions of a college court—even during their matriculation period at one institution. The new regulations are also confusing and unclear in many ways and speak in a language of legalisms unfamiliar to many students.

So, how should Wells lead her Title IX response system to comply with regulations when a primary group of stakeholders—students—may not view college court as the best solution?

TITLE IX COMPLIANCE IS MORE THAN RUNNING COURT

Wells should coordinate Title IX compliance efforts by emphasizing two key elements. First, the federal Title IX regulatory system is organized into "Four Corners of Compliance" as I have outlined in my scholarship—organization and management; investigation, discipline, and grievance procedures; impacted individual assistance; and campus culture and climate.[39] Second, the mission of Title IX, to reduce or eliminate sex discrimination and redress its effects, depends on more than grievance systems to sanction wrongdoers.

Colleges must have well-trained personnel in place to manage Title IX compliance, must have supportive measures available, and must engage in preventative culture and climate work. Merely providing grievance systems to resolve disputes and sanction wrongdoers is insufficient for federal compliance. The quest for fairness in investigation, discipline, and grievance procedures (one corner of compliance) should not dominate Title IX response efforts to the detriment of other compliance efforts. Ultimately, a well-ordered Title IX response system must rely on science-based prevention efforts, strong culture and climate work, effective supportive measures for complainants and respondents, *and* enforcement mechanisms.

No campus will simply adjudicate its way to a culture free from sex discrimination. The law specifically requires science-based prevention efforts; such efforts also comport with sound education policy. Title IX legal compliance requires broad institutional r*esponse* efforts, in several dimensions, aimed at engineering better educational communities. Campuses also have ethical, accreditation, and business responsibilities to create safe and responsible learning environments; college court is insufficient in itself to meet these expectations.

THE BEST LEGAL COMPLIANCE SOLUTIONS ARE OFTEN NON-LEGAL

Wells faces challenges under these regulations. She can expect that every choice reflected in this case will be met with opposition, in and out of court. Her professional time may be diverted to litigation management and regulatory review. Wells and her team, however, can remind the community that Title IX responses to sex discrimination are multifaceted. The best way to reduce burdens related to running college court is to prevent discrimination that could lead to a grievance; prevention also reduces the likelihood of litigation and regulatory intervention. The best strategies for Title IX legal compliance are non-legal solutions—increased emphasis on science-based prevention efforts and strong culture/climate work.

Peter Lake is professor of law, Charles A. Dana chair, and director of the Center for Excellence in Higher Education Law and Policy at Stetson University College of Law. He also serves as a part-time senior higher education consulting attorney at Steptoe & Johnson PLLC.

CHAPTER 5

Responsibilities to Justice-Involved Students in Higher Education

NICOLE LINDAHL-RUIZ AND REBECCA M. TAYLOR

This case introduces ethical considerations regarding colleges and universities' inclusion and support of students with histories of involvement in the criminal legal system.

Growing awareness of injustices within the United States criminal legal system, from policing to incarceration, is raising questions about the responsibilities of societal institutions to address their roles in perpetuating historical and contemporary inequity. In the realm of higher education, students and faculty at many campuses have advocated for reexamining relationships between colleges and police departments and divesting from contracts that rely on prison labor. Yet one intersection of higher education with the criminal legal system has remained underexamined in mainstream discourse: the inclusion of students with criminal convictions.

Exclusion of individuals with convictions from higher education is a widespread phenomenon that affects many potential students and often goes unquestioned. Examining this issue raises an important ethical question: If colleges and universities understand themselves to hold a specific responsibility to redress their involvement in perpetuating societal inequities, how should they structure policies and practices regarding the inclusion of justice-involved students?[1]

INTERSECTIONS BETWEEN HIGHER EDUCATION AND THE CRIMINAL LEGAL SYSTEM

Understanding the reach of the criminal legal system and its intersections with higher education is a necessary first step in considering the ethical questions that arise regarding the inclusion of justice-involved students. Through decades of "tough on crime" policies that began in the 1970s, incarceration rates and the number of justice-involved people across the country skyrocketed.[2] The US now incarcerates more people than any other country in the world, holding only 5 percent of the world's population but 25 percent of the world's incarcerated population. More than 70 million people in the US have criminal records—roughly the same number that hold a bachelor's degree; among working-age adults, nearly one-third have an arrest or conviction record.[3]

As the number of people with conviction histories has ballooned, their ability to access higher education has been restricted significantly. In 1994, all but a handful of the approximately 350 college programs operating in prisons nationwide shut down after incarcerated people were prohibited from accessing Pell Grants, the primary source of funding for these programs. Barriers to higher education for people with convictions in the community also increased through the imposition of mandatory criminal background checkboxes on college applications and prohibitions on receiving federal student aid for some individuals convicted of drug-related crimes.[4]

These barriers to access are far-reaching. Three independent national studies conducted between 2009 and 2014 found that a majority of private institutions (60 to 80 percent) and public institutions (55 percent) require undergraduate applicants to respond to questions about criminal background in the admissions process.[5] One survey found that over three-quarters of those that collected the information reported using it in the admissions process, and of these, over half have no written policy and offer no training regarding how it should be used.[6] Another study found that applicants who disclosed low-level felony convictions were 2.5 times less likely to be admitted than comparable students without convictions.[7] Moreover, evidence suggests that many prospective justice-involved students are deterred from completing the application process when criminal background questions are asked.[8]

Because of racial and economic bias within the criminal legal system, policies that exclude prospective students on the basis of past convictions can perpetuate existing inequities. Researchers have documented racial bias at every stage of an individual's trajectory through the criminal legal system—from policing to pretrial experiences to sentencing to parole to post-conviction collateral consequences.[9]

These biases exceptionally impact Black people, who are imprisoned at 5.9 times the rate of white people, and are compounded for individuals from low-income backgrounds.[10] Consideration of criminal background information thus can extend existing inequities in access to higher education.

In recent years, efforts to expand access to higher education for justice-involved people have gained some traction. In December 2020, as part of an economic stimulus bill, Pell Grant eligibility was restored for incarcerated people. This legislation builds on a 2015 pilot program launched by the Department of Education under Obama and expanded during the Trump administration, which provided Pell Grants to a limited number of incarcerated students. In the context of admissions, the Ban the Box campaign has called for the removal of questions of criminal background from college applications.[11] And on college campuses, justice-involved students and their advocates have organized student recruitment and retention centers. Despite this momentum, emerging initiatives and programs often lack sustainable sources of funding and are inconsistently available.

ETHICAL CONSIDERATIONS FACING COLLEGES AND UNIVERSITIES

As college and university administrators consider whether and how to expand inclusion, they confront a number of complex ethical considerations. They may believe that concerns about campus safety, the relevance of moral character in admissions, or fairness in allocating resources justify excluding justice-involved students. As they weigh each of these concerns, administrators also face evidence regarding the individual and societal benefits of higher education for justice-involved people, as well as potential harms of exclusion.

Safety

It is widely accepted that colleges and universities must prioritize safe learning environments. Administrators may assume that applicants with conviction histories should not be admitted because they will make campus less safe. Safety concerns are the primary reason many colleges ask for criminal background information in the application process.[12] They are often used to justify automatic exclusion of individuals convicted of violent or sexual offenses (55 percent of state prison populations) and may be used to exclude those convicted of nonviolent drug offenses (14.8 percent) or other non-serious offenses.[13]

In recent years, awareness of the prevalence of campus sexual violence, in particular, has grown, as has acknowledgment of the physical harms to survivors and the psychological challenges they may face continuing to pursue their education on campus. Many colleges have responded with harsher consequences, including expulsion, for students found responsible for sexual misconduct through campus-based investigations. Given the importance of reducing sexual and other forms of violence on campus, it may seem logical for higher education institutions to exclude applicants based on prior convictions, particularly for crimes categorized as violent or sexual.

A 2016 meta-analysis of research on the connection between admitting justice-involved students and campus crime concluded that, while high-quality research is scarce, the existing evidence does not support the effectiveness of exclusion for improving campus safety.[14] Colleges and universities that use criminal background information in the admissions process can compound existing racial inequities through reliance on convictions that stem from a racially biased criminal legal system. They also risk inequitable decisions based on admissions officers' personal biases. Researchers recently tested whether admissions officers would exhibit racial bias in reviewing applicants who reported low-level felony convictions (e.g., burglary).[15] They found that Black applicants disclosing these convictions were more likely to be rejected than their white counterparts at colleges with higher campus crime rates. These findings suggest that admissions decisions may be biased by racial stereotypes linking people of color, and Black men in particular, to criminality and violence.

Finally, the forms of higher education that emerged in carceral settings after cuts to Pell Grant funding have included internet or paper-based distance learning, prison-based classes composed of on-campus and incarcerated students (for which incarcerated students do not receive credit), and a small but growing number of in-prison, degree-granting programs.[16] Prison-based programs provide indispensable opportunities to incarcerated people and may present an option for engaging justice-involved students that avoids campus safety concerns. However, when institutions offer prison-based programs while maintaining exclusionary policies in on-campus programs or offer credit for integrated prison-based courses only to on-campus students, they risk perpetuating segregation and inequitable educational opportunity for incarcerated people.

Administrators thus face a vital question: How, if at all, should concerns about campus safety inform decisions about inclusion of justice-involved students?

Moral Character

College and university administrators may feel a responsibility to consider moral character in the admissions process. Regarding an applicants' worthiness to access educational opportunities—both to learn and to contribute to knowledge production—colleges may assume that moral character is a relevant criterion in admissions and financial aid decisions and that a criminal history is a valid indicator of moral failing. Colleges and universities may also want to weigh character as one means of upholding their missions of fostering ethical learning communities. Some education scholars are advocating for more formal character assessment in admissions processes on these grounds.[17] However, most admissions officers work without clear guidelines. For most applicants, moral character considerations in admissions are not systematic, but are instead weighed as one element of a holistic review of an applicant at the discretion of the reviewer. Justice-involved applicants, in contrast, may face automatic exclusion.

In the context of some professional programs at the undergraduate and graduate level (e.g., teacher preparation, social work, law), admissions officers may also feel an ethical obligation to deny admission to students who may be barred from practicing after graduation due to moral character requirements imposed by professional licensing boards. Legal restrictions in licensing and employment are variable and number in the hundreds in most jurisdictions; they range from requiring background checks to automatically barring participation in certain professions or business practices.[18] While these restrictions are in place, admissions officers may feel it is unethical to admit students who will spend time and money pursuing degrees in fields in which their convictions could prevent them from practicing.

These concerns point to an important question: What are the implications of moral character considerations for the development of policies regarding the inclusion of justice-involved students?

Fairness

In addition to weighing the qualifications of individual applicants, colleges and universities also arguably hold a responsibility to distribute educational opportunities fairly. Administrators may assume that admitting or providing financial aid to a person with past convictions is unfair to other qualified applicants without convictions. The hundred most selective undergraduate institutions accept under a third of their applicants, with the most selective universities accepting no more than 5 percent.[19] For these programs and for competitive graduate programs, admissions officers must determine how to allocate scarce slots.

Concerns about fair allocation of resources arise differently at broad access public institutions like community colleges. Rather than a scarcity of admission slots, these institutions often have limited resources to support the diverse needs of large student populations. Funding a support center for justice-involved students, for example, may mean diverting funding from other student needs, such as those stemming from housing instability, work or childcare responsibilities, or learning differences.

Whether allocating admission slots, financial aid, or campus resources, administrators may face challenges from students, parents, or funders who are concerned that distributing these scarce resources to justice-involved students is unfair to others. How should administrators weigh and respond to concerns about fairness when considering the inclusion and support of justice-involved students?

Serving Students and the Public Good

Colleges and universities arguably bear a responsibility to serve both students and the public (or common) good. In considering this responsibility, administrators can turn to the growing body of research that articulates the benefits of education for justice-involved people, their communities, and US society writ large, as well as the harms of exclusion.

A 2013 meta-analytical study found that individuals who participated in college programs while incarcerated have 51 percent lower odds of committing new crimes or being returned to prison on parole violations.[20] Additional benefits of higher education for justice-involved people include finding meaningful work, achieving economic self-sufficiency, and contributing to their families and communities. When justice-involved individuals access higher education and attain degrees, they often establish careers addressing conditions that lead to crime and violence. These career paths may unfold in drug counseling, reentry, youth mentoring, and community organizing, among other fields in which direct experience with the justice system is increasingly recognized as an asset.[21] Moreover, when justice-involved students pursue academic careers, their scholarship contributes to knowledge formation from marginalized perspectives.

Alongside these individual and societal benefits of inclusion, the potential harms of exclusion extend beyond compounding racial bias to include denial of educational opportunity and its residual impact on individuals and communities. Additionally, the requirement to disclose criminal history may impose a uniquely stigmatizing toll on applicants—extending punishment beyond the legal system as college administrators "readjudicate" the penalties for their past convictions.[22] How, then, should college and university administrators weigh the potential harms of excluding justice-involved students and the broader benefits of inclusion alongside concerns about safety, moral character, and fairness?

As college and university communities grapple with their roles in perpetuating historical and contemporary inequity, they face an essential question: What responsibilities do they hold to serve justice-involved students?

COMMENTARY

Educating to Foster Justice

Vivian D. Nixon

RACE IN THE BOX

There is no limit to the number of ways a college or university can ask an applicant to disclose criminal history: Have you ever been convicted of a crime? Have you ever been convicted of a felony? Have you been convicted of a felony in the last ten years? Have you ever been arrested? Have you ever been incarcerated? If the answer is yes, the next step is anyone's guess, but the application fee will not be refunded.

This case study describes the unprecedented nature of incarceration in the US. More than 70 million people have some type of criminal record, many of these lifetime indictments are attached to people in communities that have endured generations of racialized policing and prosecution. At the same time, efforts to improve conditions and increase programs in prisons recently succeeded in lifting the 1994 ban on Pell Grants for incarcerated students.

A growing number of people with criminal records seek postsecondary degrees to improve their life chances and reduce the stigma of criminalization. Ironically, stigma meets them at the admissions office. Social justice advocates oppose the use of criminal record histories to summarily dismiss applications or unduly influence admissions decisions. Colleges and universities are called to demonstrate integrity, fairness, and active pursuit of justice in admissions policy and practice.

Institutions of higher learning have a responsibility to acknowledge harms done to Black communities as well as the extended damage to all people through militarized policing and hyper-criminalization. These practices leave a trail of criminal records and collateral consequences including discrimination in college admissions.

Lurking behind these issues is the failure of the US and its most prominent institutions to address the structural racism that has morphed into a monstrous criminal legal system. Demands to dismantle unjust criminal legal systems and reckon with all the communities harmed by them are linked to structural racism. Questions about fairness, safety, and the responsibility that higher education institutions have to all applicants who have criminal records must be examined through the lens of ethical responses to racial inequity.

FAIRNESS

If an applicant's qualifications are evident, the institution honors the principle of fairness by making decisions based on the unique merits that the student demonstrates in stages of the application process. But when criminal records serve as an easy and immediate reason to reject one of two equally qualified applicants, the institution places itself in the role of the criminal legal system, which has already extracted the required recompense. In too many cases, criminal records exist because of injustice in the legal system. To expect potential students to display qualities of basic decency is reasonable. But arguments that a criminal record counts as the deciding factor between two equal candidates opposes fairness. A system corrupted by structural racism should not function as empirical evidence of a person's character. Criminal records are, at best, a reflection of an applicant's past actions. Records are not a window into the applicant's present moral character. Alternatively, an applicant who has means, but lacks integrity, can purchase false evidence of academic merit.[23]

SAFETY

Since criminality is often confused with Blackness, "the box" can appease people for the wrong reasons. Asking about convictions on the application reassures tuition-paying parents. It doesn't make campuses safer. Safety on campus is important, but screening applicants for criminal records would not have prevented the ten most horrific campus crimes in modern US history.[24] The ethical objective is to protect people on campus rather than predict who might be a threat. Trained professionals should design, promote, and implement systems that foster a culture of safety on campus and beyond. Practices that work on most campuses are recognizable and common. Safety is often about paying attention to the details of systems that are in place. Institutions should provide visible and consistently located safety teams, access to technology with no dead spots, accurate vehicle registries, threat alert systems, campus-sponsored local transportation, and transparency about incidents.

If institutions of higher education own public safety as their responsibility and then actively promote and create, in partnership with professional safety staff, a safe environment, it is no longer the duty of educators and admissions professionals. They are freed to review criminal history information thoughtfully in the context of applicants' cultural and ethnic diversity, depth and breadth of life experience, and the institution's responsibility to contribute to the making of a just and equitable society.

DISCRIMINATION

We know that acts of discrimination occur at every stage of the criminal conviction process. But discrimination against Black people in American society does not start with the criminal legal system. Scholars across disciplines link four distinct eras that are the fruit of American racism's great progenitor—chattel slavery. From that tree fell decades of discrimination under reconstruction, Jim Crow, deindustrialization, and mass criminalization.[25]

Intentional or not, decisions based on criminal records can function as a surrogate for decisions based on race. New iterations of anti-Blackness now impact all aspiring students who have criminal records. When criminal records are used as a surrogate for race, institutions can control the number of Black admissions while avoiding accusations of race-based discrimination. As our society becomes increasingly diverse, white people will get caught in the throes of anti-Blackness. That may be what we are witnessing in this moment of resistance.

The great orator and abolitionist Frederick Douglass understood knowledge to be his "pathway from slavery to freedom."[26] White power structures of the time also understood education's ability to create advantage. Surrendering privilege does not come easy, so neither abolition nor reconstruction resulted in educational equity for Black people. Instead, the 1896 Supreme Court case *Plessy v. Ferguson* sanctioned school segregation, effectively preserving inequity until 1956. Today, inclusive admissions criteria employed by some public university systems and affirmative action policies—proposals intended to make access a reality for the masses—are under attack. Denying access to higher education based solely on the existence of a criminal record is a discriminatory, scaffolding act of structural racism.

JUSTICE

Institutions of higher education have an essentially common mission to shape good citizens. The power to deny education is a grave responsibility. Criminal history records are saddled with what Khalil Gibran Muhammad has called "the lawlessness of the law itself."[27] Blatant disparity in the execution of law has labeled one-third of Black men in the US as convicted criminals. To say that this is an accurate indicator of insufficient college readiness or moral character only compounds injustice. Institutions of higher learning have a responsibility to counter the cumulative impact of structural racism, a corrupt and enduring system from which many institutions of higher learning have profited. Black people are outrageously overrepresented in the criminal legal system. Such injustice expands the responsibility of institutions of higher learning. Colleges and universities must think beyond simple service delivery to the practice of establishing justice.

Vivian D. Nixon leads College & Community Fellowship, a New York nonprofit creating equity and justice through higher education, antiracism, economic development, and civic engagement for women affected by criminal legal systems (CLS) and their families. Released from the New York CLS, 2004; MFA, Columbia School of the Arts, 2020.

COMMENTARY

The Carceral State of Affairs and Systemic Barriers

Tiffanie Agee

While we often hear that the US incarcerates more people per capita than any other nation; at a rate of 698 per 100,000, the sheer scope of the impact of these numbers can be hard to grasp.[28] The Prison Policy Initiative recently released an extensive report providing context:[29]

- 19 million people have been convicted of a felony; 77 million people have a criminal record of some kind.
- 3.6 million people are on probation, and 840,000 are on parole.
- Black youth represent only 14 percent of the population under eighteen in the US, whereas 35 percent of girls and 42 percent of boys in juvenile facilities are Black.

In data from 2010, incarceration rates per hundred thousand people varied widely across racial/ethnic categories:[30]

- 2,306 Black/African American
- 1,291 American Indian/Alaskan Native
- 1,017 Native Hawaiian/Pacific Islander
- 831 Latinx
- 450 White (not Latinx)
- 115 Asian

Additionally, adults in poverty are three times more likely to be arrested than those who are not, and those earning less than 150 percent of the federal poverty level are fifteen times more likely to be charged with a felony.[31] These numbers show that poverty and race are two of the strongest predictors of incarceration, not criminal activity or behavior. US society envisions itself as one rooted in freedom and equal access for its citizenry; however, millions of Americans live limited lives within the confines of the enduring destructive conceptualization of "criminal" activity.

While interning during my final year of law school, I met an older Black man housed on death row who had been convicted of capital murder. My work partner and I sat rapt and took notes as his story unfolded with keen clarity, but fraught with emotion and pained inflection. Two hours passed quickly, as his story spanned over thirty years in prison. He had gone to jail at seventeen years old and was never released again. Though we sat in an open cafeteria, the air hung stale and unforgiving as we listened to his anguish. Sadly, once we understood more about his case, we realized we could not provide the help he needed and wrote him a letter apologizing that our organization could not accept his case. He responded to us with a letter of his own, thanking us for listening and for allowing him the emotional space to express his frustrations, particularly when he detailed the numerous executions that had taken place since his arrival. He expressed this was the first time since his incarceration someone had taken the time to sit and listen to his side of the story.

Now, as a criminal defense attorney, I represent people convicted of doing bad things, brutal things, things that make you believe in monsters that go bump in the night. And yet, when I sit across from those same people and listen to their stories, I don't feel the way one might assume I would. I am neither afraid for nor concerned about my safety; in fact, I am comfortable, having a normal conversation between two people. Entering the prison itself presents more discomfort. I have personal rules of engagement, each of which maintain that I do not reduce the totality of my clients' humanness to a set of behaviors defined as criminal activity. Often what takes shape through multiple interactions are my clients' personalities and personhood, in the midst of the legal reality that these attorney-client interactions were caused by alleged violations of our laws, breaches of the moral code. Our laws exist as the confluence of regulation, collective moral authority, and sovereignty of self. I find myself often defending my own moral compass when I explain the types of cases I take or the clients I represent because people will make judgments about my character for providing legal counsel to "criminals."

In legal terms, until someone is convicted, they are presumed innocent, but social classifications and linguistic systems often diminish the legal power behind this concept. An adjudication of guilt strips one of this presumption of innocence and triggers both state control of one's physical person and a relinquishment of one's identity. Substantively, the text of state criminal codes defines specific behaviors as criminal, assigns punishment or sentences for these behaviors, and classifies people based on the type of crime committed. Instead of limiting the punitive impact of committing a crime to a sentence, these legally established categories serve as instruments of resource management and control of autonomy.

State-sanctioned custodial control of one's autonomy pervades the lived Black American experience. Though we are decades beyond Jim Crow laws, scores of people remain entangled in a punitive state simply because of artificially constructed labels such as *criminal* or *felon*. Once classified with either label, two truths emerge regarding one's identity: that person at some point deviated from the collective moral compass, and society has a vested possessory interest in the resources consumed by that person as a result of this violation. At its core, these identifiers categorically create a sociocultural paradigm that collectively functions as a mechanism of resource control that manifests the fallacy of our own moral distinction and superiority.

CLASSIFYING IDENTITY FOR USE IN ADMISSIONS PROCESSES

By denying access to those with past encounters with the criminal justice system, colleges and universities, whether inadvertently or deliberately, extend punishment beyond state-sanctioned sentencing by using classifications that unjustifiably reduce these applicants' humanity and autonomy. Requesting an applicant's criminal history insufficiently addresses these issues if the person reviewing the application lacks personal proximity to the justice system. To directly address the inequity experienced by this vulnerable population, institutions of higher education must embrace that: (1) the current system perpetuates punitive measures rooted in self-appointed moral sovereignty, and (2) inclusivity requires a boundless definition of humanity. There must be a willingness to define one's own morality without the dehumanizing othering of someone who may have committed a crime.

If the gentleman I met in that prison cafeteria applied for admission to college, would the substance of his story matter? Or does a murder conviction render him ineligible for admission? Answering these questions necessitates asking ourselves what mechanisms empower us to gauge another's moral compass. Simply relying on a criminal conviction to define this elevated moral position presupposes, at minimum, an innate infallibility of the justice system and the validity of the facts established by the conviction itself. These presuppositions create immovable barriers for potential students under control of the justice system.

When one loses the right to autonomy because of externally created categories defining the breadth of their morality, which then becomes their identity, inclusivity requires removing questions of morality from the equation. The starting point of one's eligibility for access to educational resources must begin within the unquestioned absolute—one's innate and unalienable humanity.

Tiffanie Agee, a local of Birmingham, Alabama, graduated from Texas A&M University and then earned both her JD and LLM in Business Transactions from the University of Alabama School of Law. She interned at both the Southern Poverty Law Center and the Equal Justice Initiative. Since beginning her legal career in 2015, her cases have ranged from complex criminal matters to civil disputes. She has won the release of clients with overturned convictions and is one of few attorneys in Alabama who accepts appointments to capital murder appeals.

COMMENTARY

Complexities and Constraints for Public Four-Year Universities

ASHLEY FLOYD KUNTZ

College admissions are ethically fraught in the US. The majority of our postsecondary system is not open access, nor is it provided free on demand to students. Many students will be turned away from one or more institutions for any number of reasons—lower grades, standardized test scores, lack of extracurriculars, problematic recommendations, or other criteria that are subject to bias and often say more about inequities and systemic disadvantage in our society than they do about a student's preparedness for college or capacity to succeed.

Every admissions decision—from which high schools to visit, to which admission criteria to prioritize, to who receives the best scholarship and financial aid packages—is imperfect and exclusionary. Universities have limited resources, and many rely on predictive analytics to govern distribution of the resources they do have. Prospective students often operate unaware of the ways they are sorted and analyzed by score bands and high school rigor, subjected to "gapping" in financial aid offers, or given preference based on whether they live in emerging or established markets. Given the known social benefits of a college education, we should give serious ethical consideration to admission practices and make them fairer, where we can, for all students, including formerly incarcerated individuals.

ETHICS IN CONTEXT

However, any adjustments to admission policies and practices will be made in highly complex contexts with existing constraints. While the case provides context for understanding these decisions in relation to the US legal system, it is largely silent on the institutional contexts that will shape admission policies. Here, I focus on a single context—public four-year universities—for these reasons: (1) they serve the vast majority of students, (2) they are accountable to the public both in a general sense and in the special sense of state legislatures, and (3) they generally operate within multi-institutional systems of higher education. Additionally, excluding the fewer than thirty "public ivies" with large endowments and ample prestige, most public universities exist in competitive markets under increasing political pressure and/or with strained budgets.

Public universities generally will not have sufficient space or resources to admit everyone who applies, and many will receive tens of thousands of applications. Thus, enrollment policies and practices are developed with efficiency and transparency in mind—most commonly, GPA and test scores are used to streamline admission decisions. These universities may also operate within the context of systemwide policies or legislative constraints meant to ensure that students from every high school are offered admission (e.g., Texas HB 588 "Top 10%"; Florida's "Talented Twenty"). Finally, they may be subject to statewide articulation agreements with community colleges.

PUBLIC DECISION MAKERS

This case raises a number of interesting ethical questions directed at "college and university administrators" or "admissions officers." However, for public universities, the reality is much more complex. There are no single deciders, either within the campus or outside of it. Assume a senior enrollment leader wanted to remove "the box" from the admission application. Doing so would require approval from the president's cabinet. Deans would likely weigh in, especially those leading professional schools with licensure limitations related to prior convictions. Even with internal consensus, this decision would be subject to board approval—from the university's board, a systemwide board governing multiple campuses, and/or a statewide superordinate board. Notably, some universities wield less power in systems and are more sensitive to legislative overreach, so the outcome of such efforts may differ based on who does the asking.

Thus, I worry the questions raised in this case assume that any single enrollment official, university, or board has much greater power than actually exists. The majority of public universities likely will not be in the position to unilaterally change course on an admission policy, much less one as politically contentious as increasing access for justice-involved students.[32]

ASKING CONTEXTUALLY GROUNDED QUESTIONS

With this in mind, I want to offer a set of supplemental ethical questions related to admission for justice-involved students, ones that I think are especially salient to public universities.

If the state legislature or governing board requires public universities to ask about prior felony convictions, how can enrollment leaders ensure that such information is reviewed as fairly as possible? Who should have access to that information and at what point in the admissions process should they have it? The Department of Education's *Beyond the Box* report offers some helpful recommendations.[33]

What opportunities exist for universities to expand access to incarcerated individuals? How might public universities be uniquely equipped to work with state boards and legislatures to provide educational programs for students now that the federal Pell Grant ban has been lifted?

Whether or not students are asked to report prior convictions, gaps in their educational background will likely be noticed (and often interpreted as negative) during the admissions process. At more selective universities, how can enrollment leaders train staff to read these gaps for all students and understand what they say and do not say about applicants?

Finally, how can university leaders respond to public concerns for campus safety? As the case notes, there have been no more than a handful of empirical studies assessing links between admitting students with convictions and campus safety. So little data is unlikely to convince concerned students, especially those more likely to be victims of crime. For example, given that 26 percent of undergraduate women are subjected to rape or sexual assault, prospective students may reasonably ask whether the university considers prior convictions for these crimes.[34] Additionally, in light of growing numbers of hate crimes, Black, Jewish, and LGBTQ students, who are more likely to be targeted, may reasonably ask their public universities what can be done to make campus as safe as possible.[35] Asking about prior convictions may not be the answer. However, telling students to set aside their concerns because there is no evidence that they will be less safe also isn't the answer, especially when there is so little evidence at all.

ACCOUNTABILITY AND ACTION

No single policy shift (including removing the box) will fully address the need to expand educational opportunities to justice-involved students or any other population more likely to experience marginalization in college admissions. University administrators may have little, if any, power to override state or systemwide policies. They can, however, create internal practices that demonstrate greater respect for the inherent dignity of all applicants, and they can respond to public concerns surrounding access, fairness, and safety with that same level of respect.

Part of this work requires a fundamental shift in the types of students we imagine as worthy of recruiting and retaining. Too often, universities design admission processes for a normalized default—a high school senior seeking immediate entry into college. Applicants falling outside of this norm are commonly designated as "other" or "nontraditional" and may be eligible for fewer institutional scholarships. Justice-involved students are susceptible, as are people who spent time working, parenting, caretaking, or addressing psychological or physical health challenges. University leaders may be unable to shift system- or state-level policies, but they can ground their enrollment practices—from recruitment materials to application requirements to new student orientations—in a different mindset, one that values a diversity of lived experiences and actively welcomes and includes all students.

Ashley Floyd Kuntz is a clinical assistant professor of higher education at Florida International University. She began as an admission and financial aid counselor and has served in a variety of administrative roles at both private and public universities.

COMMENTARY

Punishment as Exclusion from Higher Education

Shaeeda Mensah

This case asks: "If colleges and universities understand themselves to hold a specific responsibility to redress their involvement in perpetuating societal inequities, how should they structure policies and practices regarding the inclusion of justice-involved students?" The very need to pose a question of this sort highlights the reality of the *collateral consequences* of mass incarceration—the broad set of legalized forms of discrimination to which an individual can be subjected upon being convicted of an offense.[36] These include, but are not limited to, the denial of voting rights, access to social welfare services, and access to institutions of higher education. Thus, individuals are subject to continual processes of discrimination and alienation, even after completing the terms of their punishment. This case foregrounds the fact that punishment, for many people in the US, is indefinite. Institutions of higher education that reject applicants on the basis of prior convictions perpetuate this indefinite nature of punishment.

In exploring ethical implications of policies that allow for discrimination against individuals with criminal records in college admissions, the authors note that administrators are often tasked with building and maintaining ethical and safe learning communities. Accordingly, administrators sometimes see the exclusion of individuals with prior convictions as aligning with their task to uphold safety and morality. At the crux of this line of reasoning is one of the assumptions highlighted in the case—that a relationship exists between past convictions and flaws in moral character.

Using conviction records as an indicator of moral character in admissions rests on two related assumptions: (1) that a person who has a conviction has done something wrong and is of flawed moral character, and (2) that a person without any convictions is innocent of wrongdoing, and thus lacks such flaws. Yet the realities of the criminal justice system highlight the faults in this line of reasoning.

RACISM, CONVICTIONS, AND WRONGDOING

Studies of policing and arrest practices highlight the fact that Black people are disproportionately targeted by police. One way that this emerges is in police officers stopping, frisking, and sometimes arresting Black subjects for actions that would often go unaddressed when committed by a white person. Actions like standing in a group are seen as suspicious when committed by Black youth, for example, but not when done by white youth.[37] Similarly, the popular phrase "driving while Black" references the assumption that being Black and driving a nice car is often treated as a punishable offense. What results is that Black subjects are punished more harshly than whites for similar or identical actions. Once stopped by a police officer, a Black person is likely to be arrested for any attempt at questioning the officer's intentions or failure to comply with any aspect of the officer's demands. This difference means that Black subjects are more likely to find themselves directly subject to formal criminal justice policies than white people.

In addition to being disproportionately subject to interactions with the police, Black people fare worse if subjected to a jury trial. Each person accused of a crime has an option to be tried by a jury of their peers, but who counts as a peer is ambiguous. When faced with the reality that a jury may be predominantly white and the dominant association of Blackness with criminality, Black defendants are forced to reckon with the reality that they would fare better if they pled guilty and accepted a plea bargain, even if innocent.[38] Consequently, Black defendants will have higher rates of criminal convictions, even when innocent. Accordingly, they will disproportionality risk denial of admission from colleges that use convictions as an indicator of moral character.

I have been intentional about discussing Black individuals in general, and not Black men or boys in particular. Though less attention has been paid to the experiences of Black women when compared to those of white women, it becomes clear that they also face high levels of discrimination in the criminal justice system. For example, when convicted of offenses, white women are often cast as victims, and their victimization shapes the understanding of their criminal activities.[39] Black women, on the other hand, when accused of crimes, are not seen as victims and are likely to be cast as aggressive, violent, and "real" criminals.[40] Colleges and universities must attend to these intersections of race and gender as they determine ethical admissions policies.

CLEAN RECORDS AND INNOCENCE

Coupled with the hyper-punishment of Black subjects is the tendency to underpunish or fail to punish white individuals for their criminal offenses. In a class that I taught on racism and the criminal justice system, several white students disclosed that they had committed criminal offenses but were not charged because of law officials' willingness to acknowledge the impact a conviction would have on their future. In fact, a 2014 hashtag #crimingwhilewhite resulted in more than 300,000 white people publicly recounting times they committed crimes but were not punished for their actions.[41] College campuses are likely already filled with individuals who have committed criminal offenses. However, since they have not been formally punished, their criminal acts are not used as a basis for making decisions about their moral character and their morality is not called into question as college administrators make decisions about their applications. Thus, criminal records offer a valid indicator of neither actual past criminal activity nor moral character. These records cannot justifiably be used in making decisions about college admissions.

While it is undeniable that institutions of higher education have obligations to their learning communities, there is no clear link between upholding this obligation and denying entry to individuals with former convictions. The practice of denying students admission on the basis of criminal convictions stands to disproportionately affect Black students. Additionally, and more generally, the practice perpetuates the indefinite nature of punishment. Given the research on education and reductions in recidivism, institutions that are committed to the formation of a more just world might actively recruit students with past convictions.[42] This is especially pressing, given the continuous decline in education programs offered in prisons. Doing so would benefit those students as well as our communities and would reduce injustice. Additionally, institutions of higher education would do well to offer re-entry programs and/or classes to ensure that students with former convictions have the support to thrive not only as students, but as well-supported and resourced individuals.

Shaeeda Mensah is a visiting assistant professor of philosophy at Franklin & Marshall College. Her areas of specialization are social and political philosophy, philosophy of race, and feminist philosophy. Her research considers the social, political, and epistemological implications of the marginalization of Black women's experiences in analyses of state violence.

COMMENTARY

Whiteness, Temporal Arbitrarity, and Academic Justice

Nassim Noroozi

In this commentary, I will examine temporal arbitrarity as a manifestation of whiteness in our theorizing of the world and its relation to the notion of justice in academia.[43] I define *temporal arbitrarity* as a willful identification of two pasts for others and a discretionary accounting of one of them as tangential and the other as central. In academia, this selection is done by a person/group with the authority or wherewithal to determine others' pasts as tangential or cardinal. As a result, this arbitrary selection of different pasts determines these others' presents.

Temporal arbitrarity as whiteness is not an anthropological observation. It is rather a concern and an inquiry about (1) whether its presence in our everyday theorizing has a substantial role in maintaining the systemicity of injustice, (2) whether we are responsible to tackle this arbitrariness when thinking about manifold aspects of struggle, and (3) whether lack of vigilance about it can entail far-reaching consequences. I explore the implications of attending to temporal arbitrarity for academia through a series of examples.

EXHIBIT ONE: CRIMINAL PAST AS DECISIVE

When he was seventeen, Nathan Formann, an African American teenager, committed an armed robbery during which someone died. He was sentenced to a lengthy prison term. While in prison, he earned bachelor's and master's degrees. Formann's intense interest in his field—forensic anthropology—culminated in publishing two articles in prestigious

> journals. Formann applied for and was accepted into a PhD program at an Ivy League school. However, his admission was rescinded because of his record of incarceration; when questioned on the matter, the board mentioned that Formann's presence could potentially upset wealthy donors or parents.

In the fictional example above, a decision-making body in an elite, primarily white institution deemed Formann's *criminal past* as decisive and his *scholarly past* as tangential. Here, the lens of temporal arbitrarity reveals how authorities identify two pasts: a scholarly one according to which Formann was initially granted admission, and a criminal past for which he had already served his time and yet according to which his admission was rescinded. With this decision, academia becomes an additional tribunal for a (formerly incarcerated) published scholar rather than a site where he can continue the trajectory of his scholarly past.

EXHIBIT TWO: SCHOLARLY PAST AS DECISIVE

> "When I read Heidegger's books, I 'knew'—but didn't particularly care—that he had been a Nazi . . . though his ideas felt vivid and present, his biography belonged to the past . . . It's always been safe to assume that Heidegger, being a Nazi, was also an anti-Semite (though not necessarily a 'virulent' one, whatever that term might mean)."[44]

As exemplified in this quote from Joshua Rothman, temporal arbitrarity is also evident in the—often hidden—logic of inclusion and presence of certain philosophers in academia, namely those with criminal pasts. In contrast to Formann's example, Martin Heidegger's scholarly past tends to be identified as central. His inclusion as a classical thinker of the Western canon implies that his criminal past—one that has been contaminated by Nazism—is assumed as tangential. What has remained central is Heidegger's scholarly past as a philosopher of *Being and Time*.

Here, when decision-makers engage in temporal arbitrarity, it does not lead to the exclusion of Heidegger from academia, nor from the horizon of intellectual thought. Instead, it leads to attempts to justify the unconditional inclusion of white scholars in academia. Rothman writes that philosopher Babette Babich framed these decisions about Heidegger as follows: "Philosophy professors . . . had to defend the thinkers that mattered, even if they had said or done terrible things, because it was so easy for a thinker to disappear from the intellectual landscape. . . . 'Heidegger's not taught very often as it is.'"[45] Rothman's translation of Babich's plea is, "Don't throw the baby out with the bathwater."[46] As such, it highlights temporal arbitrarity in her reasoning regarding Heidegger—a philosopher with an intellectual-past-as-cardinal.

Louis Althusser's inclusion in the Marxist theoretical sphere reveals a similar trend, as his criminal past of having murdered his wife has not led to his academic exclusion. For Althusser, temporal arbitrarity functions not only to prevent erasure, but also to situate the tangential past as an issue of professional intellectual interest, thus leading to more scholarly work.[47] Among Marxist scholars, questions about whether they should continue to employ Althusser's philosophical ideas in light of this offense are often followed promptly by suggestions of closer examination of Althusser's case and not his dismissal. As William S. Lewis muses, "How should this fact [of him having killed his wife] effect the reception of Althusser's work, and how should those who find Althusser's reconceptualization of Marx and Marxism usefully respond? . . . It is more than appropriate to think about the relation of his biography to his ideas and to the history of their reception."[48] This invitation from Lewis for a nuanced look, as opposed to exclusion, highlights an implicit acceptance of his criminal past as tangential and his scholarly past as central: "For those of us who find Althusser's rethinking of Marxism of theoretical or practical relevance, a pressing moral and political question is, therefore, *how* can we continue to think with Althusser [emphasis added]."[49]

TEMPORAL ARBITRARITY AS WHITENESS IN ACADEMIA

The implications of temporal arbitrarity diverge in the examples of Formann, Heidegger, and Althusser. While the latter two have the possibility to outlive their perceived *tangential* criminal pasts without having served time, the former faces an impossibility of outliving it, since it is deemed cardinal. Thus, temporal arbitrarity de/legitimates presences and accesses and directs the trajectory of personhood to different paths for different ethnicities. Temporal arbitrarity as whiteness thus reinforces existing systemic inequities.

This manifestation of temporal arbitrarity as whiteness in academia reverberates the temporal arbitrarity embedded in the logic of colonial education manifested in the history of Indian Residential Schools. That logic presumed the present state of one ethnic group (e.g., the British) as the ideal future for the present state of another ethnic group (e.g., the Native Americans), because the latter's present states were identified as *savage* or as belonging to the primitive times of humanity.

One wonders whether the two have a common denominator: the persistence of a "misanthropic doubt" (a form of questioning the very humanity of Non-white people) in their identifications of presents/pasts as central, tangential, savage, or ideal.[50] One also wonders whether systemic oppression feeds off of the aforementioned persistence, and continues to contribute to the impossibility of outliving the legacies of temporal arbitrarity as whiteness—hence the necessity of thinking about temporal arbitrarity as a weighty issue of justice in academia.

Nassim Noroozi is a visiting lecturer at Concordia University's Faculty of Arts and Sciences. She is trained in philosophy of education. Her research focuses on ethics of resistance in today's colonial context. Her work specifically examines the relationship between the phenomena of time, colonization, and resistances against it.

COMMENTARY

College Admissions in the Carceral State

ERIN L. CASTRO AND CAISA ELIZABETH ROYER

The physical prison is perhaps the most well-known aspect of punishment culture in the US. The image of vertical bars springs to mind for most people at the mere mention of punishment, but the prison itself represents just a fraction of the massive carceral state, a concept largely absent from the social imagination. The carceral state is the collection of attitudes, behaviors, structures, and systems that prioritize discipline and death. The inclusion of requisite disclosure and use of prior legal punishment (or criminal) histories in college admissions is a manifestation of the carceral state.[51] Indeed, the same carceral logics that make it rational to prevent individuals with criminal records from accessing public welfare benefits, voting, or gaining employment are exactly those that make it reasonable to discriminate against individuals in the college admissions process.

Now, many readers may be thinking, "Okay, but asking someone about previous criminal activity during the admissions process is not discrimination. Crime is a threat to everyone's safety, especially on college campuses." However, colleges and universities are not making evidence-based decisions about crime or the threat of crime when requiring applicants to disclose prior legal or criminal histories during admissions. Reliable and consistent longitudinal data make at least one thing clear: screening applicants for criminal history does not make campuses safer.[52] The reliance on screening for prior criminal history during admissions, then, only extends a barrier that excludes already marginalized and underrepresented populations from pursuing higher education.

SCREENING FOR DISADVANTAGE

When institutions of higher education require disclosure of prior criminal history during admissions, they ask a range of different questions. Some ask specifically about prior *convictions*, whereas others ask questions about whether an applicant was *arrested* or *charged* with a crime, and others include broad questions that include academic disciplinary charges. The framing of these questions can broaden or narrow the scope of scrutiny, which shifts the breadth of impact of carceral logics. Nevertheless, none of these questions accurately or appropriately assesses risk to institutions of higher education, and all are inherently built on information created by systems that disproportionately affect people based on their race, ethnicity, gender, and class. US prisons are filled with people who were born into the grip of poverty, a violence that is wholly unequal.[53]

Incarceration, punishment, and criminalization have become the answer to an array of social challenges in the US, replacing what should be a strong and reliable network of resources and supports for communal welfare. Instead, the latest data indicate that race and class strongly correlate with involvement with the legal system and lifetime likelihood of imprisonment. Individuals born into marginalization are at the most risk of incarceration, including those with mental health challenges, histories of substance misuse, and trauma—all experiences mediated by race and class. More than a third of incarcerated people in prisons (37 percent) and almost half of incarcerated people in jails (44 percent) had at one time in their lives been told by a mental health professional that they had a serious mental health disorder, including major depressive disorder, bipolar disorder, post-traumatic stress disorder, personality disorder, schizophrenia, and related psychotic disorders.[54] The toll of systemic racism on the health and well-being of Black people is staggering, with ample evidence demonstrating a link between trauma exposure and increased likelihood of arrest and incarceration for Black adults.[55] This means that members of Black communities who have been subjected to trauma have a greater chance of being incarcerated as adults.

In fact, disproportionate impacts based on race and ethnicity are built into every stage of the US criminal punishment system. The police are more likely to instigate an investigatory stop against and arrest Black individuals than white individuals.[56] Prosecutors are more likely to charge

People of Color—overwhelmingly Black and Latinx—with crimes, and those charges tend to be more aggravated.[57] If convicted, Black defendants and defendants of Color are more likely than white peers convicted of similar offenses to receive harsher sentences.[58] For example, Black youth are more likely to be charged and convicted as adults, which means it is less likely that their criminal records will be sealed and more likely those records will appear on a criminal background check compared with white juvenile defendants.[59] The racist nature of the criminal punishment system makes it far more likely that a Black or Latinx applicant to a college or university will have something to disclose in response to a question about their prior criminal history and thus that they will be exposed to additional review or rejection by the institution of higher education.

FAIRNESS IN THE CONTEXT OF CARCERALITY

The carceral state criminalizes existence, especially for those living in poverty. Rather than exclude individuals trapped in the punishment system, colleges and universities must resist the contours of the carceral state by proactively and meaningfully recruiting individuals directly impacted by these systems. Because of the inherent racist and classist dimensions of carcerality, the work of equity and diversity on college campuses must include space for people who have been stigmatized with legal records. The uninterrogated collection of information from these records during the admissions process is an endorsement of the carceral state and only further exacerbates inequity. Attending to the notion of fairness demands that colleges and universities stop using legal histories in the admission process.

Erin L. Castro, PhD, is an associate professor of higher education and codirector/founder of the University of Utah Prison Education Project. She directs the Research Collaborative on Higher Education in Prison.

Caisa Elizabeth Royer, JD, PhD, is a postdoctoral research fellow with the Research Collaborative on Higher Education in Prison. Her research focuses on how social perceptions affect decision-making in legal contexts.

CHAPTER 6

Free Tuition for All

Weighing the Promises and Pitfalls

REBECCA M. TAYLOR AND JOY MOSLEY

In this case, the student representative to the board of trustees of a public higher education system weighs whether to support or oppose new state-level legislation that would create a free tuition program.

Over the past few years, the idea of a statewide tuition-free college program available to all residents had gone from a pipe dream advocated by only a few to a real possibility with bipartisan support in the state legislature and broad public appeal.[1] Gabriela Diaz had recently been elected governor. A long-time state representative known for working across the aisle to support the state's working people, she had campaigned on an education and economic opportunity platform. Central to her campaign was a call to provide free access to the state's public colleges and universities.

On the campaign trail, Diaz regularly drew large crowds. Whether talking to residents of the state's rural agricultural communities or its urban centers, she often shared her personal story of growing up with hardworking Puerto Rican parents, aunts, and uncles who struggled to make ends meet, of believing in the promise of a college education to help her and her family gain stability, and of taking out student loans to fund her education—loans she was still repaying. Connecting her own experiences to those of students and families across the state, Diaz would close her speeches with the rallying call, "Every person in this state who wants to pursue an education and improve themselves, their families, and their communities should have that chance and shouldn't have to go into debilitating debt to do it! It's time to make education work for all of us!"

This message resonated with voters. Across the state, 60 percent of college students were graduating with student loan debt, with an average debt burden of $28,000. Loan default rates had increased steadily in the last decade as many struggled to find stable, well-paying jobs. Students and their families were becoming increasingly wary of the risk of taking on debt to go to college, unsure of whether it would pay off in the long run. This wariness was felt by both public and private colleges and universities in the state. Enrollments in state universities had been decreasing in recent years, contributing to generalized concern about the future of higher education. Recognition was growing that bold changes were needed to make college more accessible and to protect the future of higher education.

When Governor Diaz took office, she told state legislators that if they could agree on a free college tuition program and get it to her desk, she would sign it. Free tuition bills had been introduced in the State House of Representatives previously, but they had never garnered enough traction to move forward to a vote. When the new legislative session opened, the atmosphere felt different. Many members had been hearing their constituents' excitement about the governor's platform, and they arrived motivated to get a bill through the House and over to the State Senate. Not only was the idea of free college popular, but many representatives shared a belief that more students attending and graduating from college would benefit the state civically and economically.

Sam Chu, an MBA student at the state's flagship research university, was eager to see the legislature make progress. They had recently been appointed by Governor Diaz as the student representative on the board of trustees, the fifteen-member governing body for the state's public colleges and universities. Sam was excited to serve on the board, especially at a time when so much attention was being given to access and affordability. They had seen friends decide against attending college because of the costs. Although sharing these concerns, Sam knew college graduates earned higher wages and were less likely to be unemployed; they thus decided that taking out loans was worth the risk.[2] Having worked for a few years at an urban development organization, they also saw the way college affordability impacted economic decisions. Sam had met many people who were still renting apartments rather than investing in a home because they lacked savings for a down payment and worried that the rising costs of college were impacting long-term financial health for their generation and for the state as a whole.

At a board meeting, Sam learned from one of the other members that a small bipartisan group of state representatives had begun drafting a bill to bring to the House floor. The legislators started by reviewing evidence from the free tuition program enacted in Tennessee in 2014. Tennessee Promise, which quickly gained widespread public support, allows all resident students to attend one of the state's public community or technical colleges tuition-free for up to two years. The tuition support comes in the form of a last-dollar scholarship, which covers students' costs after they have exhausted all aid available from other sources (e.g., Pell Grants, other scholarship programs). In 2015, one year after the program launched, Tennessee saw a 25 percent increase in the number of first-time students enrolling at its two-year colleges and a 9 percent increase in the number of low-income students attending college.[3]

Considering the successes of this program and others, including the Excelsior Scholarship program in New York, the bipartisan group drafted a bill to create a new College Promise Scholarship program.[4] The program would similarly provide last-dollar tuition support to students after they had already taken advantage of other existing scholarship and grant programs. However, rather than limiting the program to public two-year colleges, the new program would allow students to use the scholarship at public four-year colleges or universities as well. It would be open to all students who met state residency requirements and wouldn't have any merit-based eligibility criteria. Each student would be eligible for up to four years of funding, and scholarship recipients would be required to live and work in the state for a year after completing their studies.

The bill's authors hoped that this approach would match the demands they were hearing from their constituents while retaining the economic benefits of the program within the state. By including both two- and four-year institutions, they hoped to attract more students and boost enrollments across all of the state's public institutions. Once the authors introduced the bill in the State House of Representatives, its text became public. As attention to the bill grew, concerns about the details emerged. Sam followed the response to the bill carefully.

One concern voiced early and often was how the state would pay for the program. The bill included the creation of an endowment, the interest from which would be used to fund the scholarships. The endowment fund would be built with a portion of proceeds from the state lottery, which had been used to help fund education for over twenty-five years. Up to this point, a third of the lottery proceeds had gone to education, with the rest going to prizes, operations, and marketing for the lottery. Education funds had been divided between a higher education scholarship program for students who met an academic threshold in high school and various forms of support for K–12 education, such as salary increases for teachers. If the new bill passed, the previous merit-based scholarship program would be phased out and the higher education portion of the lottery proceeds would be redirected to the College Promise Scholarship endowment.

The state comptroller's office issued a report identifying concerns about whether the endowment plan would be adequate. Fiscal conservatives were alarmed and raised further questions: What if the program's popularity grew more quickly than anticipated? Or what if an economic slump led to a reduction in lottery participation and decrease in interest generated from the endowment? As the plans for paying for the newly proposed program began to generate debate, Allies for Economic Justice (an advocacy group actively involved in state politics) challenged the reliance on the lottery in the first place. Long critical of the lottery as a regressive tax on the state's poorest residents, they argued instead for a new wealth tax that would shift the burden of paying for the program from the state's lowest-income residents to its wealthiest.

Sam watched as more people came forward to voice their concerns. Advocates for low-income students challenged the proposed structure of the program. Some pointed to evidence that Tennessee's program primarily supports high-income students and fails to address affordability barriers for lower-income students.[5] They asked how this program would be different. Would it benefit students with the most need, including the 15 percent of residents and 21 percent of children living below the federal poverty line in the state?

Education Tomorrow, an education policy think tank, released a projection that students in the top half of the income distribution would receive a greater share of the program's benefits than students in the bottom half. They argued that, rather than improving access for the students with the most need, the proposed College Promise Scholarship program would actually limit the availability of resources to support the students who most needed assistance. They proposed an alternative—a first-dollar program that included living expenses and had a firm income threshold.

Others defended the current structure, countering that it was the best way to expand access for all students and boost enrollments. They argued that a first-dollar scholarship would have less impact overall because other funds available to support the lowest-income students would be left unused. They hoped that a universal program would also shift public opinion about college and result in more people seeing a college education as within their reach, including first-generation college students and those from low-income backgrounds. Moreover, they argued that increased enrollments at the state's struggling colleges and universities were much needed and any amendments that would limit enrollments were counterproductive.

An undocumented student advocacy group, Free to Learn, joined the debate by publishing an op-ed in the *Capitol Times*. The piece supported the new program but called for a guarantee that undocumented students, a growing group that already represented four percent of state residents, would be eligible for the Promise Scholarship.

A few days later, the *Capitol Times* published a joint letter from the presidents of some of the state's small private colleges, including the leaders of several historically Black colleges. Both public and private higher education institutions had seen decreasing enrollment numbers, and the hardest-hit institutions had been small private liberal arts colleges. HBCs had been particularly hard-hit, as financial struggles caused by general enrollment declines were compounded by the racial wealth gap, which impacted their endowments and donations from alumni. In the last few years, several had closed permanently. The presidents together supported the bill's aim of making college more accessible for students across the state and called on the legislature to amend the bill to allow students to use the scholarship funds to attend private institutions as well.

A week later, several letters to the editor challenged the joint letter, expressing concern that including all private institutions would unjustly funnel funds that should go to support the public system to instead benefit elite private schools. Reading these letters, Sam was conflicted about how to weigh the seemingly competing interests of various groups of students in the public system, which Sam represented on the board of trustees, and the myriad concerns of justice and fairness that were emerging.

As demands for amendments to the bill proliferated, several faculty at the state's public colleges and universities entered the debate. Some called for their representatives to vote against the bill, pointing to concerns that the scholarship program would widen the divide between public and private institutions. They worried that it would create new burdens for faculty, who would be expected to teach larger classes and, at the same time, would limit resources available for increases in faculty salaries. They anticipated an acceleration in the deprofessionalization of higher education, in which colleges and universities would offer fewer and fewer tenure-track faculty lines and instead hire faculty on contingent contracts, which were often underpaid and ineligible for benefits. For these reasons, they argued that a free college program should be passed only with accompanying funding increases for faculty support.

Student and academic affairs professionals expressed similar concerns about the likely increase in demands they would face to support a growing student population. How would already understaffed financial aid, advising, counseling, and residence life offices be able to support students effectively without more resources?

Sam observed the debate over the bill and realized that, despite the popularity of the idea of free college, disagreements over the details might derail efforts to get a program started. Several amendments had been introduced but had not gathered enough support to be incorporated into the bill. Many of the challengers shared a core desire to make college more accessible and affordable and to advance equality of opportunity. They wanted students across the state to grow up believing that college was a real option for them and to be able to earn a degree without being overburdened with debt, but they disagreed about how to accomplish this goal. Many free college advocates worried that if the bill couldn't pass now, they might not get this far again for many years. History had repeatedly demonstrated it was much easier to amend an imperfect program once it was in place than to enact a new one.

Up to this point, the board of trustees had been silent on the issue. Given the uncertainty surrounding the bill, the board decided to weigh in. Believing that the board's statement would be a decisive factor in whether the bill passed or not, the chairperson decided to draft a concrete recommendation. At the next board meeting, each member would vote yes or no on the bill in its current form, and the majority of the votes would form the basis of the recommendation to the House.

As the day of the meeting approached, Sam was conflicted. What was best for students? For the system as a whole? How should the state balance the complex interests of the higher education system, including its two- and four-year public and private colleges? How should the various ethical issues raised about the free tuition bill be weighed, including those of justice, fairness, and inclusion? Would this imperfect bill, all things considered, be better than the status quo?

COMMENTARY

Beyond the Slogan: The Need for Equity-Driven Free College Programs

JAIME RAMIREZ-MENDOZA AND TIFFANY JONES

Crushing student loan debt, increasing default rates, decreasing enrollments: this scenario illustrates why policymakers proposed the College Promise Scholarship program. However, the current proposal offers a version of free college that is heavy on rhetoric but fails to target the students who have the greatest financial need and the most to gain from higher education. In order to unlock the true potential of their program, the board's recommendation must look beyond the "free college" slogan that inspires students to enroll and center on equity to ensure the new policy delivers on its promise and provides financial benefits for all students, especially those who struggle the most to pay.

CURRENT DESIGN HIGHLIGHTS THE IMPORTANCE OF EQUITY

Promise programs have been shown to increase enrollments, and there are elements of the proposed bill that would do so equitably.[6] For instance, by covering both two- and four-year institutions for up to four years, this promise program would allow students to choose an institution that meets their needs and create an affordable pathway to earning a bachelor's degree that has higher economic payoffs. Furthermore, the new bill would phase out the state's current merit scholarship program. This is an equitable step in leveling the financial aid playing field, as merit-based aid disproportionately benefits White, affluent students because they are more likely to afford to take standardized tests multiple times, pay for tutors, and attend better-funded schools with more Advanced Placement courses compared to their non-white, low-income peers.[7]

However, there are also elements of the bill that could have negative implications, one of them being its last-dollar approach. Advocates are correct to challenge this structure, as studies have found that some last-dollar programs actually benefit middle- and upper-income residents more than their low-income peers. Furthermore, the residency requirement could disproportionately impact students of color who may have to look out of state for employment due to discrimination in the labor market. Lastly, using lottery funds is not the most secure funding source, as studies have shown states that go this route end up decreasing their overall spending in education over time.[8]

While an equity-centered free college program would help make college more affordable, it won't solve all the systemic issues that perpetuate persistence and graduation gaps for historically marginalized students. This is highlighted in the case by the faculty and student affairs professionals who voice concerns about larger classes and increased advising demands with no financial or structural support to serve the students equitably.

THE EXCLUSION OF CERTAIN STUDENT POPULATIONS SPEAKS VOLUMES

While inclusion of undocumented students is a step in the right direction, the lack of accessibility for other marginalized student groups is worrisome and could end up exacerbating the same inequities the state is trying to fix.

For instance, the bill has no language on whether adults, returning students, or part-timers are eligible for the program. Given that 37 percent of college students are twenty-five years or older and millions more have some college and no degree, this oversight could exclude a big portion of today's students.[9] If the board wants to avoid the mistakes of the New York Excelsior program—which excluded one-third of all City University of New York undergraduate students with its full-time enrollment requirement—it should also include this population.[10]

Additionally, there was no mention of previously and currently incarcerated individuals. The criminal legal system disproportionately impacts millions of Black and Latinx people who will eventually be released without the necessary job skills to be competitive applicants. Including them would provide an affordable pathway to an education that will increase their employment options and earnings potential, reduce recidivism, and move the needle on overall postsecondary attainment while addressing socioeconomic inequities in education and employment.[11]

RECOMMENDATIONS

In addition to including the student groups mentioned above, the board's statement should support creating a dedicated funding stream via modifying existing state wealth taxes or creating a new wealth tax. That funding would be used to transform the promise program structure to a first-dollar model with an income cap so that it benefits students who need it the most. Furthermore, the statement should emulate the Tennessee Promise lottery funding structure, which puts the reallocated funds into an endowment that accrues interest over time, buffering the program from low lottery sales. This endowment should go toward a new statewide student success initiative that includes supporting faculty and student affairs professionals, with an emphasis on institutions that enroll more low-income students and students of color, including those who enroll part-time.[12] Lastly, the board should recommend that the state track student outcomes and disaggregate data by race, income, gender, first-generation status, persistence, and transfer rates to better understand who is being served by these programs and whether they are helping to shrink or expand racial equity gaps.

CONCLUSION

If Governor Diaz wants to make good on the promise of making college affordable for all, then the board must make recommendations that go beyond the "free college" slogan and center on equity.[13] Only then can the state unlock the full potential of its free college program and take an important first step in building a highly educated workforce. This will forge an affordable pathway in which students—especially students from low-income backgrounds, students of color, adult learners, undocumented students, and currently and formerly incarcerated students—are no longer forced to shoulder crushing debt to pursue their college dreams.

Jaime Ramirez-Mendoza is a first-generation, low-income Latino scholar who is currently a policy analyst at The Education Trust, where he focuses on equitable policies around college affordability and access. He holds a master's degree from Harvard and did his undergraduate education at the University of California, Davis.

Tiffany Jones is the deputy director for measurement learning and evaluation at the Bill and Melinda Gates Foundation. She is formerly the senior director of higher education policy at The Education Trust, where she promoted legislation to improve access, affordability, and success for low-income students and students of color. She has a PhD from the University of Southern California.

COMMENTARY

Context Matters in State Higher Education Policy Making

PAUL G. RUBIN

Sam Chu has two important decisions to make: (1) Should they support the free college proposal? and (2) If so, what should be the characteristics of the policy? Many states are currently tackling similar questions as they try to improve rates of college enrollment and degree attainment while contending with increasing costs of attendance and mounting anxieties about accumulating debt. Moreover, as research shows that financial concerns disproportionately influence the educational decisions and outcomes of individuals from traditionally underserved populations, these policy choices have equity implications that can impact a state for years.[14] Nevertheless, as seen by studies examining policy nonevents, ensuring alignment between policy goals and broader state contexts offers the greatest likelihood for successful adoption of new policies regardless of their success in other states.[15] For these reasons, Sam must consider the specific context of their state in order for any policy solution to be effective. Grounded in research examining influential state-level characteristics on higher education policy making, I will offer questions for Sam's consideration to help them decide on their vote.[16]

HOW IS HIGHER EDUCATION VIEWED IN THE STATE?

An underlying factor that Sam should reflect on centers on the views of state officials and the broader citizenry vis-à-vis the purpose and goals of higher education. Based on voters' positive response to Governor Diaz's campaign platform and the legislature agreeing to review a free college proposal, it can be reasoned that there is general agreement across the state regarding the importance of higher education and that finances should not be the sole barrier for individuals to attain (at least some) postsecondary education. However, other than these inferred viewpoints, the case does not offer much insight into how the people of the state view higher education to aid Sam in their decision-making.

For example, it would be appropriate for Sam to consider the college-going culture of the state, including the awareness of and interest in pursuing postsecondary education and prevalence of college access programs.[17] As one of the established benefits of free college centers on expanding interest in pursuing postsecondary education and increasing enrollments of students from traditionally underrepresented populations, there may be less value in enacting a free college program than pursuing an alternative policy depending on the existing college-going culture.[18] Specifically, if the desire to attain higher education remains high in their state but students are enrolling elsewhere due to cost, Sam may determine that a focused need-based grant program is a more targeted solution to decreasing debt levels than supporting free college. On the other hand, if the declining enrollment at the state's institutions is indicative of a negative shift in the state's college-going culture, free college may be the better option to reinvigorate interest in pursuing postsecondary education.

Sam should also think through how state legislators and citizens view the aims of higher education. This includes whether institutions should focus on teaching workforce-related skills and providing vocational training or offering a more liberal-arts-based curriculum. In part, these preferences can be connected to the growing partisan division in opinions toward higher education nationally, but they may also reflect state and local priorities regarding economic and industry needs.[19] Further, these differing positions may relate to broader perceptions of the value of two-year versus four-year credentialing that could influence where legislators and citizens offer their support. Ultimately, by considering how their state views higher education, Sam will be able to understand if free college is a better option than the status quo and which sectors should be included in any proposed policy.

HOW IS THE STATE'S HIGHER EDUCATION SECTOR ORGANIZED AND GOVERNED?

In addition to understanding state perspectives on higher education, Sam should also consider the more practical organization and governance of their state's postsecondary education sector. Specifically, it would be helpful for Sam to identify whether the public two-year and four-year sectors are organized under a single agency, how the state manages its financial aid and college access programs, and how private institutions formally interact with the public sector. Previous research has found that differences in state-level governance play a significant role in the policy process.[20] These governance features may provide insights to opportunities and additional potential barriers for a free college program in the current case.

For example, if the current state financial aid program is separated between public and private sectors or only supports certain types of institutions, the proposed free college program will likely need to be managed by a separate entity to bridge these silos. The Tennessee Promise program, for instance, is administered by the Tennessee Student Assistance Corporation (TSAC), which includes representation from the governor's office, public and private higher education sectors, students, and the state citizenry.[21] Therefore, the state's willingness and capability to establish such an entity may answer (or further complicate) the questions Sam is currently debating.

MOVING FORWARD

Given the variety of existing free college programs, Sam will have many choices to consider if they decide to support adopting the new policy.[22] However, despite the significant attention directed toward free college, it is critical that Sam reflect on whether this policy aligns with their state's values and perspectives on postsecondary education and is feasible given existing organizational arrangements. Ultimately, although goals of equity and inclusion should rightfully guide Sam's decision, bearing in mind their state's context is equally important when deciding the best policy solution moving forward.

Paul G. Rubin is an assistant professor in the Department of Educational Leadership & Policy at the University of Utah. His research examines higher education policies aimed at improving college access and degree attainment for traditionally underserved populations, and state and institutional factors that influence the policy-making process.

COMMENTARY

On Ethical Obligations and Student Representation

WINSTON C. THOMPSON

This case appears ethically thorny as one considers the stakes, political strategies, and constitutive responsibilities of making the best choice. That said, I believe the case becomes somewhat clearer when we refocus our attention, moving away from seeking a version of the bill that might stand as the *best* choice (as one might pursue when considering an abstract puzzle of social or political theory) and favoring instead the more minimal pursuit of a *good* choice as compared to the status quo alternative (as one might be inclined to aim at in real-world circumstances of incomplete knowledge and shifting variables).

In what follows, I will highlight how a good choice might be made, focusing attention on Sam Chu's role as a student representative. I believe Sam has good reason to view this role as one that calls for a special focus, even as they bracket other known concerns. Building on this, I offer a particular recommendation for Sam's present action.

ETHICAL AND PROCEDURAL OBLIGATIONS OF A REPRESENTATIVE

While it is tempting to engage ethical cases with the assumption that all parties have similar, general ethical obligations to others, it is hardly radical to suggest that some ethical obligations arise from the particularities of one's circumstances. In this case, one of Sam's circumstances that deserves our attention is the fact that they are a student representative.

In a complex democratic system, representatives have specific obligations to those they represent. While philosophers and theorists disagree about the contours and mechanisms of representatives' accountability to their constituents, the general facts of that accountability are without serious contestation.[23] Representatives are obliged to give voice to their constituents, reflecting their aims in democratic decision-making processes. Still, Sam is in an ethically contentious situation due to the fact that their role—student representative—is not an elected position. Sam does not have a clear mandate from voters who elected them on the basis of campaign statements or shared views about issues likely to emerge.[24] Toward more clearly demarcating the ethical limitations of Sam's role, I would like to consider the contrasting role obligations of another person in the case: Governor Diaz.

GOVERNOR DIAZ'S SPECIAL DUTY TO REGULAR REEVALUATION AND POTENTIAL IMPROVEMENTS

Unlike Sam, Governor Diaz has been elected by voters to serve as a custodian of the public will. Although the case does not provide conclusive details about her election and public support (though she seems popular, partially due to her attention to tuition), we can assume that Diaz is beholden to multiple constituents, comprising the general state population. As such, she is bound by a far greater number of concerns than Sam. Governor Diaz cannot bracket the interests of one or another group. She ought not continually speak on behalf of one segment of the population. She cannot wave away issues of implementation and resource management. Whatever decision is reached during the upcoming meeting and eventual vote on the bill, Governor Diaz should commit to reviewing the decision and addressing ongoing concerns (potentially including the "first-dollar" variants of the plan, expansion to private colleges, etc.). In this, we can begin to recognize the very specific set of obligations held by Governor Diaz—an elected official, responsible to all state citizens for very many of the interrelated issues of design and implementation—in relation to the proposed bill.

In contrast, the substance of Sam's decision is far less complicated.

SAM'S SPECIAL DUTY TO REPRESENT STUDENT INTERESTS

As an appointed representative, Sam surely must articulate student interests. But Sam has good reason to be cautious in representing others. Rather than making very specific or nuanced decisions on the basis of demonstrable constituent faith in Sam's judgment, Sam might attempt to channel a more general synthesis of student will into a form of endorsement or dissent related to the decisions ahead.

Taking this seriously, we do well to focus attention on the specifics of Sam's obligation to speak on behalf of student interests (thereby inclusively representing current, future, and potential students) within the board of trustees. In this, Sam may need to bracket considerations that (while perhaps personally held or apparently compelling to a broader population) sit outside this obligation to forward student interests.

Among those concerns that may need to be set aside, Sam should not prioritize background logistical or institutional concerns about the lottery system, faculty funding, or support for student and academic affairs professionals. These are surely important but are not issues that Sam must solve (or prioritize, if these are not voiced by students). This is not to suggest that Sam ought to be oblivious or insensitive to these issues. On the contrary, in a complex system of interlocking institutions, Sam ought to be aware of these concerns and has duties to consider how actions in one domain indirectly impact others. But they ought not feel a primary obligation to endorse only those proposed courses of action that clearly satisfactorily address all related issues. Simply put, their scope of responsibility is relatively limited as one representative within a larger decision-making body.

As student representative, Sam should surely take into account the matters forwarded by student advocates and groups like Education Tomorrow. These concerns, regarding the possibility of aggregating advantage for high-income students to the detriment of other students, more immediately link to the views articulated by students. Therefore, Sam ought to focus on how these concerns weigh on an obligation to represent the interests of the constituents. They should ask: What do the students qua students seem to want and need in this decision? How can I represent those students who are not present in the board's deliberations? What would a *good* choice for students look like in this moment?

SAM SHOULD SUPPORT THE DRAFT BILL

In closing, I would like to offer some remarks on the substance of Sam's choice.

I recommend that Sam support the current bill. Again, they are an unelected representative of student interests. They need not solve all possible shortcomings of the bill (transforming it into the *best* version of itself); rather, they are obliged to represent broad student interests in the service of an outcome that students might recognize as *good*.

As noted earlier, Sam should not aggressively push for student interests above all other concerns. But they ought to make a case specifically representative of student interests. Substantively, Sam should prefer a bill that does not aggregate advantage to the detriment of low-income students. But it is not clear that their current choice can appropriately articulate this preference. Were they to decline the current bill in the service of holding out for ideally desirable revisions, the status quo is, at least, temporarily, maintained. A focus on Sam's accountability to students suggests that it would be better to support the current bill, even while planning to advocate for improvements in future. Choosing a *good* result now might provide opportunities to pursue the *best* results later.

Winston C. Thompson is an associate professor of philosophy of education and associate professor of philosophy (by courtesy) at The Ohio State University. Thompson's scholarship focuses on normative ethical and social/political questions of justice, education, and the public good, with recent efforts analyzing dilemmas of educational policy.

COMMENTARY

"Free Tuition" Means Two Very Different Things

NICHOLAS C. BURBULES

This debate around "free tuition for all" mixes two different policy goals.[25] One is "more students attending and graduating from college" and helping students who "decide against attending college because of the costs." The other is "[e]very person . . . who wants to pursue an education . . . should have that chance." The first emphasizes affordability for those already qualified and ready to attend college; the second emphasizes removing all barriers, financial and otherwise, to anyone who wants to attend college. Slogans like "free tuition [or free college] for all" confuse those two objectives, and as a result, they create certain expectations that can have counterproductive effects for both students and the higher education system as a whole.

IMPACT ON STUDENTS

For students, the expectation that everyone who wants to pursue college should be able to may be counterproductive. Providing access, or an opportunity, is not the same as guaranteeing success. While it is a good thing to create high expectations and encourage an aspiration toward higher education, for many students, the main impediments to higher education are *not* cost-related. Success is limited by a lack of adequate academic preparation in high school (or even earlier), poor counseling, and students' abilities and dispositions. Once these students arrive on campus, many will need compensatory instruction and significant academic advising and support. This is an unfunded cost borne by the institution, and not all schools are well-equipped to provide these services effectively.

Students' choices of majors create more or less challenging avenues to completion. At my university, there is a holding category for struggling students with no majors and no particular plans for one; at many schools, there are "majors" that are less demanding so that students can end up with something on their transcripts. Studies consistently show the employment and salary benefits of a college degree, but a reform that increases participation while cheapening the standards of completion could actually reduce the value of that degree.

Addressing the cost side without a more extensive analysis of the pathways—and impediments—to access and success is not only a waste of resources, it could be counterproductive to what we actually want to achieve. As former University of Michigan president James Duderstadt writes, universities are poorly equipped to help the demographic groups whose demand for higher education is growing the fastest.[26] A better investment for many students may very well be attending a two-year school that is better equipped to deal with their lack of preparation and then seeking to transfer into a four-year school.

IMPACT ON HIGHER EDUCATION

Another area of unintended consequences is the impact of the expectation that college should be accessible to everyone on the higher education system itself. Such an expectation could create pressure to lower or change admission standards, even at selective schools. Other schools will become "open access" to anyone who can pay, which could include for-profit schools that will absorb public subsidies without producing quality results.

As university budgets are becoming more dependent on undergraduate tuition, competition for students is increasing. A free tuition policy will accelerate this competition even further. Universities will do more to promote and publicize their teaching mission, which could have direct implications for faculty workload and time commitments. As noted in the case study, the already-growing shift from tenured faculty to untenured teaching staff would likely accelerate. Some schools, of course, already have a heavy emphasis on undergraduate teaching. Others are more geared toward research and graduate and professional education. Many schools would be forced to put more resources into compensatory programs and support for underprepared students. But not all schools have, or should have, the mission of serving a broad array of students.

Many universities today depend on a mix of in-state, out-of-state, and international students paying different levels of tuition. A program funded primarily on a state-by-state basis would affect this mix; some schools would be forced to prioritize in-state students and limit recruiting out-of-state or international students. On the student side, students may be limited in their ability to use their support to attend an out-of-state school. International students who are not part of this program could expect even higher tuition costs.

As funding for universities depends more on public funds supplied via state legislatures, one can expect greater demands for state oversight and regulation. Several state governments have already made inroads into institutional autonomy—numerous examples point to increased public funding coming with regulatory strings attached. What sorts of cost controls or audits would be imposed from the outside to ensure that public funds are being used "efficiently"? This could entail greater external involvement in academic program decisions, including admission standards, and greater pressures to demonstrate increased graduation rates. How would such pressures distort internal processes of evaluation and grading?

Finally, the current tuition model—flawed as it is—allows institutions to adjust prices to accommodate rising costs. In a state-subsidized tuition model, schools would not have the same flexibility to do this (except, perhaps, by gouging out-of-state and international students).

RECOMMENDATION ON THE PROPOSED BILL

We need to decide which of the two models I identified at the outset is our priority. If we aim to ensure greater affordability for those prepared to attend and complete college successfully, we should emphasize increasing merit- and need-based scholarships. It is not obvious that a completely free option would engender the level of student commitment necessary to persist and finish (as massive open online course [MOOC] providers found, adding even modest fees increased persistence and completion rates). Greater financial assistance through work-study options may have added benefits for many students.

If, on the other hand, the goal is to turn higher education into a free, open-access entitlement, then we should focus on developing multiple pathways of access that take advantage of the diversity of schools within the overall higher education system. Free access to community college, improved transferability, bridge programs, tuition reductions at some schools that are currently crying out for students, and more clearly delimiting the complementary missions of different kinds of schools would all be part of such a plan.

Finally, we need to go beyond a focus on college attendance in the traditional sense if we are truly to improve access to success for the many types of student who desire it (including older students who may be more mature and better prepared to pursue educational opportunities): lifelong learning programs beyond just a focus on four-year institutions; innovative workplace, adult, and continuing education programs that are not part of this proposal; and innovative uses of technology to teach larger numbers of students at lower cost. (Together, I call these "ubiquitous learning.") It is not clear that attendance at a four-year campus is the pathway best suited for the needs, abilities, and career aspirations of a broad range of students.

Nicholas C. Burbules is the Edward William and Jane Marr Gutgsell Professor in the Department of Educational Policy, Organization and Leadership at the University of Illinois, Urbana-Champaign. His primary research areas are philosophy of education; the ethics of communication; and technology and education. He is currently the editor of Educational Theory.

COMMENTARY

Designing a More Progressive Promise

FEDERICK NGO

As the governing body for public institutions, and with an expressed interest in access and affordability, the board of trustees should focus their recommendation on two goals: avoiding regressive policies that benefit students from wealthier families and maximizing student success. This case response will summarize research on how these goals can be achieved through policy design of aid programs.

AVOIDING REGRESSIVE POLICIES

Regressive aid policies are those that benefit wealthier families more than poorer families—something policy design can help to avoid. Although the College Promise Scholarship program (CPS) replaces the merit aid program, which has regressive tendencies (see, for example, increased car sales after Georgia HOPE scholarship income caps were removed), it is concerning that CPS itself does not have income-eligibility criteria.[27] Need-based aid directly benefits low-income students and has been found to be more effective as a college access tool than merit-based aid.[28]

CPS is also a last-dollar scholarship, which can be regressive in practice. Since last-dollar scholarships are applied after preexisting aid like Pell grants and state aid are applied to tuition, low-income students cannot use Pell aid to cover additional college costs (e.g., food, housing, books). Indeed, research on last-dollar programs finds that recipients often receive no additional financial support. Also, while racially minoritized students are more likely to participate in last-dollar programs, they are less likely to receive aid from them.[29] Additional expenses have to come out of pocket, which is one reason that last-dollar scholarships may not ultimately increase college enrollment.[30] Furthermore, if last-dollar scholarships cover only tuition costs, students may choose less pricey institutions, including less selective institutions that have lower degree completions rates.[31]

MAXIMIZING STUDENT SUCCESS

It is not surprising that private institutions are vying to allow students to use CPS dollars at their institutions—promise programs appear to change the institutions in which eligible college students enroll. The earliest free college programs in two-year colleges often drew students from four- to two-year institutions.[32]

Should the policy then allow public promise dollars to subsidize enrollment in private institutions? While one might argue that it is in the best interest of the state to reinvest public dollars back into public institutions by delineating eligible institutions, this may not actually be in the best interest of students. A merit-aid program in Massachusetts that provided high-achieving students tuition waivers at in-state public colleges actually led students to *forgo* college quality and attend less selective institutions.[33] The scholarship program ultimately *lowered* the college completion rates of recipients. College quality does matter for college completion, and more selective institutions are more likely to graduate their students.[34] Therefore, some amount of the scholarship should apply at all public and private institutions. For-profit colleges should not be included, due to their low completion rates and predatory practices.

At the same time, private colleges cost more, and with a last-dollar scholarship—one that covers the cost of tuition—they could be incentivized to engage in raising tuition to capture the guaranteed revenue from increased aid dollars. This phenomenon is known in higher education finance as the Bennett Hypothesis. Although there is no clear evidence of this behavior, what would prevent colleges from raising tuition in response to last-dollar scholarships is to target those programs toward low-income students ("Bennett Hypothesis 2.0"). If financial aid is restricted to low-income students and instead offered in first-dollar form, then colleges may be less likely to engage in Bennett behaviors.[35]

Provided there are only state residency and no citizenship requirements, CPS will open doors for low-income undocumented students who face obstacles to college access and success even in states with in-state resident tuition policies.[36] Any iteration of CPS should allow undocumented residents to be eligible for these funds.

Lastly, the proposal makes scholarship recipients commit to living and working in the state for a year after completing their studies. The effects of these strings and commitment devices for financial aid programs are not as well known, but place-based programs can motivate students to stay local.[37] Yet there is one major equity concern. CPS will restrict Promise graduates from competing fully in the job market and garnering competitive wages, which may disproportionately affect mobility for students from lower-income backgrounds. It may be more equitable to offer an income or tax incentive to stay, rather than to inflict a payback penalty for leaving.

RECOMMENDATION

The research findings described above suggest that including income-based eligibility criteria will improve the design of the policy and counteract its regressive components, as was the case with Oregon's Promise program.[38] This will prevent the policy from becoming an unnecessary subsidy for wealthy families and prevent colleges from attempting to raise tuition prices to capture more aid revenue. The scholarship should also be an adequate first-dollar scholarship so that it truly reduces the full cost of college for low-income students. Students should be able to use it at both public and private institutions, and the first-dollar amount should cover most of the tuition cost at public institutions. Moreover, policy makers should be concerned that per-student resources will fall as enrollments increase. The faculty are right—these access programs need to be complemented with more institutional support, especially in a context of declining state appropriations for higher education.

Without these policy design elements and with limited lottery revenues, the CPS proposal may be more regressive than progressive and not fully achieve its goals of access and affordability. The board should recommend incorporating more policy design elements that truly achieve access and affordability for those students and families who need it most.

Federick Ngo, PhD, is an assistant professor at the University of Nevada, Las Vegas. He studies higher education policy with a focus on community colleges. He also conducts research on college access and success for underrepresented and racially minoritized students.

COMMENTARY

Reimagining the Higher Education Narrative

JENNIFER M. MORTON

Free college tuition is framed as either an inclusive step in supporting higher education for all or an inefficient and inequitable policy that will benefit those who are already better off. Given the serious and persistent inequalities in access to educational opportunities in the United States, we have good reason to worry about the anticipated effects of free college tuition on the distribution of already limited educational resources. Arguably, students who are already advantaged in our unequal educational system will also benefit most from this program. This policy might redirect money away from the K–12 system, even though younger students stand to benefit the most from increased educational investment. Moreover, those students who are the least well-served by the K–12 system are less likely to attend college and benefit from this policy. Finally, this policy might have concerning impacts on the higher education system—perhaps proving the death knell for struggling private universities that serve historically underrepresented groups. Without minimizing these valid critiques, I want to urge us to reconsider what is missed by evaluating this policy solely on distributive concerns. Policies also express our values as a society. I will argue that free college could enable all students, regardless of economic background, to adopt a more student- and values-centered narrative, rather than a meritocratic or parental investment narrative.

MERITOCRATIC AND PARENTAL INVESTMENT NARRATIVES

This expressive dimension of our policies is often revealed by the narratives students have about education. At least two such narratives pervade the discourse on higher education. The meritocratic narrative tells us that it is the hardworking, smart students who deserve admission to college. Merit-based scholarships exemplify this idea. This narrative has been challenged by what we have learned about the correlation between a family's socioeconomic status, a student's zip code, and educational outcomes.[39] In its place, many now see college as a family investment. A student's future, according to this second narrative, depends on a family's capacity and willingness to cultivate it. This narrative is more accurate in some sense—as we know from decades of research in the social sciences, a family's ability and willingness to invest in a child's education does have consequences for that child's future trajectory.[40] But this narrative tethers a student's future to their family's ability and willingness to invest in them far into adulthood.

In her book *Indebted*, Caitlin Zaloom focuses on the financial sacrifices made by families who are sending their children to college but who are too wealthy to qualify for Pell grants or other forms of need-based aid yet not well-off enough to pay for college tuition outright.[41] Zaloom shows how these families are squeezed by ever-rising tuition costs. Families take on second mortgages; stop contributing to retirement; or, in some dire cases, empty out retirement accounts to invest in their child's future. Many of these parents try to shield their children from knowing the full extent of their sacrifice, preferring to maintain the illusion that they can provide their children with a boundless future. A further pernicious aspect of this narrative is that it ties students' college decision to parents' views of what that education ought to be like. In his book on higher education, Paul Tough describes well-off families that are so invested in where their children attend college that they manage every aspect of their children's lives to ensure their admissions into the "right" schools.[42]

A STUDENT- AND VALUES-CENTERED NARRATIVE

One might ask why, when so many low-income students struggle to pay for public higher education, we should be concerned with the *narratives* that we have around higher education. My conjecture is that the existing narratives harm all students. The current policy, despite its imperfections, will help erode those pernicious narratives.

We know that the meritocratic narrative harms students because it portrays merit as divorced from the socioeconomic circumstances in which talent and ability are developed. But the parental investment narrative harms low-income students as well. As I argue in my book *Moving Up Without Losing Your Way*, low-income and first-generation students are often torn between doing what they need to do to succeed in college and playing critical support roles to loved ones.[43] Families are put into the difficult position of needing to rely on their adult children to play these support roles and feeling guilty about not being able to provide the education they think their children deserve. Free college wouldn't necessarily eliminate these trade-offs, but it would empower students and their families to think of these decisions differently.

When a good public option is available for free to all students, a student's choices about higher education are less dependent on their family's views of education, willingness to invest in them, or ability to do so. Many working-class students will still be unable to afford college despite not having to worry about tuition (and we should urge legislators to enact more generous policies after this one is adopted). Some students might choose to prioritize their commitment to supporting their families over going to college. Others might succumb to parental pressure to attend the school of their parents' dreams. Some might be willing to let their parents decimate their retirement accounts to go to the college of their dreams. But in all cases, these students will be making these decisions as adults contending with the costs and benefits that their choice entails, not as an extension of their family's investment. The proposed policy moves us away from thinking about college as "a family's decision." It should be an adult student's decision. There is no better time for students to engage in the kind of ethical reasoning that they will have to undertake as citizens—reasoning that considers the costs and benefits of their decisions to their communities, families, and to themselves—than in deciding on college.

Jennifer M. Morton is an associate professor of philosophy at the University of North Carolina, Chapel Hill. Her book Moving Up Without Losing Your Way: The Ethical Costs of Upward Mobility *was published by Princeton University Press in 2019 and won the American Association of Colleges and Universities' Frederic W. Ness Book Award.*

CHAPTER 7

HBCUs and the Ethical Dilemmas of Meeting Contemporary Expectations

JOHN TORREY AND COREY REED

This case study presents a presidential search at a fictional historically Black college and the ethical choices members of the board of trustees and the Presidential Search Committee must weigh in choosing a candidate.

THE COLLEGE

Baker-Baldwin College, founded on February 6, 1880, is a historically Black, liberal arts college in the small city of Cypress, Tennessee.[1] The college is in a consortium with similar HBCUs, such as Rust College, Stillman College, Talladega College, and Lane College, all of which share missions of emphasizing undergraduate instruction, Southern-Black history, and community development. The pillars of Baker-Baldwin's mission statement are to:

- Provide a quality education for our students both inside and outside of the classroom
- Foster a learning environment that encourages self-expression, creativity, and the discovery of purpose
- Inspire our students in civic leadership and community engagement
- Develop innovative and critical thinkers
- Promote Christian values, established through the church in which the institution was founded

Baker-Baldwin is a historic institution that Black students could attend prior to the desegregation of Cypress University in 1968. The college's current enrollment is approximately twenty-two hundred undergraduates, many of whom come from Cypress and the surrounding areas of eastern Tennessee. Roughly 80 percent of its current students identify as Black or African American.

THE PRESIDENTIAL SEARCH CRITERIA

With the retirement of President David Cross, Baker-Baldwin is searching for a new president. The Presidential Search Committee consists of several members of the board of trustees, as well as faculty and student representatives. The committee is led by Regina Coffie, a philanthropist, retired university administrator, and HBCU alumna who is known nationally for her pioneering work in education reform at the federal level. Under Ms. Coffie's leadership, the committee is searching for a candidate who can do the following well:

- Preserve the ideals of Baker-Baldwin, while successfully navigating the recent 15 percent drop in enrollment amid national economic upheaval due to the COVID-19 pandemic and the resulting financial pressures to colleges and students
- Address concerns voiced by faculty (and affirmed in a vote of the faculty senate as a priority for the presidential search) about both their job security and working conditions, including concerns about increased teaching loads due to faculty loss
- Demonstrate the ability to engage the student body as it pertains to student activism, students' social and emotional well-being, and the growing tension between the police and Black communities of Cypress amid the Black Lives Matter movement following the death of Shawn Perry, a former Baker-Baldwin student, who was killed by the police in 2019
- Respond to the student government's "issue of focus" (affirmed by a student vote) regarding the treatment of queer, gender-nonconforming, and all other students on campus whose appearances diverge from the traditional image expectations that the institution upholds

THE CANDIDATES

The three finalists for the position include:

- *Mr. Donald Block:* An HBCU alumnus, native of Cypress, and former chief financial officer for a major national bank who helped rescue the corporation when it was in financial crisis. Mr. Block holds an MBA and represents the business interests of the community and city. He is a major advocate for Baker-Baldwin in the corporate world and a leader in Cypress's business industry. He has previously raised $1.1 million for Baker-Baldwin.
- *Dr. Harriet Taylor:* A well-known Africana historian who transitioned into administrative leadership roles at a West Coast college. She rose from being a faculty member to dean of Humanities and Social Sciences and from dean to provost. Dr. Taylor has received local and national awards for both her research and her ability to lead faculty—representing their needs and inspiring their participation—even in tough financial times.
- *Dr. Theodore Davies:* An academic specialist in administration of small, liberal arts institutions and an alumnus of Baker-Baldwin. Dr. Davies holds a doctorate in higher education administration. He has written several articles on HBCUs, the benefits of small colleges, the profitability of "school image" on HBCUs, and shifting models for institutional survival. He worked as an administrator of three colleges prior to applying for this position (one community college, one large public university, and one HBCU similar to Baker-Baldwin).

THE PERSPECTIVES OF SEARCH COMMITTEE MEMBERS

The Presidential Search Committee consists of eleven members: chairperson Regina Coffie, six standing board members, two faculty representatives, and two non-voting student representatives. In discussions of the merits of the candidates after their interviews, disparate perspectives became apparent on how to weigh various values and priorities for Baker-Baldwin.

Jamal Hall, Student Representative

The student body takes great pride in Baker-Baldwin College. Many of us come here searching for somewhere we can be our authentic selves, feel protected from the racism of the world, and discover our vocations and purposes in life. There has been debate among the students regarding what it is like attending Baker-Baldwin. Some claim it is the safe haven they have always wanted. Others, especially students who identify as queer or who dress in ways society deems "thuggish" or "unladylike," have stated that Baker-Baldwin can be a hostile and uncomfortable space. Due to the queer phobias and respectability politics that our school promotes via dress codes, hair expectations, and consistently mandating suits/dresses at certain functions, some students don't feel like this is home. It is the belief of the majority of students surveyed that we have an obligation to make sure that our next president is willing to tackle these issues.

When I posed these concerns to the three candidates, Mr. Block seemed to think that these were minor issues and an "easy fix." His only concern was the appearance of the institution to the donors, both those more liberal and those more conservative in their stances on gender/sexuality.

Dr. Taylor gave a very strong answer to my question, stating, "Baker-Baldwin's mission encourages self-expression; thus, the self-expression and identities of its students should be both respected and protected. That protection includes students feeling comfortable on campus regardless of their appearance, feeling safer from the racism in the world, and feeling like this is their home where they can be themselves."

Dr. Davies was well aware of some current trends among all universities regarding gender and sexuality inequalities and the unique ways these issues arise in church-based HBCUs in the South. He cited research about how colleges and universities do better when diversity is embraced, and spoke on how he, as an alumnus, takes pride in the type of home Baker-Baldwin is.

Based on the level of care shown in Dr. Taylor's response to our primary concerns, along with her emphasis on the preservation of faculty and pushing an agenda of social justice through her "Shawn Perry Plan," we, the student representatives, recommend Dr. Taylor for president.

Dr. Carol Knight, Faculty Representative

Our students make very clear and important points. As faculty, we interact with them daily, and from conversations with them, we are aware of the varying degrees of safety they feel. Our students need and deserve a president who is going to see those problems and address them.

The faculty's primary concern has been the financial stability of the institution and how that will affect the faculty's jobs and workload. Most of us teach three courses per semester, while still fulfilling demanding research and service requirements. Faculty are worried about increased workload, and our non-tenured faculty are fearful for their jobs. The main question we had for the candidates was: "In light of COVID-19 and our already fragile budget as a small, liberal arts institution, what is your plan for addressing the financial realities while protecting the faculty?" We also asked, "Do you see a path to financial stability without raising tuition on our already burdened students?"

Mr. Block gave a complex response, suggesting that we continue to diversify the student body, recruiting more non-Black students. He suggested directing more energy to building partnerships with industries in the city, funneling our graduates to their companies and providing specialized training to our students in exchange for increased financial support. He also proposed an evaluation of our degree programs and potentially consolidating or eliminating majors with low enrollment. With Baker-Baldwin only offering eighteen majors, and each major already having a skeleton faculty, this worries us, especially with the growing trend of universities and colleges eliminating the humanities and social sciences.

Dr. Taylor demonstrated her reputation of championing faculty, guaranteeing that she would do everything in her power to keep every tenure-track and tenured faculty member we have while maintaining workloads. Her plan for ensuring that, however, was a bit vague. She referred to heightening our reputation as a premier liberal arts college and gaining more students from outside the region, but that idea was not developed further.

Dr. Davies, however, gave a surprising response, stating that the way to grow retention, especially in times of crisis, comes down to presenting Baker-Baldwin to prospective and current students as an institution actively invested in creating economic and educational opportunities for Black students. He recommended that we increase and incentivize dual-degree programs with our high schools, that we bring more students to campus for Homecoming week, that we create financial incentives for students who do their entire four years at Baker-Baldwin, and that we take a public stance as a safe space for our students regarding racial prejudice trends in the United States. It was clear that Dr. Davies understands the legacy and culture of Baker-Baldwin and the proud traditions that honor our namesakes and celebrate our community. He offered promising ideas about how these traditions should inform how we focus the marketing of the school.

Although Mr. Block demonstrated a great financial plan and Dr. Taylor seemed the most connected with faculty interests, we feel the best overall candidate is Dr. Davies.

Princeton Hayes, At-Large Board Member and Senior Partner at Wright, Hayes, & Associates

First, I want to publicly thank our students and faculty for their contributions. As one of the lawyers on this board, my perspective always has legal repercussions in the background. As a private institution, Baker-Baldwin has more flexibility than most in making decisions for itself about how it wants to operate. However, it also carries an increased burden as a tuition-driven institution. How "bought-in" our donors, students, and alumni are has direct implications for our finances. All our decisions should have a stakeholder mentality, which is why the students' perspectives are just as important as the donors'. My question to the candidates was how each of them would balance these three stakeholder groups.

Mr. Block gave the most formal of the responses. He stated that the funders that are most likely to take their money elsewhere are those that have set ideas of what Baker-Baldwin alumni should be. One of Baker-Baldwin's goals has been to change the assumptions society has concerning young Black people. Those appearance values are held by the institution and its donors alike. Major policy changes could result in loss of those donors. Some of them have an ideal standard of what Baker-Baldwin graduates should look like, act like, and speak like, beyond gender performance. He proposed that we attempt to maintain the commitment of all students, alumni, and donors by making compromises instead of stark changes in the issues voiced.

Dr. Taylor gave a completely opposite response, claiming that our students and faculty are a priority that should always come first and supersede financial influences. When I asked her about donor expectations, she claimed that restrictive expectations of how Black students engage the world are, in and of themselves, anti-Black. A school that focuses on Black liberation, as HBCUs have since their inception, should take students as they are and reject respectability politics. Her proposition was to emphasize maintaining the student population necessary to make financial ends meet, including increasing alumni giving via student sponsorship (i.e., alumni sponsoring students who are going into their projected fields so that mentorship can intertwine with alumni giving).

Dr. Davies's proposition was to conduct a critical examination of our donors, look at what percentage of support each donor contributes, and make some projections about how many new donors we would need to substitute any we might lose. This way, we can focus on the students and keep the money necessary for the school to function. For these reasons, my recommendation for president of Baker-Baldwin is Dr. Davies, who gave the most reasonable approach to financial stability of the three.

Bernadette Price, At-Large Board Member and CFO of Total Enterprises, a Mass Distributing Company Located in Cypress

I am going to keep this short; our financial position should not be taken lightly. Baker-Baldwin has tried changing SAT/ACT and GPA requirements to attract more students. It has tried gaining grants to balance the financial deficit. Although this year's enrollment is expected to drop around 15 percent, primarily due to COVID-19, Baker-Baldwin has experienced small losses in both alumni giving and student enrollment over the last decade. Compared with 2010, we are looking at about a 21 percent drop in enrollment. We need a president who takes that seriously. Campus issues are real and important, but Baker-Baldwin's fiscal reality should be our number-one priority. While we are able to survive for the near future, we are not financially stable enough to have any significant donor loss.

I found Mr. Block to be the most upfront about that reality, giving real financial propositions with foreseeable gain. I found Dr. Taylor to be a bit of an idealist and visionary, which is great in times of excess, not in times of loss. Dr. Davies's plan is possible, but also fragile. What if our highest donor, Sizzle Soda Co., lowers its giving or divests? It is not likely that we could make up that kind of money. Sizzle Soda has donated so much and hired so many alumni because it has an expectation regarding the professionalism of Baker-Baldwin students and alumni. The company has also shown itself to be very pro–law enforcement. The ideals that Dr. Taylor exemplifies would have major repercussions for this school financially. We should err on the side of caution, and Mr. Block does that the best. He is my recommendation for president.

The committee ultimately chose to elect Dr. Theodore Davies as the next president of Baker-Baldwin College, but many ethical questions remain, including:

- How should Baker-Baldwin balance advocating for its students' concerns while also navigating financial issues and donor expectations?
- How should Baker-Baldwin promote students' freedom of expression and appearance while preparing them for industries with preconceived notions regarding what "Black professionals" are like?
- How should a school that is historically and predominantly Black align with the Black Lives Matter movement while having ties to the larger public?
- Should there be any presentative/performance expectations on graduates from HBCUs?
- Did the committee make the right choice of president?

COMMENTARY

W. E. B. DuBois Speaks to HBCUs: "Whither Now and Why"

NATASHA MCCLENDON AND JOYCE E. KING

> *Transforming education for and about people of African ancestry in order to go beyond "inclusion into a burning house," as James Baldwin once put it, is a formidable task. To attack the roots of our miseducation, cultural annihilation, and economic subordination, we must undo the system of thought that has justified our predicament. Thus, Black Education is more than a "minority issue."*
>
> —Joyce E. King, 1990[2]

A CONFLICT BETWEEN ALTERNATIVES

Is the problem financial first and foremost? Is this case about the education that Black students need? Is education fundamentally about getting a job? Should a Black college abandon its historical legacy by recruiting non-Black students to solve its financial challenges? If an ethical dilemma is a "conflict between alternatives" where, no matter what one does, "some ethical principle will be compromised," do these strategic choices entail compromising any ethical principles?[3] In this historic moment when African Americans are navigating the dual pandemics of a deadly global virus and white supremacy racism, both threatening us with extinction, what ethical principles should inform decisions regarding the kind of education that HBCU students need and deserve?

Framing Baker-Baldwin's institutional challenges within "Westernity's" mainstream conception of educational purposes neglects the reality regarding the Black existential condition in this society.[4] While the scenario presents seemingly inevitable "no-win" situations or "dilemmas as choice" between a rock and a hard place, our concern is not only for the survival of the institution but also for the survival of African American people.[5] This commentary will name the ethical principles the committee should consider in setting Baker-Baldwin's future direction.

AN AFROFUTURIST CONCEPTIONS OF ETHICS

We evoke *Afrofuturism* to illuminate ethical principles that merit consideration.[6] Theoretically, Afrofuturism is informed by metaphysics, ethics, and digital hermeneutics in the humanities and sciences, plus Black people's history of self-determination and resistance. As a social imaginary, Afrofuturism merges the African cultural ethos of *Ubuntu* ("I am because we are") with a theology of sufficiency (not Western culture's individualistic hyper-prosperity) within our tradition of collective struggle.[7] Black studies theorists articulate this ethical educational principle: Black communities aspire to collective struggle for collective betterment. Afrofuturism invites us to imagine differently while engaging with the wisdom and heritage of African diasporic cultures to promote and uphold Black thought and communal well-being.

In *The Mis-Education of the Negro*, Carter Woodson argued that graduates with the "wrong kind" of education will be a disadvantage to the race.[8] Following Rodney King's infamous 1991 beating by Los Angeles police, Sylvia Wynter emphasized that Woodson had asked what is wrong "with a system of education whose scholarly curriculum not only served to strongly demotivate Black students and to lead to their dropping out, but which also socialized white students to be lynchers (and policemen-beaters) of black Americans when they become adults?"[9]

In a commencement address titled, "Whither Now and Why," W. E. B. DuBois stated, "The correct attitude toward vocations must be taught increasingly within our schools to ensure that students learn ways to support, build, and sustain their communities."[10] Beyond the narrow but pragmatic goal of preparing students to "get a job," economist Jessica Gordon Nembhard offers a justice-centered "real world" principle: the importance of preparing Black students for democratic economic participation enabling them to transform workplace racial and economic inequities.[11] Linking this principle to our conception of HBCU students' professional success is akin to the ethical social imaginary that Native American scholar Daniel Wildcat connects to the indigenous knowledge that humanity needs to survive not global warming but "global burning." Wildcat asserts that "the magnitude of the changes that need to be made in how we, humankind, think and live are immense. . . . The most difficult changes [required are those in] worldviews and the generally taken-for-granted values and beliefs that are embedded in modern, Western-influenced societies."[12]

Although HBCUs represent only 3 percent of colleges and universities in the US, their graduates make up 80 percent of Black judges, 50 percent of Black doctors and lawyers, and 25 percent of the nation's STEM graduates.[13] If HBCUs are producing a large percentage of graduates who attain lucrative and fulfilling careers in high-demand fields, are HBCU leaders and decision-makers ethically obligated to consider not only how well-prepared their graduates are for individual success but also the mindset *to choose to contribute* to the well-being of the Black community—and humanity?

The crux of the issue presented in this case might seem to be how Baker-Baldwin can/should sustain itself financially. Although we recognize the real financial challenges HBCUs are facing, we also see the source of funding as an ethical issue, aligned as well with the necessity for Black thought, which is integral to all facets of HBCU leadership and decision-making. Thus, we return to DuBois's unapologetic commitment to Black thought and Black well-being: "What I have been fighting for and am still fighting for is the possibility of all Black folk and their cultural patterns existing in America without discrimination, and on terms of equality."[14]

How HBCUs answer and enact this Black Lives Matter imaginary, no matter which presidential candidate the committee selects, is the actual ethical dilemma.

Natasha McClendon is a doctoral candidate in the Educational Policy Studies program at Georgia State University. Her research explores institutional and student-defined student success within higher education, Black aesthetics, and visual research methods. She is also interested in policy analysis that integrates Black aesthetics to investigate how policies are visually communicated.

Joyce E. King, PhD, holds the Benjamin Mays Endowed Chair at Georgia State University. She was the 2015 president of the American Educational Research Association, an American Council on Education Fellowship recipient, and senior academic affairs administrator and faculty at both HBCUs and PWIs. Her publications include eight books and numerous refereed articles.

COMMENTARY

An Ensouling Education

RASHAD RAYMOND MOORE

For 140 years, Baker-Baldwin College has prided itself on providing a historically Black liberal arts education for generations of students. Founded in 1880, when Black students were not allowed to attend nearby Cypress University, Baker-Baldwin has a long-standing legacy of producing creative, expressive, innovative leaders. Today, the college is working to preserve the ideals of its early founders, who built the institution on Christian values, while also meeting the challenges of decreasing enrollment, financial pressures, and loss of faculty. The Black Lives Matter movement has ignited a new wave of student activism that challenges policing and demands a place for queer, gender-nonconforming students in institutional life. Students are demanding that Baker-Baldwin change its policies and structures in order to ensure that they can live as their authentic selves on campus.

Although Baker-Baldwin was established by the work of the church, it is not a church. The school's allegiance must always be to its students and not the traditions, customs, and doctrines of a religious institution. Historically Black institutions often feel obligated to maintain respectable values and appearances that do not meet the needs of current students. Baker-Baldwin is in the opportune position to ensoul its students with an educational experience that is agential and affirming. I offer three suggestions for how Baker-Baldwin can promote the well-being and flourishing of its students: (1) provide space for students to disrupt old traditions and create new ones; (2) provide a moral education that is rooted in the history of the college, and (3) provide an affirming atmosphere where students can experience the joy of belonging.

DISRUPTING OLD TRADITIONS

First, the college must remain open to the possibility of change as students continue to demand and disrupt traditions. Students play an important role in maintaining the health and relevance of an institution. Through acts of disruption, students exercise their agency by questioning norms, protesting policies, and challenging the restrictions that prevent them from living their authentic lives on campus.

While the histories of HBCUs are often told from the top down, the archives also bear witness to the ways students and alumni have challenged institutions from the bottom up. There is no university without protest and truth-telling. Baker-Baldwin would do well to take seriously the demands of its students to live and learn in a place where they can be their authentic selves. Too often, historically Black colleges have been committed to the politics of respectability to meet the approval of white philanthropic individuals and organizations. To remain strong and relevant, Baker-Baldwin must make the needs of its students its top priority rather than the respectability politics of its board.

The history of HBCUs also tells the story of student-led and alumni-supported disruptions that have called institutions to task for stifling freedom of expression on campus. For instance, W. E. B. DuBois was a staunch critic of his alma mater, Fisk University, because of its strict culture of discipline that choked student freedom in order to acquiesce to Southern genteel sentiments of white philanthropists. In his essay, "Diuturni Silenti," DuBois argues that freedom of spirit, self-knowledge, and recognition of truth are the three pillars of a great university.[15]

RITUALS AS MORAL EDUCATION

Second, Baker-Baldwin can provide students with a moral education through rites of passage designed to aid in identity and character development. HBCUs like Baker-Baldwin have preserved the memory of former Black professors and figures through monuments, statues, and graves. Although the college has roots in the Christian faith, it can still forge a moral education that transmits values of excellence, discipline, and integrity without proselytizing.

For example, Morehouse College relies on its institutional narrative to inform its mission and philosophy of education. New Student

Orientation at Morehouse is a week filled with ceremonies that mark the beginning of the student's journey as a Man of Morehouse. Students are initiated into Morehouse's story through a series of workshops and rituals on the history of the college and its key figures in order to cultivate a sense of urgency, excellence, and a commitment to social justice. Baker-Baldwin, like Morehouse, can use its campus to offer a counter-narrative of Black life that is not marred by the negative stereotypes and tropes found in dominant culture.[16]

JOY AND BELONGING

Finally, Black colleges are a part of the cultural fabric of Black America. Amid the trauma and rage of anti-Black racism, HBCUs are a symbol of the joy and hope of Black America. Black colleges are *more* than institutions of higher education. Although their primary purpose has been nurturing thinkers and supporting research endeavors, Black colleges symbolize the power of joy, hope, and creative resistance in the face of racism, violence, and anti-Blackness. Black teenagers and college-age students are surrounded by the negative realities of police brutality, mass incarceration, and the pressures that face every urban Black community. The Black college stands a beacon of hope, a reminder that there is another way.

The HBCU Homecoming experience is one of the major rituals of joy. Every year, thousands of Black folk travel to the South for Homecoming at HBCUs. Whether they graduated, attended, or not, they make their way to Black college campuses to be "baptized in blackness."[17] Homecoming week is filled with concerts, comedy and fashion shows, and worship services and culminates in the Saturday football game and tailgate festivities. To some, the event may seem like a distractive debauchery, but to many Black alumni and community members, it is an eschatological experience in real time—a gathering of Black folk away from the pressures of anti-Black racism, a chance to catch one's breath and be strengthened by collective journey before returning back into the cold world. However, with the global COVID-19 pandemic still looming into the fall, the annual gatherings were canceled in 2020, leaving thousands mourning and reminiscing via social media and virtual gatherings.

After a weekend of reuniting, celebrating, dancing, laughing, and reminiscing, thousands of Black alumni take the joy of Homecoming home with them. They return to classrooms, pulpits, boardrooms, courtrooms, and communities with a reinvigorated hope; they serve their people with a little extra love. Homecoming reminds us that "*We gon' be alright!*"

In a political climate that is marked by unrest, a resurgence of white nationalism, and precautious isolation, the true measure and value of a college will now be determined by its ability to meet not only contemporary expectations, but the needs of a community navigating collective trauma and uncertainty. It is the experience of being nurtured in a community that affirms Black life, normalizes Black achievement, and creates endearing relationships, maintained by joy that will last long after graduation.

Rashad Raymond Moore is a doctoral student in philosophy and education at Teachers College, Columbia University. An alumnus of Morehouse College and Union Theological Seminary, Rashad is a passionate teacher, preacher, and scholar. His research interests are centered on the history and philosophy of African American education, as well as concepts pertaining to joy, becoming, and imagination. Rashad is the senior pastor of the First Baptist Church of Crown Heights in Brooklyn, New York.

COMMENTARY

How Baker-Baldwin College Can Envision Its Advancement

Tryan L. McMickens

Small tuition-driven institutions of higher education face many challenges and opportunities, and in the unprecedented year 2020, they are operating in the context of the COVID-19 pandemic, skyrocketing unemployment, renewed anti-Black racism, and a faltering economy. Baker-Baldwin College, a historically Black small institution in Cypress, Tennessee, is no exception. Its president is retiring, and a presidential search committee has chosen Dr. Theodore Davies as its new leader. In this commentary, I discuss student success strategies that could address the long-standing challenges facing Baker-Baldwin. I also offer perspectives from a historical lens to help inform readers' understanding of the ethical dimensions of the case in addition to offering contemporary lessons for Dr. Davies.

STUDENT SUCCESS STRATEGIES

No college can operate without students, who are unarguably the primary beneficiaries of higher education. Baker-Baldwin can have a multifaceted, effective, and robust student success model where strategic enrollment and retention management is centered to address the long-standing declines it has seen over the past decade. This is the right approach because most people on and off campus affiliated with the college ought to play a role in enrollment and retention management—including public affairs, public safety, food service, grounds/maintenance, residence life, budget office, academic deans, faculty, alumni, friends, provost, president, and the board of trustees.[18] This strategy prioritizes the key to making the institution remain viable and thrive when the onus is shifted to most of its constituents. It sends a signal to the local Cypress community and current and prospective donors that progress is being made in recruiting students, retaining students, and ultimately graduating them. This strategy would also address the concerns raised by a faculty representative on the presidential search committee, Dr. Carol Knight, about the financial stability of Baker-Baldwin, because transparency, ongoing reporting, and accountability will be part of the model.

I believe the student success mantra to be especially true for HBCUs because they are responsible for producing the majority of our Black teachers, veterinarians, lawyers, engineers, judges, and medical doctors. According to the UNCF, HBCU graduates' lifetime earnings will be $1 million more than if they had only a high school diploma, and within ten years post-graduation, they will be earning more than $71,000 a year. HBCUs like Baker-Baldwin College transform the Cypress community, the state, the nation, its students' families, and Black communities at large.[19]

A HISTORICAL LENS AND LESSONS ON FUNDRAISING EFFECTIVENESS

Benjamin Elijah Mays, a legendary president of Morehouse College who mentored Martin Luther King, Jr., said, "To be president of a college and white is no bed of roses. To be president of a college and black is almost a bed of thorns."[20] HBCU leaders have navigated and negotiated segregation, Jim Crow, economic depressions, lack of resources, and insufficient funding since their inception in the 1800s. HBCU leaders have always had to make a way out of no way while managing institutional, individual, and sociocultural oppression.

Mary McLeod Bethune, founder of Bethune-Cookman University, a political activist, educator, and educational leader, is a relevant figure from whom to draw implications for Baker-Baldwin College. More specifically, lessons from Bethune's fundraising success in the early 1900s are applicable to this case. Bethune started the college with only $1.50 in a dilapidated rental house, making a down payment of 50 cents and then paying $11 monthly. In an earlier analysis of her fundraising success, Shaun Harper and I found that Bethune was politically visible and engaged, politically astute, shameless, and skillful at cultivating politically beneficial relationships.[21] Her national visibility was a result of speeches and essays that she published and circulated throughout the US. She challenged white supremacy even as she sought interracial alliances. She held membership in many organizations and became the first Black woman to serve as head of a federal agency. Her involvement on multiple fronts in education, child welfare, and housing brought her into contact with a wide range of influential people, including influential philanthropists and US presidents. Most notably, Bethune was unabashed in the way she communicated and interfaced with philanthropists by remaining frank about the financial hardships threatening the college and unashamed to ask high-profile donors and strangers for large chunks of money. As we argued, "The evidence does not suggest that Bethune seemed to care much about African Americans being caricatured as poor and in need of White salvation; in fact, she used it to her advantage. Contemporary HBCU presidents, understandably, may deem improper this particular strategy. Yet, it is important to keep in mind, as Bethune did, that benefactors will not rescue an institution if its financial hardships are kept secret."[22]

A lesson that Dr. Davies could use from Bethune for his short- and long-term fundraising strategies is to contend with the politics of race and fear of political backlash. For example, it would behoove Dr. Davies to engage the nation publicly and be at the forefront of social movements like Black Lives Matter while also addressing the atrocity that happened in Cypress when the police murdered Shawn Perry, a former Baker-Baldwin student. Privately and simultaneously, Dr. Davies could reason with wealthy and powerful persons to advance causes important to him. Harper and I contend that Bethune engaged in what critical race theorists describe as interest convergence: "helping White persons recognize how they would benefit from advancing causes that help people of color."[23] This strategy would also be useful for Dr. Davies as he navigates the aftermath of Perry's murder and helps the students heal and develop healthy coping mechanisms while continuing to help Baker-Baldwin maintain and even exceed its financial priorities.

I am an eminent associate, a donor committed to providing substantial philanthropic support, to my undergraduate alma mater Tuskegee

University. I give at this level because of the institution's historic and contemporary mission, its proud traditions, and the ways that the faculty and staff develop leaders. I am equally moved by how its campus culture is implicitly and explicitly focused on preparing students to respond productively to racism, face life's challenges, and engage with the community.[24] Baker-Baldwin shares these attributes, and by building on them, it can continue to embrace its mission, achieve its vision and strategic priorities, attract and retain new students, and seek and cultivate new revenue streams to drive growth and improve its impact.

Tryan L. McMickens is a tenured associate professor at Suffolk University. His research agenda examines education inequities and marginalized college students. He earned bachelor's degrees in sales and marketing/business administration from Tuskegee University, a master's degree in higher education from Suffolk University, and a doctorate from the University of Pennsylvania.

COMMENTARY

Creative Imagination as a Grounding for Presidential Service

Illya Eliphis Davis

Many of the characteristic problematics faced by HBCUs are exacerbated by functioning ideologies that imply academic ineptitude and/or purport that HBCUs are functionally deficient. Both allegations lack merit and are founded on precarious presuppositions rooted in historical bigotry and racist predilections. Nonetheless, the merits of HBCUs are uniquely attributable to their cultural, social, historical, and political significance, intentionally and purposefully imbued by the schools. The merits are qualitative and substantive, and not merely historical.[25] HBCUs have consistently provided historical contexts for their students that often galvanize Black students to engage in social and political commitments and actions that exemplify this history. The criteria for the new president of Baker-Baldwin College must be attuned and committed to these concerns and needs. Baker-Baldwin's students opine for these fundamental qualities that identify HBCUs' uniqueness and relevance. The criteria for selecting an HBCU president must engage in imaginative ways of sustaining the social and intellectual relevance of the institution as well as cultivating students' commitment to remaking life-worlds through progressive social intervention.

MAPPING THE TERRITORY

In this case study, John Torrey and Corey Reed have provided an astute disclosure of the traditional presuppositions regarding practical criteria that have guided diverse college presidential searches, and by implication, they have given account of the character of higher education's vocational ambitions. They have delineated a particularly descriptive account of the evaluative and functional qualifications that they aver exemplify many extant HBCU presidents. They propound a uniqueness for the HBCU milieu. The candidates for president portrayed in the case study reflect formulaic *ideal types* that reveal an impoverished treatment of the progressive and creative institutional requirements requisite for many HBCUs. Fundamental to this engagement is a thoroughgoing creative imagining to refine the qualifications of the presidential candidates. In what follows, I will provide a description of the general tasks and complexities that are endemic to institutions of higher education in general, as well as an account of a uniqueness that is discernible within the HBCU context. These values serve as fundamental organizing principles, functioning as prescriptive guides for vetting the new president.

Baker-Baldwin must secure a new president because of the retirement of its recent president. The search committee is led by a competent alumna who recommends criteria that should be included in the assessment of candidates for the position. The new president should be adept at shoring up a fledgling enrollment and financial volatility; recalibrate the school's public image; and buoy efforts to strengthen the academic vitality through culturally contextual instruction and social advocacy. Two candidates have higher education experience, Dr. Taylor and Dr. Davies, while the third candidate, Mr. Block, is a businessman. They have varied foci for moving the college forward in positive directions.

CONCURRENCES AND VARIANCES

Prevailing assessments of higher education in general in the US are replete with forecasts of financial uncertainties associated with volatile and declining enrollment, concerns about unstable funding from corporate and governmental sources, prognostications of practical irrelevance and utility, and portentous assessments of possible culpability of expanding asymmetrical socioeconomic structures that appear to promote a contemporary plutocracy. These are authentic concerns that are viewed with greater suspicion of adequate redress when faced by HBCUs in comparison to HWCUs. If true, the Baker-Baldwin president has this added deficit to overcome when addressing these problems. The fundamental insight gleaned is this: because the HBCU most often has to disproportionately demonstrate competence and fidelity to the academic domain in general, it is incumbent upon the HBCU president to assuage these critical challenges through administrative rectitude, social relevance, and HBCU competence. This contextual competence is perhaps the animating virtue that keeps the HBCU president centered within the appropriate peculiarities of place and time.[26] Baker-Baldwin must prioritize its unique mission to serve Black students who come from divergent social contexts, yet are galvanized by sociopolitical and cultural forms of lived experiences—real and potential. Financial competence is paramount. But a "corporatization" of academic initiatives and institutional growth indices can lead to a marginalization of the purported centrality of the intellectual development of its students.

Baker-Baldwin must be circumspect regarding the prioritization of the business model promoted by Mr. Block. The virtues of HBCUs have traditionally been linked to the consequential and purposeful social intercourse that they nurture. There is mounting concern over what is viewed as the commercialization of colleges and universities, a critique levied from within and without the academy. The forms of commercialism are encompassing. There is a diffuse and pervasive sentiment in academic culture that some forms of marketing invite a language and attitude of the market, which is interpreted as corporatization. The language of "branding/rebranding" for purposes of recruitment further fuels the notion that the academic quarters have given way to market vernacular. Mr. Block's neoliberal proclivities toward co-opting a language that tends to the dehumanization of students by "branding" them fails to enlarge the students' humanity. The search committee should not choose a candidate better suited to serve as the institution's financial manager at the expense of maintaining a careful balance of financial aptitude and fidelity to the academic standards resonant with the aims and aspirations of its students and faculty.

FIDUCIARY FIDELITY

A moral virtue of the new president should be exemplified in the promotion of intellectual refinement of the students, academic freedoms for the faculty, and a curriculum conducive to developing cultural competencies.

Both Drs. Taylor and Davies aim to demonstrate profound fiduciary commitment to the students and would continue to foster the values of academic exactitude. These values buoy more receptive environs that embrace multifarious forms of diversity in the student population. Progressive imagining by Baker-Baldwin's new president should actively, if not proleptically, assure the faculty of its centrality to the fundamental sustainability and reputation of the college. Baker-Baldwin's robust liberal arts curriculum is appropriate to imbue the students with the intellectual wherewithal that facilitates addressing desired social transformations. Taylor and Davies find resonance with this scheme. The students' desire for a president attuned to developing a community that is invested in diverse modes of subjective expressions of identity, as well as versed in the cultural and social complexities within and without the college, is accounted for through progressive instruction and a curriculum designed to allay political and social conflicts.[27] This is enabled by infusing the value of imagination in the governing procedures of the president. Both Taylor and Davies appreciate cultivating students' social progressivism. Baker-Baldwin is not in need of candidates harboring messianic complexes, where foreclosure of the possibility for growth and maturity of the institution is reducible to one individual's musings. This will be a concerted effort. In choosing a president, the search committee must not ignore the redeeming attributes that ground the institution in the virtues its students and faculty have come to love.

Illya Eliphis Davis is the dean of Freshmen and Transition Programs, director of the Morehouse Accelerated Academic Program & Pre-Freshman Summer Enrichment Program, and professor of philosophy at Morehouse College. His research and teaching focus on Black intellectual traditions, Africana philosophy and race, philosophy of religion, philosophy of language, and moral philosophy.

COMMENTARY

HBCUs Are Rising: Contending with the Myths, the Legends, and the Realities

Steve D. Mobley, Jr., Travis C. Smith, and Jamila Lee-Johnson

(RE)SETTING THE TONE

As we analyzed this case, we immediately began to nuance the myriad factors at play. It is critical to note that HBCUs have been controversial since their foundings, and their cultures have been shaped in the womb of a country that perpetually struggles with *how* and *if* they are truly invested in the educational interests of Black Americans.[28] For example, the US Supreme Court has questioned their value in landmark cases (e.g., *United States v. Fordice* and *Adams v. Richardson*); policy makers in Alabama, Georgia, and Mississippi have also championed mergers with historically White intuitions (HWIs) and closures of HBCUs altogether.[29] Conversely, this case also illuminates how HBCUs often have to confront their own tendencies to inculcate socially conservative cultures. Conservative values, practices, and traditions are not relegated to a specific sector of HBCUs.[30] However, many of these institutions endorse traditionalist beliefs that affect myriad HBCU stakeholders who do not yield to particular mores that these colleges strive to uphold.[31] Thus, as critical HBCU scholars, during our appraisal of this case, we heavily considered how HBCUs are often forced to navigate tradition and legacy, White supremacy, and public perceptions that are mired in anti-Black fallacy.

"TELL THEM WE ARE RISING"

A significant detail that should not be overlooked within this case is that Baker-Baldwin's presidential search committee identified several vital issues that were pertinent to the search. These directives called up how HBCUs have perpetually been purveyors of social change and racial uplift—and how this must continue at Baker-Baldwin. These specific criteria also illuminated the reality that HBCUs are among few educational spaces that both sustain and place Black culture at the forefront.[32] In tandem with reconciling financial and enrollment management concerns, the search committee made it very clear that the next president must be able to: (1) preserve the ideals of Baker-Baldwin amid the COVID-19 pandemic, and (2) be adept in discussing and engaging Baker-Baldwin constituents in contemporary conversations regarding anti-Blackness, racism, and White supremacy.

While COVID-19 is a formidable force that the world now has to reckon with, the presence of systemic racism has been an everlasting pandemic that HBCUs *and* Black communities have been forced to reconcile and navigate. It is no secret that, since their establishments, HBCUs have had to combat anti-Black ideological violence that is a direct by-product of the historical oppression and racism of which these institutions were born.[33] Thus, the ways in which the new president leads Baker-Baldwin in traversing Black struggle *and* triumph will be critical and emblematic in how the institution evolves in community *with* various Black stakeholders.

Finally, it is quite encouraging that with regard to COVID-19, a prospective HBCU president has models for how they can traverse these dual pandemics (e.g., North Carolina Agricultural & Technical State University, Elizabeth City State University, and Alabama State University). Black communities have succumbed to this pandemic at alarming rates, yet HBCUs are once again at the forefront of providing refuge. Unfortunately, many HBCU students, staff, faculty, and administrators have either experienced loss or succumbed to the virus. However, HBCUs have credited high compliance rates and low COVID-19 numbers due to their communal cultures and a collective responsibility that is very knowing of the toll that the pandemic has had on Black, Latinx, and Indigenous communities.

ALL BLACK LIVES MATTER

A final directive from the presidential search committee was for the incoming president to be able to address the student government's "issue of focus" regarding the treatment of queer, gender-nonconforming, and all other students whose appearance goes against the image expectations that the institution upholds in its conservative values. As this case revealed, there are errant anti-Black practices that manifest on HBCU campuses that have been veiled under the guise of tradition and policies that directly impact their students (e.g., dress codes and student codes of conduct). The aforementioned conservative ideals that arise on HBCU campuses in efforts to "fix" or "protect" their students heavily affect their experiences during matriculation and even upon graduation.[34] Thus, we support the choice of Dr. Theodore Davies and believe he would acknowledge that ALL Black Lives Matter (e.g., heterosexual, queer, cisgender, gender-nonconforming, and trans* students).

HBCUs do not represent a singular ideal of Blackness. Rather, within these distinct spaces, Blackness has always been (re)imagined and given space to be performed in its infinite possibilities.[35] This is key because, as Blackness continues to evolve, HBCUs must respond to shifts in Black communities as well. As Dr. Davies ascends to the presidency, he must critically assess and reevaluate the hetero-patriarchal norms of Baker-Baldwin as he has committed to honoring "the proud traditions and namesakes" of the institution.

Steve D. Mobley, Jr., is an assistant professor of higher education administration at The University of Alabama. His scholarship focuses on the contemporary placement of HBCUs. Particularly, his research underscores and highlights the understudied facets of HBCU communities including issues surrounding race, social class, and student sexuality.

Jamila L. Lee-Johnson is an inclusive excellence lecturer in the Department of Curriculum and Instruction at the University of Wisconsin-Whitewater. Her scholarship focuses on the experiences of Black women in higher education, specifically undergraduate Black women's leadership at HBCUs.

Travis C. Smith is a clinical assistant professor of student personnel in higher education at the University of Florida. His scholarship focuses on Black student involvement at historically Black colleges and universities. Particularly, his research examines and highlights the understudied experiences of HBCU students regarding leadership, race, gender, and class.

COMMENTARY

Boards, Budgets, and Black Lives: Baker-Baldwin's Great Balancing Act

Felecia Commodore

Baker-Baldwin is a liberal arts HBCU amid an institutional transition consisting of new presidential leadership, new economic challenges, and shifting ideas on campus and in greater society. Baker-Baldwin is navigating enrollment challenges, financial challenges, and possibly shifting institutional focus and identity. As the board and new president move forward in Baker-Baldwin's next great era, major considerations exist. Currently, Baker-Baldwin is determining how to navigate heightened US racial tensions as well as instructional delivery challenges due to COVID-19. Like many US institutions, enrollment has become a major concern during the pandemic. This strain occurs as Baker-Baldwin has already been experiencing enrollment challenges. It is imperative that institutional leaders set a vision for their campus community, communicate that vision, and inspire and motivate community members to buy-in and implement said vision. In this context, I present three major areas of consideration Baker-Baldwin's leadership should engage as they attempt to lead this institution in building upon its great legacy.

CULTURALLY SUSTAINING STRATEGIC PLANNING

Baker-Baldwin must be intentional in developing both a short-term and long-term strategic plan. The first part of this process will be ensuring that the new president, board chair, and the rest of the board build a trusting, transparent relationship that includes collective work and communication. If there is no trust present between a president and a board or there are tense president-board relations, the institution suffers.[36] Being that Baker-Baldwin must address some large issues to continue its success, it is a necessity for the board and new president to have a solid relationship. With this relationship as foundation, the president and board need to engage with key leaders and campus constituents to devise an institutional strategic plan. However, this cannot be a generic plan. The current stressors and challenges presented by COVID-19, declining enrollment, and issues of equity must be centered in the strategic planning process in order for Baker-Baldwin to successfully navigate its changing campus culture. A governance model that Raquel Rall, Demetri Morgan, and I have proposed—Culturally Sustaining Governance (CSG)—can serve as a guide.[37] CSG is a decision-making approach in which boards work to recognize the assets and strengths of each of the campus and community members and leverage those traits to help propel and strengthen institutional transformation. Through employing this model, board members consider culture by way of equity as a central piece of their decision-making.[38]

This approach to strategic planning bodes well for the institution moving forward. Baker-Baldwin must face the very serious fiscal and enrollment situation before them. However, as their student body and faculty have called for attention to the various socioeconomic statuses of students, some students' lack of sense of belonging, and social and racial justice issues affecting the community, the board must make fiscally solvent *and* equity-centered decisions. Engaging in CSG allows for that opportunity. For instance, regarding instructional delivery during COVID-19, the institution has an opportunity to take inventory of its infrastructure capabilities. This includes understanding the needs and access challenges that may exist for its students.

Some of the challenges Baker-Baldwin is experiencing, such as enrollment, are not unique but rather reflect national trends. Nevertheless, Baker-Baldwin is experiencing these trends in its own way. Therefore, the institution must engage in a nuanced, multifaceted approach. Though many of the faculty provide anecdotal data about student concerns and barriers to success, leadership needs disaggregated data to help inform decisions. Together, this data, an understanding of student experiences, and Dr. Davies's expertise may lead to a strategic enrollment plan that adapts to the current challenges but keeps Baker-Baldwin's unique identity in mind.

BALANCING BUDGETS AND BUILDING BRANDS

Trustee Price brings a sobering perspective to the search committee discussions highlighting Baker-Baldwin's current financial deficit and projected 15 percent enrollment decrease. These financial and enrollment deficits should not be taken lightly, as financial issues are often the top issue in accreditation challenges for HBCUs. The board and president must consider creative ways to cut costs and expenditures and hold steady or increase income. This is not new territory for HBCUs, which have always engaged in creative and entrepreneurial imagination due to wealth barriers created by systemic racism. Opportunities may exist in development and consortium membership.

Leadership must continue to hold good relationships with current donors while procuring new donors and partnerships. The current awakening regarding inequities and racial injustice position Baker-Baldwin well to attract philanthropists willing to invest in the HBCU sector. Having leadership that will not simply sell the institution as a brand but rather position it as a value proposition will bode well for the institution's place in the higher education marketplace. To successfully make that value proposition, the data mentioned in discussing strategic planning will be crucial. Additionally, another area to conserve costs and expenditures is by using the consortium. Though it is not clear what the consortium entails, course sharing or even resource sharing opportunities, if present, could aid in cutting costs. Collaboration has historically proven itself to be a tool HBCUs can engage during lean times. Collaborative efforts also showcase the HBCU community's creativity and collective economics.

Though these strategies speak to fiscal issues, financial challenges are not the same as enrollment issues, even at a tuition-dependent institution. Nestled in the strategic planning process, Baker-Baldwin's leadership should consider a targeted, data-driven enrollment management plan, including a plan to rebrand. This does not necessarily mean a complete overhaul but rather using various forms of data to identify strengths and opportunities for niche building. The niche approach has proved beneficial for several HBCUs. This opportunity exists and can be accomplished while staying true to Baker-Baldwin's institutional mission. Part of brand building includes examining and evaluating campus climate and culture.

TRANSFORMATIVE TRADITION

There is a difference between tradition and poor practice. The former can build intergenerational bonds, inspire, and provide a sense of collective identity. The latter can cause miscommunication, ineffectiveness, and even harm. Baker-Baldwin's leadership should evaluate its practices, determining which are community- and institutional-building traditions and which should be discontinued. Doing so will take much conversation and education. Leadership has an opportunity to bring various campus constituencies together for dialogue, allowing student issues with inclusion to be addressed. This also provides an opportunity for Baker-Baldwin to consider how to build on its legacy and traditions in ways that speak directly to this moment of awakening to US racial injustice.

As an HBCU, Baker-Baldwin likely already has elements and tools needed to equip students to navigate heightened racism as well as to fight against racist, white supremacist structures. HBCUs have long been fertile ground for activism. From young Black women HBCU collegians fighting for Black women's suffrage in the early 1900s to those currently fighting to ensure justice for the murder of young Black people, HBCUs are not new to empowering students to speak out against an anti-Black society and to speak truth to power. Leadership should see the current racial tensions not as a challenge but as an opportunity. HBCUs, from their very foundation, were created for moments like this. Baker-Baldwin has new leadership and new challenges, but strong resolve and strong community members. A leader who can honor what exists while casting a vision of what can be, in a way that engages stakeholders and achieves buy-in, will be a leader who takes Baker-Baldwin into its next great iteration.

Felecia Commodore is an assistant professor of higher education at Old Dominion University in Norfolk, Virginia. Felecia's research focus areas are leadership, governance, and administrative practices focusing on HBCUs. Felecia's research interests also lie in decision-making processes and the relationship of Black women and leadership in higher education.

CHAPTER 8

Community-Campus Relationships and the Public Good

REBECCA M. TAYLOR AND ALICE REZNICKOVA

In this case, the newly hired director of a community partnership initiative at a small Midwestern college evaluates possible program models to advance sustainability and justice.

Pruitt College recently launched an initiative, Partnership for Plainview, to be led by the new Center for Community Partnerships (CCP).[1] The initiative had grown out of a series of Presidential Town Halls in which students, faculty, and staff had discussed the role of serving the public good in their mission. The conversations were far-reaching. Questions were raised about Pruitt's responsibility to prepare students to be democratically engaged members of society; about the quality of Pruitt's relationships with the local municipality, businesses, and community organizations; and about their wide-ranging impacts on Pruitt's hometown of Plainview, as well as on the surrounding region through everything from emissions to procurement practices. Partnership for Plainview represented a narrowing of this vision; its goal was to strengthen Pruitt's efforts to provide robust and innovative community-engaged learning experiences for students and to reimagine the role of local communities in these learning experiences.

Aria James was hired to direct the CCP in a dual administrative and non-tenure-track faculty appointment with a three-year contract. Aria, a first-generation college graduate, had gone on to earn a PhD in sustainability education from the flagship public research university located in the state capital, her hometown. While completing her doctoral program, she had worked as a community liaison in the Center for Development and Social Change at the university. During her interview at Pruitt, Aria had emphasized the importance of critical community engagement and reexamining the balance of power in community-campus partnerships. Her vision for Partnership for Plainview was grounded in her conviction that efforts to promote the public good should be rooted in the values of sustainability and justice—requiring a broad societal transformation that involves reconceptualizing progress as a society and redistributing power and resources across communities. She believed colleges and universities should prepare students to take up this cause for the betterment of their local communities and broader society.

Before accepting the position, Aria learned that Plainview, though primarily populated with white, multigenerational Midwestern families, included a small number of Latinx families and a growing community of Somali refugees. Stretching beyond the town limits were a number of rural, predominantly white agricultural communities as well as a small area of recognized tribal lands of the region's First People. Beyond them, within a few hours' drive, several midsized cities, including the state capital, dotted the map. These cities, which boasted a wider array of industries, were home to sizable Black and Latinx communities, which included both multigeneration US-based families and newer refugee and immigrant families. Plainview, like many small towns in the Midwest, was predominantly politically conservative, with approximately 70 percent of residents voting Republican in the last two presidential elections. Across the entire region, communities were struggling to weather an economic decline that had begun decades earlier and been worsened by the 2008 recession and the COVID-19 pandemic. In recent years, several landowners in the region had leased their property to sand-mining operations, hoping to benefit from increased demand for natural gas.

Aria also learned that Pruitt—a moderately selective private college with around eighteen hundred students and a medium-sized endowment—was navigating an enrollment decline that had begun a decade earlier. Historically, Pruitt had enrolled mostly white middle- and upper-middle-class students from suburban communities across the Midwest. As enrollment and retention dropped, the admissions office had begun to recruit more heavily in the surrounding area—targeting both rural and urban communities. These efforts were bolstered by a new scholarship program for students from underrepresented backgrounds. With this change in recruitment strategy, the college was gradually becoming more economically and racially diverse, while also experiencing increasing political polarization among students on campus.

With this context in mind, Aria and the CCP team (an administrative assistant shared between several offices and a few student interns) conducted an inventory of community-engaged and publicly oriented learning experiences currently provided at Pruitt. They learned that students had ample opportunities to participate in volunteerism and philanthropy with local community organizations ranging from events organized by Greek life to staff-led days of service. On the curricular side, all students were required to complete one community-engaged (CE) course before graduation. To fulfill this requirement, courses had to address the core objectives of teaching students to: (1) collaborate effectively with a community partner to address a goal or need of the partner, (2) identify diverse perspectives on social issues, and (3) improve their communication skills.

From reviewing syllabi and talking with students, faculty, and community leaders, Aria gathered that the quality and approach to community engagement of these courses varied. Most CE courses required students to volunteer a set number of hours in a local organization and journal about their experiences. Student feedback was divided: some enjoyed it; others considered it a waste of time. When asked to describe what they took away, many students focused on how they enjoyed helping others and getting off campus. Community partners reported disparate experiences with the CE courses. While some described effective collaborative partnerships with faculty and students that continued to develop over the years, others mentioned faculty who were hard to reach and students who were underprepared to interact with communities different from them.

Aria contemplated the best way forward. She knew the college had only committed to funding Partnership for Plainview for its first three years. During their initial conversations, Pruitt's senior leaders had emphasized the ways the CCP could be leveraged to promote recruitment and retention and to bolster their efforts to solicit new donations in the future. Aria knew that the sustainability of Partnership for Plainview itself was key to its potential long-term contributions to the public good. She was wary of trying to do too much, but also wanted to be bold and have a positive impact. Aria knew she would have to navigate these various aims in order to build a sustainable and impactful program. With these constraints in mind, she decided to explore options for building on the existing CE requirement, given its established presence on campus.

One option had been voiced by a number of faculty in the college's growing pre-professional programs. They were interested in expanding the CE requirement beyond the traditional service-learning model by incorporating internship opportunities. Parker Brown, a business professor, was the first to propose this idea to Aria: "If you ask me, the two most important ways Pruitt can contribute to the public good are preparing students to succeed in the real world and supporting economic development in Plainview. Both of those goals can be achieved through internships. We already provide internship opportunities, but some of them lack a robust classroom component. With your support, we could diversify the types of organizations we support and improve the quality of the internships across the board." Aria imagined that positive internship experiences could encourage more students to stay in Plainview after graduation and could enhance fundraising opportunities for Pruitt, providing resources to build out Partnership for Plainview in the future. The CCP could help develop relationships with potential internship placements and work to ensure both students' and community partners' interests are met.

An internship model would put the interests of the community partners first, but at the same time, opportunities for students to do transformative work in sustainability and justice might be limited. Some internships might even actively undermine these aims. The local chamber of commerce and its affiliated businesses had expressed interest in creating formal structured opportunities for students to work with them for course credit during the academic year, rather than providing only a limited number of opportunities over the summer. One idea they proposed was collaborating on a plan to attract more businesses and high-end housing to the area to promote local commerce and tourism. Aria worried that the project could exacerbate gentrification and worsen conditions for people who were unhoused or experiencing housing instability in the area. She had also talked with a representative from a local heavy machinery manufacturing industry who was developing a proposal for a new industrial park, which could exacerbate air and water pollution that were already a concern with the sand-mining and agricultural activities in the region. If Partnership for Plainview took up the call for more internship-based partnerships, how would they navigate these potential conflicts with their vision for advancing sustainability and justice?

A second option had been expressed by a contingent of the college community who were frustrated by the variable quality of the current CE offerings. One CE course led by Ezra Madani, a popular sociology professor, had been going strong for ten years. Ezra had developed long-term partnerships with the Somali Community Development Center in Plainview and the Indigenous Community Resource Hub based in the neighboring tribal lands. Each year, these organizations proposed projects, including some research collaborations, which students further developed with Ezra's support. Each project was designed to build the capacity of the partners and their communities and to provide students with valuable project management skills and awareness of critical social justice issues in local communities.

Yet many CE courses were much less robust experiences for everyone involved. In surveying current opportunities, Aria found that most CE courses partnered with larger organizations that could take in twenty to thirty volunteers every semester, providing consistency for students and reducing burdens on faculty to find multiple placements with smaller organizations. These large organizations included a regional food bank, a popular afterschool program, and a homeless shelter. All three were run by Christian charitable organizations and focused on alleviating the consequences of regional economic downturn by providing direct services. As the need for these services was not abating, the organizations valued the steady flow of students ready to assist. These partnerships helped students build local ties, and some students continued their volunteer work even after the courses ended.

In conversation with Aria, Ezra described frustration at the lack of support available to faculty creating new CE courses: "It's no wonder that so many of these courses resort to simple volunteerism models of service learning. Doing community-based work and doing it well—in a way that involves students in real work to address the root causes of injustice in our communities—requires so much time and energy. This is what I do. I put all of myself into it. But most faculty haven't been trained to do this work, and it isn't directly linked to their research agendas. Faculty need more support, but beyond that, we should prioritize community-engaged research and teaching in promotion and tenure policies and in hiring!"

One path for the CCP would be to address Ezra's call by building up the current CE requirement. They could design faculty training workshops to support the development of high-quality community-engaged research and learning experiences for students. They could also cultivate community partner relationships with a more diverse array of organizations from local communities and connect faculty with these groups to help expand the reach of the CE courses beyond the most common large organizations.

By grounding this work in the existing CE requirement, the CCP could reach the maximum number of students, but they would be reliant on faculty to implement the resources they would offer. Aria knew some faculty members would resist taking suggestions from a non-tenure-track faculty member or simply not have time to take advantage of the resources offered. Even if faculty did engage, continuity could still be a problem. CE courses were often taught by temporary faculty members or shuffled between various department members every couple of years. This transience left community organizations with a sense that they might expend a great deal of effort to incorporate students into their work but then not be able to rely on the college for continued support. Would it be possible to foster sustainable and just partnerships within the current CE model? For this approach to succeed, would changes to hiring priorities and tenure and promotion policies be required?

The final model Aria imagined involved a more transformative approach. Amid a growing movement calling to end police brutality and systemic racism, a group of students issued a list of demands for college leadership—including severing their ties to the local police department and offering more educational opportunities that centered the aims of anti-racism and justice. Conservative student clubs on campus had challenged this call, and the local paper had published an op-ed criticizing the student activists for sowing division in the local community. The CCP could respond to the student activists' call by collaboratively designing a certificate program through which students could work with local organizations to advance sustainability and justice more explicitly throughout their undergraduate experience.

The certificate curriculum would be grounded in the principles of sustainability and justice; the learning outcomes would include project management, anti-racism, and collaborative research and project design in partnership with local community partners. One of the courses would satisfy the CE requirement. The CCP could select projects that aligned with this vision, shape these experiences with the community partners equitably, and develop long-term relationships with projects that continue building upon each other over the semesters. Rather than trying to coax faculty into doing this work, Aria could take it on herself and develop a model CE learning experience for students.

With this structure, though, they wouldn't reach as many students. And as is common with community-engaged courses, they would have to contend with students' desires to "fix" problems in the community rather than work alongside community partners to advance their aims. With a centralized approach, they might be better able to address problematic "savior" mentalities. Yet, a centralized certificate program would also engage fewer faculty, potentially losing valuable allies. Choosing projects based on criteria set forth by sustainability and justice initiatives could also make the program vulnerable to protest by the contingent of students and community members who opposed Pruitt taking a more active approach to combating issues of environmental and racial injustice. Would narrowing their approach undermine their support and thus their ability to have a long-term impact? Could they develop the kind of just partnerships they envisioned knowing the program might be cut due to backlash or shifts in staffing or funding priorities in the coming years?

With limited time for implementation and fundraising, Aria needed to establish a coherent vision for the program and undertake the lengthy process of enacting it. The three approaches she was considering varied in the number of students, faculty, staff, and community stakeholders they would engage, the type of engagement they would require, and the conception of the public good they might advance. Aria valued democratic decision-making; yet it was clear that different factions of faculty, staff, students, and community partners had divergent interests. Moreover, she was aware that despite her efforts to reach out broadly, she had not heard all voices with a stake in this initiative. This decision was complicated by the potential value conflicts embedded in the possible paths.

How should Aria move forward to advance the public good through Partnership for Plainview? How should she balance the interests of the various college and community stakeholders? What vision of the public good should guide her? How should she navigate the practical constraints that might impede realization of this vision? How does Aria's positionality within the community (including what we know, as well as what we don't know) inform the path she should take?

COMMENTARY

Letting the Public Decide What's Good for Them

Jasmine Gurneau

The United States was built on stolen land and stolen labor. In recent years, many colleges and universities have been examining their institutions' histories, either around their ties to slavery or the dispossession of traditional Indigenous homelands, and realizing they owe a lot to the communities in which they are situated. Considering this history, colleges and universities like Pruitt College have a responsibility to invest in equitable relationships with the communities in which they occupy.

As Pruitt College explores how to best advance its mission to serve the public good, I suggest that it will be crucial to understand the complex history and relationship between the college and the community, as well as to collectively co-design a framework for partnership. I will illustrate these points using the example of Western education's relationship with Native Americans in North America before introducing the concept and benefits of co-design.

HISTORY OF HIGHER EDUCATION AND NATIVE AMERICANS

For Native Americans in the United States and Canada, schooling was used as a tool of assimilation, coercing or forcibly removing children from their families to attend boarding schools miles away from home. Between the late 1800s and early 1900s, federally funded boarding schools prohibited Native American children from practicing their beliefs, language, and culture. Many forms of abuse occurred at these schools, and many children never returned home. Deep-rooted historical trauma still manifests in Native American communities today. Further, the Morrill Act of 1862, signed by President Abraham Lincoln, created land-grant institutions by directing lands expropriated from Indigenous Peoples to be sold and the profits to be used toward seed funding for the establishment of state colleges. Because many of the treaty agreements between tribes and the United States—promising health care, education, and general welfare—have not been honored, these colleges have essentially profited off the theft of Indigenous land.[2] Higher education continues to be inaccessible to Native Americans, with Natives earning less than half of the national average for both bachelor's and graduate degrees.[3] While Pruitt College may not be a land-grant institution, it occupies Indigenous homelands and exists within the context of relationships between Native Americans and the harmful legacy of Western education.

While distrust of Western education and its associated institutions exists among Native Americans, many still see education as a pathway toward cultivating the tools needed to build healthy home communities. This process can be referred to as Tribal Nation Building or the "process by which a Native nation strengthens its own capacity for effective and culturally relevant self-government and for self-determined and sustainable community development."[4] Understanding this complex history is important for any higher education institution planning to enter into partnerships with tribal communities.

WHAT IS MEANT BY "PUBLIC GOOD," AND HOW DO YOU GET THERE?

Different units within Pruitt College may all have a vision for the "public good," yet who better to help develop a vision and framework than the public themselves? An important first step will be developing a shared understanding of "public good" and equitable partnerships together with the actual public—the local municipality, business, community organizations, and tribal nations in the surrounding region.

One way to do this is by using a co-designing process. University affiliates can incorporate practices and principles from participatory design research (PDR) or community-based design research (CBDR) approaches that can promote equitable modes of learning, teaching, and research.[5] The collaborative process of co-design can aid in redistributing power and decision-making and allow for incorporating various experiences, skills, expertise, and perspectives to reconceptualize societal "progress." It was a missed opportunity not to invite local communities to the initial Presidential Town Halls; moving forward, it will be imperative that the college hosts co-design sessions with all stakeholders to discuss and dialogue what public good is and how to get there.

This process could inform a set of criteria that the college could use as a framework for building and sustaining equitable campus-community partnerships. As the university hires new faculty, creates and updates course offerings, develops new initiatives, considers and proposes new research projects, creates spending budgets, requests grant funding, or develops fundraising plans, it all can be informed by this shared framework. Co-design sessions will also need to be an ongoing practice. The community's needs will be ever-changing, priorities will evolve, and college leadership will have natural turnover. Consistent conversations will allow the college to remain informed and responsive to the needs, experiences, and vision of the communities in which the university is situated. While community constituencies are not one-size-fits-all, this framework can provide some guidance on how to engage in conversations with potential community partners.

The partnerships that Professor Madani developed are a great example of the potential of co-design. Her long-term, sustained partnerships with two organizations have hopefully led to a deeper understanding of those communities. She shares some agency with these organizations by having them propose projects, but the development of the projects seems to be furthered by students separate from the organizations. Some projects include research collaborations that have potential to address root causes of systemic issues toward long-term change making, rather than one-sided, superficial collaborations.

Fearing backlash for transforming their approach to community partnerships is understandable. A co-design process does not guarantee unanimity. Making space for different perspectives, especially those of undervalued and disadvantaged groups, will take practice and intention. Having deep and widespread engagement, enabling decision-making at all levels, and involving a broad range of stakeholders will aid in strengthening relationships, building trust, and bolstering investment or buy-in to the partnership with the college. As this process continues, a growing collective will be cultivated and, I believe, a shift in the culture will take place. This collective will broaden the base of support to protect the college and combat against any pushback that it faces. Anyone who opposes more active approaches to combating issues of environmental and racial injustice will not only be challenging the college, but all stakeholders and community members who were a part of this collective dialogue, design, and visioning.

CONCLUSION

Developing equitable, sustainable, and just partnerships begins with relationship building, shared visioning, and deepening understanding of the communities with whom the college would like to build partnerships. Acknowledging and responding to the complexity of histories, needs, experiences, strengths, and dreams is part of that work. If Pruitt College takes up its work in this way, faculty may be surprised (or not) to see that increasing internships (or, essentially, ten to fifteen weeks of hosting a minimally trained volunteer) won't quite cut it—whether there are three or thirty volunteers. Instead, they may begin to see an increase in trust, innovation, buy-in, capacity building, and a redistribution of power and resources. While colleges and universities have a history of perpetuating inequities, Aria has an opportunity to assist Pruitt College in disrupting that legacy by helping them see that they are not the only experts in the formation of a better world.

Jasmine Gurneau (Oneida/Menominee) serves as the manager for Native American and Indigenous Initiatives in the Office of Institutional Diversity and Inclusion at Northwestern University. Jasmine leads the development and implementation of university-wide initiatives related to the inclusion of Native American and Indigenous students, faculty, staff, alumni, and tribal communities.

COMMENTARY

Course-Correcting for Just Community

Alyssa Melby

This commentary is written in epistolary form to highlight the importance of relationships in community engagement efforts.

Dear Aria,

From one colleague to another, I am envious of this tremendous opportunity. Yet you were brought into a process where some decisions were already made, particularly on whose voices were heard and the initiative's priority. Pragmatically, you must choose programming soon. Given that my own role involves faculty development and the many similarities I see between our situations (first-gen women working at small private colleges in rural areas), I recommend pursuing the faculty development option, but with a few caveats to make this option as impactful and grounded in your community's priorities as possible.

The college likely hired you because of your thoughtful attention to power, relationships, and sustainability. You acknowledge that the options could both reify and challenge power inequities. Internships could reinforce capitalist notions of "economic development" if that economic development is not also concerned with justice and sustainability. Yet the small-town business owner might be your neighbor who could really use students to grow and keep their business thriving. Students devising social action projects empowers them but could shift focus to their own priorities, not those of the immediate community. Focusing on faculty continues the allocation of resources to those who already have the most power, but faculty may be in the best position to do this work long-term.

To wrestle with this dilemma, I offer the concept of *vocation*, or the calling to use one's talents for the greater good of the world. A concept rooted in Christianity, vocation can sometimes reflect a savior complex, particularly with regard to community engagement. However, I appreciate how this concept invites us (and our institutions) to consider how we position ourselves in "right relationship"—where our drive toward our own vocation does not override the dignity, needs, and vocation of others. Florence Amamoto's suggestion that we "develop [this] ability to respond" to others—"our response-ability"—starts with knowing exactly where we stand in our own beliefs and relationships.[6] While I empathize with your concern about alienating others by choosing one option over another, our students demand this response-ability from us, and frankly, our faculty and partners want this clarity too. For instance, must you say yes to every business that approaches you about internships if it is not also working toward justice and/or sustainability? Saying no may close doors to certain relationships, but perhaps those relationships aren't "right" for your and your institution's vocation. Responding fully right now to injustice is not, admittedly, likely to be reciprocal for the college, but it is what the world demands from us as we work to correct the power imbalances of our relationships. Lean into the critical commitments and justice-based values that you bring!

Speaking of relationships, Tania Mitchell explains that authentic relationships between community and campus partners are "dependent on dialogue and connection," and I agree with her that long-term partnerships should be *the* goal of critical service learning.[7] Yet relationships take time to develop authentically into long-term partnerships that possess closeness, equity, and integrity.[8] Who already has relationships with the community? Your faculty, to varying degrees of closeness. Who are likely to be around longer to build authentic relationships with partners? Your faculty. The students can and should help strengthen these relationships, but if long-term partnerships are desired, working with faculty and the relationships they bring or want to cultivate is key. Yet . . . your community is multifaceted, with very real tensions between newcomers and long-term residents—who all live on land stolen from your region's Indigenous peoples. The polarized political climate, on and off campus, makes this infinitely harder. Consider creating dialogue opportunities where people from across the community can find common values between conservative and progressive worldviews. Authentic relationships based in a sense of response-ability to each other will depend on faculty and community members finding connections.

We both know, though, that some faculty aren't good at building relationships or don't have the critical commitments to ethical community engagement. Some faculty are not well-suited for this work. *That's ok*. Just as you didn't expect all students to jump at the certificate program, not all faculty will (or should) jump at this work! A committed core of faculty can right-size this work so you can remain fully grounded in your critical commitments and also engage more students over time via your graduation requirement. Your current engaged faculty have already told you what they need in order to do this work better—more support and incentives like time, extra compensation, and acknowledgment in promotion, all of which recognize the relational labor of community-engaged (CE) courses. You already have champions to help you succeed in this option. Use their expertise and their desire to do this work better!

For instance, your faculty note the variability of CE courses where the default tends toward "simple volunteerism." Instead of dismissing direct service outright to focus solely on system-level change, this dilemma can begin to be corrected by critical reflection that "brings attention to social change through dispelling myths of deficiency while acknowledging how systems of inequality function in our society."[9] Take the food bank. Not allowing for direct service means people in the community may go hungry if students aren't there to volunteer. How could CCP move the CE courses into this critical mode? Maybe work with faculty to add an additional learning outcome focused on investigating systemic causes of social issues or encourage them to layer the direct service experience with additional actions from the Social Change Wheel, like advocacy efforts, to have students experience the multiple ways social change occurs.[10]

While envious of your opportunity, I'm not envious of the hard decisions you must make. It will take gumption and fortitude to navigate the many relationships and politics of your institution and community at large. I think faculty development is paramount, but fully acknowledge that I'm not from your community. I can't answer the most essential question: *What does* your community *need from you?* Centering the community in its many facets is a necessary ethical course corrective for years of putting faculty and institutional goals first, but so is centering the voices and needs of people who have been historically disempowered. If you keep holding the vision for a just community at the center of your decisions, you'll live into your personal values and what your community is calling you to do to exist in "right relationship."

Sincerely,
A colleague in solidarity

Alyssa Melby has served as assistant director for academic civic engagement at St. Olaf College (Northfield, Minnesota) since fall 2017. She is responsible for facilitating faculty professional development on and supporting community-engaged learning courses. She is a former community partner of higher education institutions, having previously worked in arts management and education for twelve years.

COMMENTARY

Institutionalizing Engagement for Stronger Colleges and Communities

MICHAEL J. RICH

Over the past thirty years, more than a thousand colleges and universities have increased their commitment to the civic purposes of education. While many of these institutions created centers, programs, and initiatives to further their civic missions, they have failed to achieve their desired impact. According to one authoritative assessment, achieving impact "requires institution-wide effort, deep commitment at all levels, and leadership by both campus and community."[11] Achieving the transformative effects on college and community to which Pruitt aspires will therefore require a bigger, broader, bolder, and deeper institutional commitment than the three options laid out in the case study. Here are five practices that Aria and her colleagues might adopt to demonstrate Pruitt's institutional commitment to the Partnership for Plainview.

START FROM LOCAL CONDITIONS

While Presidential Town Halls and the inventory of service-learning courses and volunteer activities are an important first step, we also need to know how Pruitt is institutionally engaged with its immediate and broader communities and how, if at all, that engagement aligns with its academic and service engagements.[12] Does Pruitt have a commitment to equitable local and minority hiring? Local and minority business procurement? Affordable housing? Business incubation? Arts and cultural development?

Most importantly, Partnership for Plainview was initially developed without any input from residents and community leaders. If this is to be a mutually beneficial partnership, it is essential that voices from a broad range of community stakeholders—residents, community-based organizations, nonprofit agencies, businesses, local governments, faith-based organizations, philanthropic and charitable organizations, among others—be heard and inform the strategic focus of the initiative. What are the most pressing problems the community is facing, and how might collaborative engagement enable the community and the college to work effectively to address these issues?

INTEGRATE TEACHING, RESEARCH, AND SERVICE

For the initiative to be sustainable, it must align with Pruitt's core academic missions. As Ira Harkavy, director of Penn's Netter Center for Community Partnerships, has noted, "[U]niversities are in a unique position to . . . [go] beyond service learning (and its inherent limitations) to strategic, academically-based community service, which has as its primary goal contributing to the well-being of people in the community both now and in the future."[13] The key for Aria and Pruitt's senior leadership will be to tie service to teaching and research to promote a deeper understanding of community needs and the most effective strategies for addressing those needs. Service that is grounded in volunteerism and alleviating individual misery (e.g., feeding the hungry, sheltering the homeless), while an important contribution, fails to fully engage Pruitt's intellectual capital to assist the community in creating and implementing solutions that address the structural factors that create the conditions that require service.

CONTINUUM OF STUDENT ENGAGEMENT

Not all Pruitt students may be interested, willing, or capable of engaging with the community at the highest levels of intensity. Requiring all students to participate in a community-engaged course, therefore, may not have the desired impact and could be harmful to efforts to develop deeper relationships with community partners. As an alternative, Pruitt should provide a continuum of engagement that provides students with opportunities for increasingly intense levels of engagement that build on prior learning and experience. This continuum might begin with a volunteer activity, move to enrollment in a course with a community-engaged learning component, advance to participation in a more focused academic program (e.g., Pruitt's proposal for a certificate program), and conclude with original research completed through an honors thesis or capstone project. Aria and her colleagues could align Pruitt's existing service opportunities and community-engaged courses to provide a foundation for a continuum organized around tracks in specific issue areas that align with community interests (e.g., economic development, hunger and homelessness, K–12 education, health, and environment and sustainability).

A continuum of engagement enables Pruitt to communicate where community engagement can lead students in terms of career paths, personal development, and the integration of their academic and cocurricular interests. For most students, connecting scholarship and service in a meaningful way is a difficult challenge and requires continued investment on multiple fronts—faculty, students, staff, community partners, and the institutional infrastructure—to strengthen the connections. Serendipity by itself will not yield the outcomes students are seeking nor those that faculty and staff aspire to achieve.

MUTUALLY BENEFICIAL PARTNERSHIPS

A fourth practice that Pruitt should embrace is involving the community as a meaningful partner in all aspects of engagement—project conceptualization, implementation, evaluation, and utilization. Moving in this direction requires deepening relationships with existing community partners and fostering relationships with new partners. It requires formalizing relationships through advisory boards that provide strategic direction and guidance. That in turn requires continuity that goes beyond reliance on individual faculty and students, whose community engagement typically lasts at best for a semester—generally too light of a touch to make meaningful contributions for community problem solving. An entity like the Center for Community Partnerships, however, can encourage continuity, nurture relationships, deepen partnerships, and ensure that commitments made to community partners are honored.

PLACE-BASED STRATEGY

The tangible impacts of engagement are strengthened when that work focuses on specific geographic areas, aligns with community needs, and directly supports the work of community partners. Focusing on specific places facilitates the integration of teaching, research, and service; provides students with a variety of engagement opportunities that build off prior learning and experience in the same communities; and develops trust and meaningful relationships with community partners. Working in specific target areas will enable Pruitt to craft stronger connections across its departments and programs, fostering collaborative work on issues that cannot be solved by a single discipline or profession. It also allows students to acquire knowledge of local conditions that can be applied and extended in subsequent community engagements. And perhaps most importantly, it provides continuity and deepens relationships with community partners that allows Pruitt to collaborate with the community to create more comprehensive solutions to the most pressing problems.

Michael J. Rich is professor of political science and environmental sciences at Emory University. His current research focuses on community building, neighborhood revitalization, and local poverty reduction strategies. From 2000 through 2014, he served as the founding executive director of Emory's Center for Community Partnerships, a university-wide initiative to strengthen community-engaged scholarship, learning, and service.

COMMENTARY

Moral Courage and the Ethics of Time and Place in Campus-Community Partnerships

Ronald David Glass

Within a three-year time frame, Dr. Aria James faces a strategic choice between three models to achieve the two goals of the center and partnership initiative: to provide robust community-engaged (CE) learning for Pruitt College students and to reimagine the role of the community in those learning experiences. Pruitt's financial survival has also been strategically aligned with a mission to serve the public good through a required CE course and with a regional recruitment strategy seeking a more racially and socioeconomically diverse student body.

I understand this case as one of moral courage in the face of strategic choices framed within the ethics of time and place. I believe the three models described in the case elide these considerations and thus undermine the intended ethical interventions into the public good that Pruitt seeks. Given Dr. James' aims to promote sustainability, justice, and social transformation, considerations of time and place should be primary, even leading her to question her positionality in the directorship and the terms of her appointment.

MAKING TIME AND PLACE FOR TIME AND PLACE

Prioritizing time and place reveals that the Pruitt initiative focuses on demonstrations of moral goodness in and for 'the' community, in part through its erasure of certain histories. The founding internal study did not allot time to address the original theft and subsequent history of the land on which Pruitt is situated, how its Indigenous people were reduced to a "small area of recognized tribal land," and what Pruitt might thus owe those communities. How did Pruitt come to possess and profit from the irrefutable public good of the land, and what ethical responsibilities might it thus have, even to the land itself?

The initiative foregrounds projects of communal improvement and moral reclamation that misunderstand the depth, extent, and cultural endurance of coloniality and injustice, and thus does not hold promise for responding with historical force. The ethics of time and place reveals that short-term reforms within ongoing structures of injustice give to some a false moral solace (and maybe career advancement) without creating possibilities for practices to emerge that are actually building new institutions. I wonder why, given Dr. James's stated values of doing grounded and transformative social justice work, she accepted a three-year term appointment in a community where she was not raised and agreed to enact a vision that elides ethically important histories and that was developed without the involvement of crucially important Plainview communities. The ethics of time and place point toward becoming answerable to these least advantaged communities in both approaching and enacting the directorship.

CRITICAL PERSPECTIVES ON MODELS OF COMMUNITY ENGAGEMENT

The ethics of time and place cast critical lights on the CE models Dr. James identifies. While the internship model ethically deepens the volunteerism of most service-learning programs, supports student academic and financial success, and contributes to economic development, it also elides key temporal-spatial ethical features. What histories of wealth accumulation, distribution, and mobilization through zoning laws, redlining, and banking practices underlie the ongoing economic structuration of Plainview and positioning of BIPOC communities? Where are worker voices and visions in conceptualizing internships? Do the internships provide moral salve for businesses and college participants to feel worthy for doing some public good in their partnership, even if the economic development and their success reinforces or leaves unchanged multiple racial, class, and other inequities?

Dr. James identifies a unique ten-year collaboration as her community engagement exemplar. The partnership between a sociology professor and the Somali Community Development Center and Indigenous Community Resource Hub enables communities to propose projects that are capacity building for both students and communities. However, she recognizes that this model requires substantial faculty professional development and support, including institutional recognition of the sizable community-centered time and place demands of forging enduring and equitable college-community relationships. Unfortunately, grant funding and institutional timelines typically ignore the ethics of time and place, thereby coercing choices that are less demanding of faculty and built around direct service volunteer projects of immediate measurable benefit.

Dr. James senses this approach requires moral courage to scale smaller and slower; the complexity and depth of long-term equitable collaborations entails serving fewer students, faculty, and community partners in fewer projects. Moreover, the model's ethical coherence can be undermined by the variability typical in community engagement, so she contains this and leverages the scale through a centralized certificate program no longer dependent on individual faculty members for curricular consistency or partnership continuity. This model seeks to become transformative through activist scholarship—engaging with current Black Lives Matter, environmental justice, and sustainability movements for a just future.

The exemplar and transformative CE models demand moral courage to be true to their motivating ethical insights that are better attuned to the ethics of time and place. These demands extend beyond structural sources of resistance and encompass persistent challenges presented by morally and politically problematic ideologies deeply rooted in the dominant culture and in quotidian self-understandings.

MORAL COURAGE IN TIME AND PLACE

Community engagement that centers student learning and near-term measurable results to secure funding and exhibit public moral leadership repeatedly produces little substantive social change. Might this be because it lacks accountability to the least-advantaged communities yet provides certifications of moral worthiness for the participating funders and college-affiliated faculty and students, without disturbing the everyday life of the dominant powers and structures in the community?

When community engagement becomes responsible and accountable through an approach and pace to work that reaches further back and forward in time and more deeply in place to more fully connect to the land and its history, then it necessarily *begins* by establishing relationships of respect, trust, and solidarity with BIPOC communities to build strategic alliances. This means making time to show up in their places on their terms.

Further, it means changing project time scales to create interventions that interrupt the entrenched dispossession and extermination of Indigenous peoples, exclusion and enclosure of BIPOC communities, and destruction of the environment. These injustices inflict episodic acute violence but endure through pervasive ongoing slow forms of violence evolved over centuries of explanations, knowledges, and practices legitimated through quotidian life in families, places of worship, schools, the media, and political and economic systems—including higher education. Community engagement that foreshortens the past and future for which it is responsible and accountable necessarily fails at accurately identifying its challenges and possibilities.

It takes moral courage to make time and place for this long-haul work of transforming the institutions of daily life and for the similarly slow and difficult inward work of grappling with the affective and epistemic embodiments of injustice in our very identities and most intimate relationships. It takes moral courage not to rush to recuperate a righteousness that repeats past White liberal assumptions of the public good of higher education, and instead make time and place to establish relations of accountability with and to historically and persistently harmed and marginalized communities and to the land itself. With that courage, Dr. James could begin truly reimagining and recreating a Pruitt committed to cultivating an antiracism, anti-oppression public engaged in the struggles necessary to achieve a more just democracy.

Ronald David Glass is professor of philosophy of education at the University of California Santa Cruz. His praxis engages education as a practice of freedom, ideological (trans)formations, and ethico-epistemic issues within justice-oriented, collaborative, community-driven research methodologies geared into public learning processes and struggles to create just, pluralistic democracies.

COMMENTARY

Defining and Supporting Service Learning

MICHAEL D. BURROUGHS

Pruitt College's Partnership for Plainview has a laudable goal: to provide innovative community-engaged learning experiences for students alongside a robust and impactful role for community members and organizations. At issue in this case, however, are at least two overarching considerations: First, what are the ends that should guide service-learning experiences? Second, what is the best means for facilitating these service-learning experiences with students, faculty, and the community? Ultimately, I will argue that choosing a path forward requires defining the kind of service-learning experience desired at Pruitt College and in the greater community and also implementing the institutional support and structure needed for successful university-community collaborations.

DISTINCT ENDS OF SERVICE LEARNING

There is a tension at Pruitt College in the form of competing notions of what service learning should aim to achieve. The institution has focused on *traditional* service learning that places students as volunteers with local community organizations through curricular or extracurricular opportunities. With this approach, students aid the work of selected community organizations and, in doing so, gain skills and meet learning outcomes. Student commitment to and formative partnership with community organizations varies greatly in traditional service-learning opportunities like these.

Now, some within the institution are calling for a more transformative and *critical* service-learning approach. Like traditional service learning, this approach involves students volunteering with community organizations; however, it also emphasizes the development of a critical consciousness regarding the fundamental inequities that lead to the need for service in the first place.[14] In addition, the critical model brings a greater emphasis on deeply integrated community-university partnerships such that community stakeholders are involved in defining relevant aims of the partnerships in question.

The tension at Pruitt College lies, in part, in the fact that the distinction between these two forms of service learning and, in turn, the values that animate these approaches have not been clearly defined. The various proposals put forward can be placed on a continuum between traditional and critical approaches to service learning and should be evaluated as such. For example, while the Parker Brown–proposed internship requirement goes beyond mere volunteerism (as it includes potentially deep partnership and learning with local businesses), it lacks the social justice focus at the heart of critical service learning. And whereas the student- and CCP-proposed certificate program includes a volunteer component for students, it is much more deliberate in its emphasis on having students understand and deploy values of sustainability and justice in their work.

SUPPORTING CRITICAL SERVICE LEARNING

Promoting meaningful collaboration and critical reflection between students and the community in which they live is laudable. But, as things currently stand, it is not clear that Pruitt College is prepared for the greater requirements needed for successful critical service learning. Consider, for example, that while a key aim of Partnership for Plainview is to advance the public good in collaboration with the community, the Presidential Town Halls to develop this outreach initiative were not attended by community members beyond the university. For critical service learning, it is key to include greater community member voices from the very start of the process so as to develop shared aims, values, and concrete project ideas.

In addition, while a community-engaged (CE) requirement is placed in the curriculum and the administration has committed funding to this initiative, there is still a problematic lack of institutional support that results in CE learning experiences that are highly variable in quality. As several publicly engaged scholars have noted, for rich and sustainable community-focused initiatives to take place, colleges and universities need to make these efforts "count" in central forms of evaluation, faculty hiring, and promotion and tenure decisions.[15] Otherwise, in the flow of demands and commitments on faculty time, the extra work needed to make these experiences impactful for and with students and community organizations will be lacking. This is not to say that high-quality work cannot exist without this structural support, but as this case reveals, it is much harder to sustain these projects apart from the supererogatory efforts of individual faculty members.

APPROACHING A SOLUTION

Simply put, if an institution states a commitment to community engagement, then it ought to also provide the means to realize that stated commitment. But while calls for practices and scholarships of engagement have increased at colleges and universities, the institutional support to make these a reality is often lacking.[16] In this case, for example, we see this lack of support in Aria's temporary (non-tenure-track) appointment and severely limited staff support in the CCP. Institutional support is even more essential in the case of critical service-learning models that aim to develop robust and collaborative partnerships between students and community organizations.

In this case, I believe the best way forward is through a hybrid solution. If a critical orientation to service learning is the goal and we know that this requires more in-depth training and attention than a volunteerism model, then it makes good sense for CCP to take a centralized leadership role, although (given their lack of institutional support) this must also be a pragmatic role. As the case demonstrates, leaving community engagement up to individual faculty will not create the consistency needed to embed this critical approach, nor will it guarantee formative collaboration with community partners. First, by starting small and adding selected CE workshops and community partner meetings, CCP could lift some of the organizational burden currently shouldered by committed faculty practitioners of critical service learning. Indeed, I've benefited from this pragmatic approach in my own work as a university-based ethics institute director—leading ethics education workshops for faculty members to, in turn, adopt useful activities and pedagogical strategies in their own courses and curricula.

Second, through the creation of a CCP-led certificate program, the critical values of sustainability and justice could be foregrounded in service-learning opportunities, and model collaborations could be identified to engage the community and serve as exemplars for CE courses. This hybrid solution would need to be strategic and measured given the many demands on Aria's time. It would not meet every need of a service-learning program, but, organized well and efficiently, it would increase the likelihood of high-quality pedagogy, formative collaboration with community organizations, and the realization of ethical and sustainable service learning for students and their community partners.

Dr. Michael D. Burroughs serves as director of the Kegley Institute of Ethics and associate professor of philosophy at California State University, Bakersfield. In these roles, he works to support and introduce ethics and philosophy in K–12 schools, prisons, community organizations, and many other locations.

COMMENTARY

Centering a New Economic Vision to Bridge Divides

TAYLOR SPICER

The Center for Community Partnerships (CCP) at Pruitt College appears to have support from the president and a contingency of students, faculty, and staff to pursue a program grounded in sustainability and social justice. Pruitt also wants the CCP to contribute to recruitment, retention, and fundraising. Aria is entering her role trying to balance these purposes and to create measurable change in three years. To work within these bounds, Aria's team will need to frame the program in a visionary yet adaptive way, tailor outreach strategies to connect on- and off-campus community members, and track and communicate about the CCP's intentional approach. The goal of transformational change is ambitious while the timescale and resources are limited, but Aria seems determined to define new relationships between Pruitt and its neighbors, while also offering students opportunities for meaningful engagement.

THE FRAMING

First, Aria needs the CCP to help dispel the assertion that Pruitt College is separate from the community. Campus decisions directly and indirectly affect wider community systems and people; therefore, work with campus departments and students contributes to community sustainability and social justice work. Additionally, Aria needs to manage expectations about how quickly students will be placed into productive roles. Building a program centered on transformational values takes time, intentionality, relationship-building, trust, and training.

Second, Aria needs to solidify the formational ideas of the CCP into a vision. The deep-rooted nature of racism, sexism, consumerism, etc., require following roadmaps developed by people who have lived experiences impacted by oppressive systems. One such framework developed by the Climate Justice Alliance outlines community values and practices that should be transformed for a "just transition" from an "extractive economy"—a "capitalist system of exploitation and oppression that values consumerism, colonialism, and money over people and the planet"—into a "regenerative economy . . . based on ecological restoration, community protection, equitable partnerships, justice, and full and fair participatory processes."[17]

Aria will face challenges to this vision. Colleges and universities reinforce extractive practices intentionally and unintentionally; therefore, the work for a just transition will challenge investment and procurement practices, staff benefits and compensation, utilities strategies, research and engagement models, and individuals' perceptions of their power and relationships. Not every campus decision maker will support this effort, but on an interpersonal scale, centering the transition of economic models could open up conversations about shared experiences pertaining to the depressed local economy, economic impacts of extreme weather events, community support networks, and more.

Third, to balance these challenges, Aria needs to resist the request to focus the CCP's efforts solely into an engaged learning format. Instead, the CCP team should develop ongoing, voluntary training modules to utilize in multiple ways—through student group orientations, courses, existing training programs, departmental meetings, etc.—to cultivate campus ambassadors. Initially, the number of students engaged will be limited, but as the CCP team trains more of Pruitt and establishes more relationships with on- and off-campus partners, the initiative should establish outreach and project management tools that allow it to become a hub for connecting trained students to community-engaged courses and internships, capstone and thesis projects, and local advocacy and volunteer opportunities identified by partners and grounded in sustainability and social justice values.

BRIDGING DIVIDES

With the framing in place, Aria's team should turn to tailored engagement strategies for on- and off-campus groups that are rooted in constructive dialogues and mutual respect. On campus, Aria's team has access to diverse professionals—facilities, utilities, food service, procurement, grounds, finance, and student life staff, faculty, and administrators. Each person holds some combination of institutional and local knowledge, professional expertise, and access from which Aria's team can benefit. The CCP can offer to connect professionals to students for analyzing proposals for energy efficiency upgrades, electric vehicle deployment, procurement waste reduction policies, etc. that could benefit Pruitt and its neighbors.

Pruitt also has a changing population of students from local families learning alongside students of diverse racial and economic backgrounds recruited from around the state. The CCP should seek out campus partners, such as student life staff and faculty, who want to intentionally facilitate programming to normalize constructive dialogue between students. Students with open communications skills will be better equipped to bridge their differences and will feel more connected to their community. Community connections often lead to caring more deeply for a place and its people, which also aligns with the CCP's purpose.

Aria's team, with a fuller understanding of Pruitt, can now approach community partners—Pruitt's suppliers, businesses, community-based organizations, governments, and the region's First Peoples—prepared to listen for the groups' histories with Pruitt, their assets and needs, and the ways they contribute to extractive and regenerative economies. If organizations see value in the CCP's approach, they can propose projects to co-create with students in a mutual way.

SHOWING VALUE

Aria's team will need to utilize formative evaluation and monitoring practices and channels for insightful and regular communication. Collecting metrics on engagement, operational savings, student deliverables, and other measures will contribute to the holistic storytelling Aria's team should prioritize to validate the CCP's vision. The more members of Pruitt are aware of the work facilitated through the CCP, the more resistance the administration will face if they want to end the program in the future.

The CCP should also assess when broader environmental justice, resiliency planning, and climate action efforts (such as Wisconsin's recent climate report) might warrant a direct partnership with Pruitt College.[18] Often these broader plans are not tailored to specific locations. Connecting to broader action plans may allow Plainview to better shape local implementation of plans, access financial and other resources, and recruit and retain students and staff by raising the status of the CCP and Pruitt.

IS THIS "NORTH STAR" GOAL WORTH IT?

Scientists have been measuring the myriad effects of human choices to extract resources from the Earth for the purpose of economic growth and personal enrichment in ways that disproportionately harm Black, Latinx, Indigenous, and lower-income people. The US labor movement in the 1970s and the environmental justice movement in the 1990s formed coalitions to challenge environmental racism and socioeconomic injustice of these extractive industries. These same industries, most centrally the fossil fuel industry, have now provoked the rise of the climate justice movement calling for a just transition that shifts power to those most impacted by climate change, who often contribute the least to it. The extractive economy that brought humanity into these crises will not show the path to a regenerative future.

But will Aria, Pruitt College, and the rest of us who benefit from the current systems relinquish our power, privilege, and comforts to humbly co-create more equitable, sustainable systems? That is the big question. Aria serves with a determination to bridge constructed divides by using her position to promote an idea of the "public good" rooted in sustainability and justice. As a gatekeeper and connector, she has agency to provide the adaptive and grounded space that just may catalyze the societal transformation that she seeks and that we all need.

Taylor Spicer is the assistant director of the Office of Sustainability Initiatives for Emory University and Emory Healthcare. Her work entails student and community partner engagement, sustainable food education and procurement strategies, program management and communications. She has a master's in development practice (MDP) from Emory University.

CHAPTER 9

An Invitation to Engage

ASHLEY FLOYD KUNTZ AND REBECCA M. TAYLOR

We close this volume with an invitation to readers to engage—thoughtfully, fervently, imaginatively—with the cases and the perspectives presented in each commentary. Following earlier volumes by Levinson and Fay, we understand the contributions here as "provocations" and "invitations to think alongside us" about equity, freedom, and inclusion in higher education.[1] When we extended a similar invitation to contributors, many asked what sorts of boundaries they should keep in mind while writing. As is evident from the diversity of perspectives included and diversity of approaches taken by authors, we gave very few parameters. Instead, we wanted scholars and practitioners to feel comfortable attending to a single feature of the case that was particularly salient to them, raising points the case did not address, disagreeing with underlying assumptions, and/or imagining alternatives not yet feasible. We invite readers to do the same.

Several factors led us to take this invitational approach, not the least of which was the context in which we were compiling this book and our own positionality within this project. Like all book projects, the content for this volume was developed over the course of several years. However, the core period of writing—both for us and for contributors—took place in the context of a global pandemic, heightened attention to systemic racism and police brutality, and democratic instability. These challenges impacted each contributor to this volume differently, and the context undoubtedly shaped our thinking about these cases. As editors, there were moments when we considered rewriting a case completely in light of unfolding events. We opted not to do so out of respect for contributors who were already burdened with other professional and familial commitments, to say nothing of the psychological distress many people experienced during this time. As White women in relatively good health, we were also mindful of the ways in which the context differentially impacted contributors with COVID-19 health vulnerabilities, those who experienced loss of income personally or within their families, and/or those who were uniquely impacted by systemic racism.[2]

We endeavored throughout the project to position ourselves as learners, recognizing that others brought academic and embodied knowledge to this project that we could not. One excellent example of this is the piece by Rashad Moore (chapter 7), an alumnus of Morehouse College, who understands historically Black colleges as symbols of "the power of joy, hope, and creative resistance in the face of racism, violence, and anti-Blackness . . . a beacon of hope, a reminder that there is another way." Another is the letter from Troy Richardson, philosopher of education and scholar of American Indian and Indigenous Studies, imagining opportunities for feminist governance to transform our responses to Title IX cases. We felt similarly about the invaluable perspective of Chanda Prescod-Weinstein (chapter 3), a physicist with expertise in dark matter and early universe cosmology as well as Black feminist science. From her perspective, in discussions of faculty activism on social media, "there is no artificial barrier for Black women scholars between misogynoir, racism, sexism, or other bigotry faced within the academe and without." Throughout the volume, the unique and situated perspectives of contributors expanded the scope of inquiry and strengthened the quality.

Ethical decisions that invoke the values of freedom, equity, and inclusion are perhaps uniquely grounded in context, and the ways readers approach these cases will shift over time as the context does. We know this to be true because it happened to us. Each of the aforementioned social crises placed new and renewed attention on injustices and vulnerabilities in our society. Even the terms we use to demonstrate respect for particular groups shifted. For example, a few months into the project, the term BIPOC gained widespread use in conjunction with the protests against police brutality and racial injustice, and we began observing its inclusion in some commentaries. With support of the press, we made the editorial decision to defer to authors and invite them to use the language that they felt was most respectful, leading to a diversity of language referencing racial and ethnic identities throughout the book. As the sociopolitical terrain shifted and we engaged anew with familiar themes of exclusion and inequity, the volume took on greater dimensionality. Conversations we had as co-editors and with contributors may not have been had in another time and place. Thus, this conclusion leans more toward a reflection and invitation to engage with the ethical issues raised in this volume than an instruction manual for how to do so. Each historical moment demands fresh consideration of how to create a more equitable and inclusive society.

ENVISIONING OUR READERS

Even with the ever-changing context, we hope this volume will be of lasting use to a number of audiences.

For faculty and students of higher education, we envision the volume—and its individual chapters—being used in instructional contexts. Diversity and inclusion courses are now commonly found in graduate higher education programs, and many of the instructional approaches outlined by Fay, Levinson, and Kanner (e.g., online/digital, small group) could be applied in such courses.[3] For example, chapter 4 may be used in courses on higher education law to prompt students to examine their own ethical stances as higher education scholars and professionals who may be asked to develop policies and practices that are (1) consistent with the law, (2) sensitive to the institutional context, and (3) respectful of all stakeholders. A course on higher education policy may find chapter 6 helpful in calling attention not only to distributive concerns of free tuition policies but also how such policies, as philosopher Jennifer Morton notes in her commentary, "express our values as a society." Or a course on leadership in higher education may turn to chapter 7 as catalyst to discuss how leaders must attend to the institution's history and culture when envisioning a sustainable future.

For college and university administrators, we envision similar uses in senior leadership retreats, book clubs, and other settings where leaders come together to think about the ethical features of educational policies and practices on their campuses. While there are occasional references to real events at US institutions, the cases in this volume are largely fictional. We hope this will free leaders to think creatively and be less hindered by whom they know or what they know about a particular situation or school. Recent events underscore the importance of prioritizing ongoing conversations among leaders about how to foster more inclusive communities so that when a crisis occurs, leaders are better prepared to respond. Chapters 2 and 3 may be particularly salient for this audience, as cases involving freedom of speech and tenure denials often come with legal ramifications and unwelcome public attention. Additionally, senior leaders may be uniquely positioned to respond to the questions raised by chapter 5 on admissions for justice-involved students and chapter 8 on campus-community partnerships.

For scholars of higher education, we anticipate these cases and commentaries will spark additional inquiry and new contributions to the literature. On more than one occasion, we found ourselves recommending to contributors that they continue to develop their ethical argument about the case topic in a longer-form article. While authors were limited to only twelve-hundred-word commentaries, their questions and imaginative approaches to these cases could have filled volumes. We look forward to reading their continued work in these domains, and we are equally eager to see other scholars take up these issues, even when they disagree with the views expressed by ourselves or our commentators.

For practitioners on campus and in the larger community, we hope this book does justice to the complexity of daily efforts to foster inclusion, respect individual and institutional freedoms, and promote equity. We intentionally invited practitioners to contribute to this volume, agreeing with the epistemological stance articulated by former AERA president and leading scholar Joyce King that "knowledge resides not only in the university and scholarly publications but also with practitioners and people who are living the problems we are examining."[4] This lived knowledge is what led Alyssa Melby, a civic engagement leader, to craft her commentary in the form of a letter to the central character, mindful of the times in which lengthy emails provide support and perspective to colleagues facing problems of practice (chapter 8). It is what led defense attorney Tiffanie Agee to highlight the "innate and unalienable humanity" of incarcerated people as she considered admissions of justice-involved students in chapter 5. And, it is what prompted Elle Shaaban-Magaña, executive director of a women and gender resource center, to note that a survivor's voice was absent in the Title IX case, which further confirmed the ways in which "we construct human objects talked about, over, through, and/or for, within these educational practices" (chapter 4). The practitioner perspective is invaluable in deliberating about cases like these.

ENGAGING WITH THE CASES AND COMMENTARIES

With these diverse audiences in mind, we offer a few suggestions for approaching discussions of the cases and commentaries within this volume. First, we found it useful to identify and interrogate our own assumptions when thinking through each case. For example, when crafting chapter 8 on community partnerships, we considered that readers might rely on assumptions about Aria James's identity and background not specified in the case to inform their judgments about the course of action she should take. The case authors deliberated about whether to identify a more narrowly defined identity for Aria or to leave some details unspecified. In this case, we opted to maintain some ambiguity with the aim of prompting commentators and readers to consider whether their response to Aria's work might differ depending on her racial, ethnic, or socioeconomic background. We asked ourselves similar questions in constructing other cases. How might changing the institutional type or various features of the social context call attention to particular ethical responsibilities on the part of the campus? How might altering (or making more explicit) the political ideology and/or race and ethnicity of central characters reveal new dimensionality in the case or prompt us to attend to different features of the case? We invite readers to identify their own assumptions prior to any group discussions as well.

Second, we ask readers to be mindful of the ways in which some people discussing the cases and commentaries will be differentially impacted by the topic. A survivor of sexual assault may have a more visceral response to the Title IX case. Someone with a prior conviction or arrest may have a unique perspective to offer on the issue of admission policies. A student who is experiencing housing or food insecurity may have a greater sense of urgency with respect to the issue of free tuition. All cases require not only intellectual engagement but also moral engagement—despite being fictional, the weight of the policies and practices discussed in this volume is heavier for some readers than for others. For these reasons, facilitators of formal and informal group discussions would be wise to consider, in advance, how to structure engagement in a way that is *invitational but not coercive*. Given the sensitive nature of some of the topics discussed, blanket requirements for participants to share their perspectives to the rest of the group may not be appropriate or advisable. Further, facilitators should be careful not to tokenize participants or ask people from particular groups to speak on behalf of all people in those groups.

Third, we encourage readers to consider the applicability of the ethical issues raised here to other ethical issues not included in the volume. For example, chapter 5 attends to the important issue of access for students with prior convictions or arrests. We know that the admissions landscape is rife with other ethical concerns, including but not limited to: predictive analytics and student privacy, international student recruitment and exploitation, and financial aid gapping and borrower debt. What would those cases look like? How would they also reflect larger structural inequities present within our society? Another opportunity would be to construct a case similar to the one on Title IX but focused instead on Title II, which protects against discrimination for students with disabilities. As with Title IX, colleges and universities must nimbly adjust their practices to accommodate new legal rulings. They also face ongoing deliberations about what may be interpreted as a "reasonable" accommodation. This volume covers only a small number of the many ethically-laden choices facing colleges and universities, and we support efforts to expand conversation from the cases presented here to others, including ones that are presently bubbling beneath the surface with less attention being given to them.

FINAL THOUGHTS

The sorts of conversations we hope this volume will foster may, at times, feel intellectually and personally risky. As Fay and Levinson note, dilemmas associated with civic discord are often avoided because of how risky it feels to "talk about contentious political issues with people we don't know well, who we don't have reason to trust, who have power over us (or over whom we have power), with whom we disagree, or in front of whom we feel we have to maintain a facade of objectivity, neutrality, or even omniscience."[5] This is true at all times, but especially in periods of great social upheaval. The cases in this volume were workshopped by authors in multiple in-person and virtual spaces. While some contributors knew each other well, many did not and had never participated in a project like this. On a few occasions, practitioners expressed concerns about feeling out of place in what was presumed to be an academic space. As always, race and gender shaped interactions, even when participants were mindful of their own positionality. Still, as we continued to engage with one another and have the conversations that felt risky to have, we gained new insights into the perspectives of our colleagues and thus into ethical inquiry in higher education.

Importantly, we as co-editors disagreed in meaningful ways at various points throughout the construction of this volume. On one case, we might find ourselves in almost complete agreement; on another, almost complete disagreement. These conversations felt risky to have with one another, not because we didn't know each other well or didn't have reason to trust one another. In fact, we have known each other for many years and collaborated together on multiple projects. We have numerous reasons to trust and respect one another. In some ways, the stakes felt higher because we wanted to preserve that foundation of friendship, mutual accord, and colleagueship. In moments like these—whether with colleagues or friends or family—there is a tendency to clam up or disengage from discussing equity, freedom, and inclusion. We are not experts on interpersonal communication, but when we found ourselves in conversations like these, we often took space to think separately before resuming conversation of a particular topic. We tended to use long-form emails or video calls to have these conversations, as opposed to text messages or comment boxes in the margins. We believe the project, as well as our own understandings, benefited from this approach to navigating ethical conflict.

Throughout the volume, readers will notice that people attend to different features of the case studies for different reasons. Sometimes, as was the case concerning Dr. Jaleesa Reese's tenure and promotion decision, contributors agreed on the action that should be taken but offered markedly different rationales. What one contributor read as a legally protected but inadvisable approach, another read as an important contribution to the field. Their point of consensus is made more compelling by the dissensus in arriving at that point. We are convinced there is great value in moments like these when we pause to consider not just what we are doing but why.

It is our hope that this volume will heighten awareness of ethically laden decisions in higher education settings and provoke deeper conversations concerning ethical ways forward. Every decision is subject to existing constraints and further contextualization. Every action is taken in a particular context mindful of its own stakeholders and institutional histories. What remains powerful about collaborative inquiry is the opportunity to engage across differences in perspective and imagine new ethical possibilities for higher education policies and practices.

Notes

CHAPTER 1

1. Hannah Hartig, "Democrats Overwhelmingly Favor Free College Tuition, While Republicans Are Divided by Age, Education," *Pew Research Center*, February 21, 2020, https://www.pewresearch.org/fact-tank/2020/02/21/democrats-overwhelmingly-favor-free-college-tuition-while-republicans-are-divided-by-age-education/.
2. Meira Levinson and Jacob Fay, eds., *Dilemmas of Educational Ethics: Cases and Commentaries* (Cambridge, MA: Harvard Education Press, 2016); Meira Levinson and Jacob Fay, eds., *Democratic Discord in Schools: Cases and Commentaries in Educational Ethics* (Cambridge, MA: Harvard Education Press, 2019).
3. Bob Fischer, *College Ethics: A Reader on Moral Issues That Affect You* (New York: Oxford University Press, 2016); Harvard Graduate School of Education, "Complete List of Case Studies," Justice in Schools, 2019, https://www.justiceinschools.org/complete-list-case-studies; Levinson and Fay, *Dilemmas of Educational Ethics*; Levinson and Fay, *Democratic Discord in Schools*; Kenneth Strike and Jonas F. Soltis, *The Ethics of Teaching*, 5th ed. (New York: Teachers College Press, 2009); and Florence A. Hamrick and Mimi Benjamin, eds., *Maybe I Should . . . : Case Studies on Ethics for Student Affairs Professionals* (Lanham, MD: American College Personnel Association, 2009).
4. Levinson and Fay, *Dilemmas of Educational Ethics*, 3–4.

CHAPTER 2

1. The university, events, and characters in this case are fictional.
2. The federally recognized term *American Indian* has a complex history, and there are regional and generational differences in its usage. When possible, it is preferable to refer to Native peoples using their specific tribal names. In recent years, there has been a shift toward using the term American Indian to refer to groups comprising individuals from multiple tribes. See https://americanindian.si.edu for additional information.

3. This approach and analysis is inspired by Sharon Stein et al., "The Educational Challenge of Unraveling the Fantasies of Ontological Security," *Diaspora, Indigenous, and Minority Education* 11, no. 2 (2017): 69–79, doi:10.1080/15595692.2017.1291501.
4. For example, when white supremacists and neo-Nazis at the "Unite the Right" rally incited violence in Charlottesville, Virginia, in August 2017, the forty-fifth US president referred to them as "very fine people."
5. Stein et al., "The Educational Challenge," 71.
6. For example, Harvard University's Louis Agassiz conducted what was considered as legitimate, scientific research on racial difference, which became the basis for the eugenics movement in the mid-nineteenth century; Craig Steven Wilder, *Ebony & Ivy: Race, Slavery, and the Troubled History of America's Universities* (New York: Bloomsbury Press, 2013).
7. I identified the process while studying professors who successfully engaged multiracial classrooms in frank, rigorous, and challenging learning about race. I developed the pedagogical approach in my courses and numerous workshops with practitioners from elementary to postsecondary; see Janine de Novais, "Brave Community, from Ethnography to Pedagogy to Post Racism," in *Encyclopedia of Educational Innovation*, ed. Michael A. Peters and Richard Heraud (Singapore: Springer, 2019), doi:10.1007/978-981-13-2262-4_108-1.
8. *West Virginia v. Barnette*, 319 US 624 (1943).
9. Thorstein Veblen, *The Higher Learning in America: A Memorandum on the Conduct of Universities by Business Men* (New York: B. W. Huebsch, 1918), 255, https://www.google.com/books/edition/The_Higher_Learning_in_America/NewDAQAAIAAJ?hl=en&gbpv=0.
10. "Free Expression," The University of Chicago, https://freeexpression.uchicago.edu.
11. Lauren Robel, "On the First Amendment," Indiana University Bloomington, https://provost.indiana.edu/statements/archive/first-amendment.html.
12. Kimberlé Crenshaw et al., eds., *Critical Race Theory: Key Writings That Formed the Movement* (New York: New Press, 1995); Marvin Lynn and Adrienne Dixson, eds., *Handbook of Critical Race Theory in Education* (New York: Routledge, 2013).
13. Michael Omi and Howard Winant, *Racial Formation in the United States* (New York: Routledge, 2015).
14. Charles Lawrence, "If He Hollers Let Him Go: Regulating Racist Speech on Campus," in *Words That Wound: Critical Race Theory, Assaultive Speech, and the First Amendment,* ed. Mari Matsuda et al. (Boulder, CO: Westview Press, 1993), 70.
15. James Leming et al., eds., *Where Did the Social Studies Go Wrong?* (Washington, DC: Thomas Fordham Foundation, 1993); Arthur Schlesinger, *The Disuniting of America: Reflections on a Multicultural Society* (New York: W. W. Norton, 1992).

16. Michael Apple, *Educating the "Right" Way: Markets, Standards, God, and Inequality* (New York: Routledge, 2006); Kristen Buras, *Rightist Multiculturalism: Core Lessons on Neoconservative School Reform* (New York: Routledge, 2008); Kathleen deMarrais et al., eds., *Philanthropy, Hidden Strategy, and Collective Resistance: A Primer for Concerned Educators* (Gorham, ME: Myers Education Press. 2019).
17. Tara Yosso, *Critical Race Counterstories Along the Chicana/Chicano Educational Pipeline* (New York: Routledge, 2006).
18. Lawrence, "If He Hollers Let Him Go," 65.
19. Lawrence, 81.
20. Mari Matsuda, "Public Response to Racist Speech: Considering the Victim's Story," in Matsuda et al., *Words That Wound*, 36.

CHAPTER 3

1. All characters, institutions, and events in this case are fictional unless otherwise noted.
2. "Percy Lavon Julian," Science History Institute, https://www.sciencehistory.org/historical-profile/percy-lavon-julian.
3. Hashtags that were not in use during the drafting of this case may be in use at a future date. The authors do not intend any connection between the case and actual usage of these hashtags on social media platforms.
4. Though the events in this case are fictional, the Algorithmic Justice League is a real entity founded by Joy Buolawmwini; "Algorithmic Justice League—Unmasking AI Harms and Biases," https://www.ajl.org/.
5. *1940 Statement on Principles on Academic Freedom and Tenure*, American Association of University Professors (1940), https://www.aaup.org/report/1940-statement-principles-academic-freedom-and-tenure.
6. Kansas Board of Regents, *Policy Manual (Rev. 06/20/18)*, http://www.kansasregents.org/resources/062018_Policy_Manual_revised.pdf.
7. Timothy Shiell, "Grappling with Collegiality and Academic Freedom," *Academe* (Washington, DC: American Association of University Professors, 2015), https://www.aaup.org/article/grappling-collegiality-and-academic-freedom#.XxtXxPhKh0t.
8. Shiell.
9. Sarah J. Jackson, Moya Bailey, and Brooke Foucault Welles, *#HashtagActivism: Networks of Race and Gender Justice* (Cambridge: MIT Press, 2020); André Brock, Jr., *Distributed Blackness: African American Cybercultures* (New York: NYU Press, 2020).
10. Hans-Joerg Tiede et al., "Data Snapshot: Whom Does Campus Reform Target and What Are the Effects?" *Academe*, Spring 2021, https://www.aaup.org/article/data-snapshot-whom-does-campus-reform-target-and-what-are-effects.
11. Peter Aldhous, "Documents Show That Arizona State Investigated a Slew of Allegations Against Physicist Lawrence Krauss," *BuzzFeed News*, October 23,

2018, https://www.buzzfeednews.com/article/peteraldhous/lawrence-krauss-sexual-harassment-report; Azeen Ghorayshi, "Here's How Geoff Marcy's Sexual Harassment Went on for Decades," *BuzzFeed News*, November 11, 2015, https://www.buzzfeednews.com/article/azeenghorayshi/how-harassment-stays-secret.

12. Moya Bailey, "More on the Origin of Misogynoir," *Moyazb*, April 27, 2014, https://moyazb.tumblr.com/post/84048113369/more-on-the-origin-of-misogynoir.
13. Robin DiAngelo, "White Fragility," *International Journal of Critical Pedagogy* 3, no. 3 (2011): 65.
14. Referring to a Black feminist hashtag designed to call out white supremacists online. Rachelle Hampton, "The Black Feminists Who Saw the Alt-Right Threat Coming," *Slate*, April 23, 2019, https://slate.com/technology/2019/04/black-feminists-alt-right-twitter-gamergate.html.
15. Toni Morrisson, *Beloved* (New York: New American Library, 1987), 190.
16. *1940 Statement*; Shannon Dea, "A Brief History of Academic Freedom," *University Affairs,* October 9, 2018, https://www.universityaffairs.ca/opinion/dispatches-academic-freedom/a-brief-history-of-academic-freedom/.
17. US Department of Education, *The Condition of Education 2018* (Washington, DC: National Center for Education Statistics, 2018).
18. *Academic Freedom and Electronic Communications*, American Association of University Professors (2014), https://www.aaup.org/report/academic-freedom-and-electronic-communications-2014.
19. Brittney Cooper, *Eloquent Rage: A Black Feminist Discovers Her Superpower* (New York: St. Martin's Press, 2018), 184.
20. Sandy Grande, "Refusing the University," in *Toward What Justice? Describing Diverse Dreams of Justice in Education,* ed. Eve Tuck and K. Wayne Yang (London: Routledge, 2018), 48.
21. Grande, 51.
22. Ibram Kendi, *Stamped from the Beginning: The Definitive History of Racist Ideas in America* (New York: Bold Type Books, 2016).
23. Aaron Fisher et al., "Structure and Belonging: Pathways to Success for Underrepresented Minority and Women PhD Students in STEM Fields," *PLoS ONE* 14, no. 1 (January 2019): 3, doi:10.1371/journal.pone.0209279.
24. Claude Steele, *Whistling Vivaldi: How Stereotypes Affect Us and What We Can Do* (New York: W. W. Norton & Company, 2011).
25. Steele, 147.

CHAPTER 4

1. The college, characters, and events in this case are fictional, with the exception of government officials and federal policy events.
2. For a summary of the 2020 regulations, see: US Department of Education, Office of Civil Rights, *Summary of Major Provisions of the Department of*

Education's Title IX Final Rule, https://www2.ed.gov/about/offices/list/ocr/docs/titleix-summary.pdf.

3. US Department of Education, Office for Civil Rights, *Dear Colleague Letter from Assistant Secretary for Civil Rights Russlynn Ali,* April 4, 2011, http://www2.ed.gov/about/offices/list/ocr/letters/colleague-201104.pdf.
4. Numerically, this is described as requiring about 75 percent certainty. This standard is used most often in the legal context when a significant liberty is at stake.
5. This standard is described numerically as requiring at least 51 percent certainty to rule on a case, or by some as 50 percent plus one or as 50.01 percent. The idea is just over 50 percent.
6. David Lisak et al., "False Allegations of Sexual Assault: An Analysis of Ten Years of Reported Cases," *Violence Against Women* 16, no. 12 (2010): 1318–34, doi:10.1177/1077801210387747.
7. John Villasenor, "A Probabilistic Framework for Modelling False Title IX 'Convictions' under the Preponderance of the Evidence Standard," *Law, Probability and Risk* 15, no. 4 (2016): 223–37, doi:10.1093/lpr/mgw006.
8. Lance Hernandez, "DU Sexual Assault Survivors Share Stories Anonymously on Instagram Account 'wecanDUbetter,'" *The Denver Channel*, January 27, 2020, https://www.thedenverchannel.com/news/local-news/du-sex-assault-survivors-share-stories-anonymously-on-wecandubetter-instagram-account.
9. See Melanie Heenan and Suellen Murray, *Study of Reported Rapes in Victoria 2000–2003: Summary Research Report* (Melbourne: Office of Women's Policy, 2006), https://www.ncjrs.gov/app/abstractdb/AbstractDBDetails.aspx?id=243182; National Sexual Violence Resource Center (NSVRC), *False Reporting Overview* (Enola: NSVRC, 2012), https://www.nsvrc.org/sites/default/files/Publications_NSVRC_Overview_False-Reporting.pdf; Lisak et al., "False Allegations"; Kimberly A. Lonsway, Joanne J. Archambault, and David Lisak, "False Reports: Moving Beyond the Issue to Successfully Investigate and Prosecute Non-stranger Sexual Assault," *The Voice* 3, no. 1 (2009): 1111.
10. Chelsea Hale and Meghan Matt, "The Intersection of Race and Rape Viewed Through the Prism of a Modern-Day Emmett Till," *American Bar Association*, July 16, 2019, https://www.americanbar.org/groups/litigation/committees/diversity-inclusion/articles/2019/summer2019-intersection-of-race-and-rape/.
11. John Dewey, *Experience and Education* (1938; repr., New York: Free Press, 1997), 25.
12. Dewey, 27.
13. See the Rape, Abuse & Incest National Network website, https://www.rainn.org/statistics/campus-sexual-violence.
14. US Department of Education, *Secretary DeVos: Proposed Title IX Rule Provides Clarity for Schools, Support for Survivors, and Due Process Rights for All*, November 16, 2018, https://www.ed.gov/news/press-releases/secretary-devos-proposed-title-ix-rule-provides-clarity-schools-support-survivors-and-due-process-rights-all.

15. Greta Anderson, "U.S. Publishes New Regulations on Campus Sexual Assault," *Inside Higher Ed*, May 7, 2020, https://www.insidehighered.com/news/2020/05/07/education-department-releases-final-title-ix-regulations#.X0cIMNnKeBo.link.
16. John Dryzek, "Leave It to the Experts: Administrative Rationalism," in *The Politics of Earth: Environmental Discourses* (Oxford: Oxford University Press, 2005), 75–98.
17. Alan Luke, "Text and Discourse in Education: An Introduction to Critical Discourse Analysis," *Review of Research in Education* 21 (1995): 13, doi:10.2307/1167278.
18. Jennifer Freyd, *Campus Sexual Assault and Institutional Betrayal: A Summary of Research* (Eugene, OR: The Freyd Dynamics Lab at the University of Oregon, 2014), 5.
19. Jennifer Freyd, "Institutional Betrayal and Institutional Courage," last modified August 26, 2020, https://dynamic.uoregon.edu/jjf/institutionalbetrayal/.
20. R. Shep Melnick, *Analyzing the Department of Education's Final Title IX Rules on Sexual Misconduct* (Washington, DC: Brookings Institution, 2020), https://www.brookings.edu/research/analyzing-the-department-of-educations-final-title-ix-rules-on-sexual-misconduct/.
21. National Academies of Sciences, Engineering, and Medicine, *Sexual Harassment of Women: Climate, Culture, and Consequences in Academic Sciences, Engineering, and Medicine* (Washington, DC: National Academies Press, 2018), doi:10.17226/24994.
22. For example, Claude Steele and Joshua Aronson, "Stereotype Threat and the Intellectual Test Performance of African Americans," *Journal of Personality and Social Psychology* 69, no. 5 (1995): 797–811, doi:10.1037/0022-3514.69.5.797; Liliana M. Garces and Uma M. Jayakumar, "Dynamic Diversity: Toward a Contextual Understanding of Critical Mass," *Educational Researcher* 43, no. 3 (2014): 115–24, doi:10.3102/0013189X14529814.
23. This distinction is similar to Berlin's positive and negative liberty; Isaiah Berlin, "Two Concepts of Liberty," in *Four Essays on Liberty* (Oxford: Oxford University Press, 1969).
24. US Department of Education, Office of Civil Rights, "Nondiscrimination on the Basis of Sex in Education Programs or Activities Receiving Federal Financial Assistance," *Federal Register* 85, no. 97 (May 19, 2020): 30152, https://www.govinfo.gov/content/pkg/FR-2020-05-19/pdf/2020-10512.pdf.
25. See Betty Reardon, *Sexism and the War System* (Syracuse, NY: Syracuse University Press, 1996); Betty Reardon, *Women and Peace: Feminist Visions of Global Security* (Albany, NY: SUNY Press, 1993); Fiona Robinson, *The Ethics of Care: A Feminist Approach to Human Security* (Philadelphia: Temple University Press, 2011); Virginia Held, *The Ethics of Care: Personal, Political, and Global* (Oxford: Oxford University Press, 2007).
26. Robinson, *The Ethics of Care*, 105.

27. Robinson, 4.
28. Betty A. Reardon, "Epilogue: Toward a Strategy of Transcending Patriarchy: Envisioning the Possible," in *Betty A. Reardon: Key Texts in Gender and Peace*, ed. Betty A. Reardon and Dale T. Snauwaert (Cham, Switzerland: Springer, 2015), 141, doi:10.1007/978-3-319-11809-3.
29. Betty A. Reardon and Tony Jenkins, "Gender and Peace: Toward a Gender Inclusive, Holistic Perspective," in *Betty A. Reardon*, 106.
30. Barbara Hudson, "Restorative Justice: The Challenge of Sexual and Racial Violence," *Journal of Law and Society* 25, no. 2 (1998): 245.
31. David R. Karp and Kaaren M. Williamsen, *Five Things Student Affairs Administrators Should Know About Restorative Justice and Campus Sexual Harm* (Washington, DC: NASPA Research and Policy Institute Issue Brief, 2020), 5.
32. Hema Hargovan, "Restorative Justice and Domestic Violence: Some Exploratory Thoughts," *Agenda* 19, no. 66 (2005): 48–56, doi:10.1080/10130950.2005.9674647.
33. Karen L. Clark, "A Call for Restorative Justice in Higher Education Judicial Affairs," *College Student Journal* 48, no. 4 (2014): 705–19.
34. Chris Cunneen and Barry Goldson, "Restorative Justice? A Critical Analysis," in *Youth, Crime and Justice*, ed. Barry Goldson and John Muncie, 2nd ed. (London: Sage, 2015), 139.
35. Tom Sebok and Andrea Goldblum, "Establishing a Campus Restorative Justice Program," *Journal of California Caucus of College and University Ombuds* 2, no. 1 (1999): 13–22, http://journal.calcaucus.com/journal-1999.html.
36. Cunneen and Goldson, "Restorative Justice?," 139.
37. Marie Keenan and Niamh Joyce, "Restorative Justice and Sexual Violence: Ireland Joins the International Debate" (UCD Working Paper Series, University College Dublin, Ireland, 2013), https://www.ucd.ie/t4cms/Restorative%20Justice%20and%20Sexual%20Violence%20Ireland%20Joins%20the%20International%20Debate.pdf.
38. Karp and Williamsen, *Five Things Student Affairs Administrators Should Know*, 7.
39. Peter Lake, *The Four Corners of Title IX Regulatory Compliance: A Primer for American Colleges and Universities* (Hierophant Enterprises, 2017), http://hierophantenterprises.com/#anchor-secondary.

CHAPTER 5

1. We use the term *justice-involved* to include currently and formerly incarcerated people and people with histories of arrest and/or conviction. However, we recognize that those no longer under the supervision of the criminal legal system may not personally identify as justice-involved.
2. Matthew Friedman, "Just Facts: As Many Americans Have Criminal Records as College Diplomas," Brennan Center for Justice, November 17, 2015, https://www.brennancenter.org/our-work/analysis-opinion/just-facts-many-americans-have-criminal-records-college-diplomas.

3. Friedman.
4. Debbie Mukamal, Rebecca Silbert, and Rebecca M. Taylor, *Degrees of Freedom: Expanding College Opportunities for Currently and Formerly Incarcerated Californians* (Stanford and Berkeley: Stanford Criminal Justice Center & Chief Justice Earl Warren Institute on Law and Social Policy, 2015), https://www.law.berkeley.edu/files/DegreesofFreedom2015_FullReport.pdf.
5. Judith Scott-Clayton, "Thinking 'Beyond the Box': The Use of Criminal Records in College Admissions," *Brookings*, September 28, 2017, https://www.brookings.edu/research/thinking-beyond-the-box-the-use-of-criminal-records-in-college-admissions/.
6. Marsha Weissman et al., *The Use of Criminal History Records in College Admissions* (New York: Center for Community Alternatives, 2020), 8–9, http://www.communityalternatives.org/wp-content/uploads/2020/02/use-of-criminal-history-records-reconsidered.pdf.
7. Robert Stewart and Christopher Uggen, "Criminal Records and College Admissions: A Modified Experimental Audit," *Criminology* 58, no. 1 (2020): 156–88, doi:10.1111/1745-9125.12229.
8. Scott-Clayton, "Thinking 'Beyond the Box.'"
9. The Sentencing Project, *Report to the United Nations on Racial Disparities in the U.S. Criminal Justice System* (Washington, DC: Research and Advocacy for Reform, 2018), https://www.sentencingproject.org/publications/un-report-on-racial-disparities/.
10. The Sentencing Project.
11. The Common Application removed mandatory criminal background questions in 2019 but continues to provide institutions the option to require criminal background disclosure.
12. American Association of Collegiate Registrars and Admissions Officers (AACRAO), *Criminal and Disciplinary History in College Admissions* (Washington, DC: AACRAO, 2019), 7, https://www.aacrao.org/docs/default-source/signature-initiative-docs/trending-topic-docs/criminal-history---college-admissions/criminal-history-report_12172019_release.pdf.
13. Wendy Sawyer and Peter Wagner, "Mass Incarceration: The Whole Pie 2020," Prison Policy Initiative, March 24, 2020, https://www.prisonpolicy.org/reports/pie2020.html.
14. Bradley D. Custer, "College Admission Policies for Ex-Offender Students: A Literature Review," *Journal of Correctional Education* 67, no. 2 (2016): 35–43.
15. Stewart and Uggen, "Criminal Records and College Admissions."
16. Mukamal, Silbert, and Taylor, *Degrees of Freedom.*
17. Brennan Barnard, "Assessing Ethical Character in College Admission," *Forbes*, June 25, 2019, https://www.forbes.com/sites/brennanbarnard/2019/07/25/assessing-ethical-character-in-college-admission/?sh=1d01688143d1.

18. "Collateral Consequences Inventory," National Inventory of Collateral Consequences of Criminal Conviction, https://niccc.nationalreentryresourcecenter.org/consequences.
19. "Top 100—Lowest Acceptance Rates," *US News & World Report*, https://www.usnews.com/best-colleges/rankings/lowest-acceptance-rate.
20. Lois M. Davis et al., *Evaluating the Effectiveness of Correctional Education: A Meta-Analysis of Programs That Provide Education to Incarcerated Adults* (Santa Monica, CA: The RAND Corporation, 2013), 34, http://www.rand.org/content/dam/rand/pubs/research_reports/RR200/RR266/RAND_RR266.pdf.
21. Nicole Solomon Lindahl, "Intimate Bonds: Dislocation, Survival, and Resistance in the Neoliberal Prison" (PhD diss., University of California, Berkeley, 2016).
22. Michelle Jones, "Biographic Mediation and the Formerly Incarcerated: How Dissembling and Disclosure Counter the Extended Consequences of Criminal Convictions," *Biography* 42, no. 3 (2019): 486–513, doi:10.1353/bio.2019.0056.
23. Eliza Shapiro and Dana Goldstein, "Is the College Cheating Scandal the 'Final Straw' for Standardized Tests?," *New York Times*, March 14, 2019, https://www.nytimes.com/2019/03/14/us/sat-act-cheating-college-admissions.html.
24. "The 10 Most Violent Acts Committed on a College Campus," College Stats, https://collegestats.org/2012/09/the-10-most-violent-acts-committed-on-a-college-campus/.
25. Loïc Wacquant, "Deadly Symbiosis: When Ghetto and Prison Meet and Mesh," *Punishment & Society* 3, no. 1 (January 2001): 95–133, doi:10.1177/14624740122228276.
26. Frederick Douglass, *Narrative of the Life of Frederick Douglass, an American Slave* (Boston: Anti-Slavery Office, 1845), 33, https://www.google.com/books/edition/Narrative_of_the_Life_of_Frederick_Dougl/gE5nZ0jDwiwC?hl=en&gbpv=0.
27. Khalil Gibran Muhammad, "A Review of Recent Historical Scholarship on Racial Criminalization and Punitive Policy in the United States" (paper presented at Roundtable on the Future of Justice Policy, co-hosted by Merritt College and the Justice Lab at Columbia University, Oakland, California, March 28, 2019).
28. Sawyer and Wagner, "Mass Incarceration."
29. Sawyer and Wagner.
30. "U.S. Incarceration Rates by Race and Ethnicity, 2010," Prison Policy Initiative, https://www.prisonpolicy.org/graphs/raceinc.html.
31. Tara O'Neill Hayes and Margaret Barnhorst, *Incarceration and Poverty in the United States*, (Washington, DC: American Action Forum, 2020), https://www.americanactionforum.org/research/incarceration-and-poverty-in-the-united-states/.

32. For example, the State University System of Florida declined to go test-optional in response to the COVID-19 pandemic. Individual campuses and their boards of trustees do not have the authority to overturn the SUS policy, which is influenced by the legislature. Scott Jaschik, "Applications Tank in State That Requires SAT or ACT," *Inside Higher Ed*, November 9, 2020, https://www.insidehighered.com/admissions/article/2020/11/09/applications-floridas-public-universities-are-down-much-50-percent.
33. US Department of Education, *Beyond the Box: Increasing Access to Higher Education for Justice-Involved Individuals* (Washington, DC: US Department of Education, 2016), https://www2.ed.gov/documents/beyond-the-box/guidance.pdf.
34. "Campus Sexual Violence: Statistics," Rape, Abuse & Incest National Network, https://www.rainn.org/statistics/campus-sexual-violence.
35. US Department of Justice, "2019 Hate Crime Statistics," FBI: UCR, https://ucr.fbi.gov/hate-crime/2019/tables/table-1.xls.
36. Marc Mauer and Meda Chesney-Lind, "Introduction," in *Invisible Punishment: The Collateral Consequences of Mass Imprisonment*, ed. Marc Mauer and Meda Chesney-Lind (New York: The New Press, 2002), 1–12.
37. Jeffrey Reiman and Paul Leighton, *The Rich Get Richer, and the Poor Get Prison: Ideology, Class, and Criminal Justice*, 11th ed. (New York: Routledge, 2016), 121.
38. Brian D. Johnson and Rebecca Richardson, "Race and Plea Bargaining," in *A System of Pleas: Social Science's Contributions to the Real Legal System,* ed. Vanessa A. Edkins and Allison D. Redlich (Oxford: Oxford University Press, 2019), 83–106.
39. Mary Welek Atwell, *Wretched Sisters: Examining Gender and Capital Punishment*, 2nd ed. (New York: Peter Lang Publishing, 2014).
40. Jill A. McCorkel, *Breaking Women: Gender, Race, and the New Politics of Imprisonment* (New York: NYU Press, 2013).
41. Rebecca M. Hayes and Kate Luther, *#Crime: Social Media, Crime, and the Criminal Legal System* (Palgrave Macmillan, 2018), 79–121.
42. Jill McCorkel and Robert DeFina, "Beyond Recidivism: Identifying the Liberatory Possibilities of Prison Higher Education," *Critical Education* 10, no. 7 (2019): 1–17.
43. I understand *whiteness* as the unquestioned objectivity that we ascribe to our formulations and reasoning without knowing how it [objectivity] is rooted in and responsible for specific historical events and formations of both geographies and tropes of thought.
44. Joshua Rothman, "Is Heidegger Contaminated by Nazism?," *New Yorker*, April 28, 2014, https://www.newyorker.com/books/page-turner/is-heidegger-contaminated-by-nazism.
45. Rothman.
46. Rothman.

47. William S. Lewis, "But Didn't He Kill His Wife?," *Verso Books blog*, May 29, 2019, https://www.versobooks.com/blogs/4336-but-didn-t-he-kill-his-wife.
48. Lewis.
49. Lewis.
50. Nelson Maldonado-Torres, "On the Coloniality of Being: Contributions to the Development of a Concept," *Cultural Studies* 21, no. 2–3 (2007): 240–70.
51. Erin L. Castro and Sydney Magana, "Enhancing the Carceral State: Criminal/ized History Questions in College Admissions," *Journal of College Student Development* 61, no. 6 (2020): 814–31.
52. Custer, "College Admission Policies."
53. Hayes and Barnhorst, *Incarceration and Poverty*; Bruce Western and Becky Pettit, "Incarceration & Social Inequality," *Daedalus* 139, no. 3 (2010): 8–19.
54. Doris J. James and Lauren E. Glaze, *Mental Health Problems of Prison and Jail Inmates* (Washington, DC: US Department of Justice, Bureau of Justice Statistics, 2006).
55. Lena J. Jäggi et al., "The Relationship Between Trauma, Arrest, and Incarceration History Among Black Americans: Findings from the National Survey of American Life," *Society and Mental Health* 6, no. 3 (2016): 187–206, doi:10.1177/2156869316641730.
56. Charles R. Epp, Steven Maynard-Moody, and Donald P. Haider-Markel, *Pulled Over: How Police Stops Define Race and Citizenship* (Chicago: University of Chicago Press, 2014).
57. Issa Kohler-Hausmann, *Misdemeanorland: Criminal Courts and Social Control in an Age of Broken Windows Policing* (Princeton, NJ: Princeton University Press, 2018); Sonja B. Starr and M. Marit Rehavi, "Mandatory Sentencing and Racial Disparity: Assessing the Role of Prosecutors and the Effects of *Booker*," *Yale Law Journal* 123, no. 1 (2013): 2.
58. M. Marit Rehavi and Sonja B. Starr, "Racial Disparity in Federal Criminal Sentences," *Journal of Political Economy* 122, no. 6 (2014): 1320–54.
59. Peter S. Lehmann, Ted Chiricos, and William D. Bales, "Sentencing Transferred Juveniles in the Adult Criminal Court: The Direct and Interactive Effects of Race and Ethnicity," *Youth Violence and Juvenile Justice* 15, no. 2 (2017): 172–90, doi:10.1177/1541204016678048.

CHAPTER 6

1. The state and its characters, organizations, and events in this case are fictionalized. Statistical descriptions of the fictional state are grounded in evidence from similar cases in the United States.
2. "Learn More, Earn More: Education Leads to Higher Wages, Lower Unemployment," *Career Outlook*, US Bureau of Labor Statistics, May 2020, https://www.bls.gov/careeroutlook/2020/data-on-display/education-pays.htm.
3. The College System of Tennessee, *Tennessee Promise Students at Community Colleges: The Fall 2015 Cohort after Five Semesters* (Nashville, TN: The

College System of Tennessee, 2018), https://www.tbr.edu/sites/tbr.edu/files/media/2018/05/TBR_TNPromise_2015_2.pdf; Ashley A. Smith, "Reports: Free College Programs Don't Benefit Low-Income Students," *Inside Higher Ed*, September 6, 2018, https://www.insidehighered.com/news/2018/09/06/new-reports-show-free-tuition-programs-may-not-help-low-income-students-much.

4. For reports on free tuition programs across the United States, see, for example, Tiffany Jones and Katie Berger, *A Promise Fulfilled: A Framework for Equitable Free College Programs* (Washington, DC: The Education Trust, 2018), https://s3-us-east-2.amazonaws.com/edtrustmain/wp-content/uploads/2018/09/05155636/A-Promise-Fulfilled-A-Framework-for-Equitable-Free-College-Programs-9.6-18.pdf.
5. Alain Poutre and Mamie Voight, *Tennessee Promise: Does It Help Students with Limited Financial Means Afford College?* (Washington, DC: Institute for Higher Education Policy, 2018), http://www.ihep.org/sites/default/files/uploads/docs/pubs/ihep_state_free_college_tennessee_promise.pdf.
6. Denisa Gándara and Amy Li, "Promise for Whom? 'Free-College' Programs and Enrollments by Race and Gender Classifications at Public, 2-Year Colleges," *Educational Evaluation and Policy Analysis* 42, no. 4 (2020): 603–27, doi:10.3102/0162373720962472.
7. Abigail Hess, "Rich Students Get Better SAT Scores—Here's Why," *CNBC*, October 3, 2019, https://www.cnbc.com/2019/10/03/rich-students-get-better-sat-scores-heres-why.html.
8. Paul Fain, "Gambling on the Lottery," *Inside Higher Ed*, September 4, 2014, https://www.insidehighered.com/news/2014/09/04/report-unintended-consequences-lottery-based-scholarships-and-how-fix-them.
9. *Today's Student* (Indianapolis, IN: The Lumina Foundation, 2019), https://www.luminafoundation.org/wp-content/uploads/2019/02/todays-student.pdf; Paul Fain, "Some College, No Degree," *Inside Higher Ed*, October 31, 2019, https://www.insidehighered.com/news/2019/10/31/new-data-36-million-americans-who-left-college-without-credential.
10. Michael Waters, "Why New York's Free College Program Is Still Costing Its Students," *Vox*, February 5, 2020, https://www.vox.com/the-highlight/2020/2/5/21113890/new-york-free-college-excelsior-tuition.
11. Satra Taylor et al., *The Promise of a Higher Education Should Be Open to All—Even Those in Prison* (Washington, DC: The Education Trust, 2020), https://edtrust.org/wp-content/uploads/2014/09/The-Promise-of-a-Higher-Education-Should-Be-Open-to-All-Even-Those-In-Prison-October-21-2020.pdf.
12. Douglas N. Harris et al., "The Promise of Free College (and Its Potential Pitfalls)," *Brookings*, September 20, 2019, https://www.brookings.edu/research/the-promise-of-free-college-and-its-potential-pitfalls/.
13. Tiffany Jones, Jaime Ramirez-Mendoza, and Victoria Jackson, *A Promise Worth Keeping: An Updated Equity-Driven Framework for Free College* (Washington, DC: The Education Trust, 2020), 8–11, https://edtrust.org/wp

-content/uploads/2014/09/A-Promise-Worth-Keeping_An-Updated-Equity-Driven-Framework-for-Free-College-Programs_October_2020.pdf.

14. Rong Chen and Mark Wiederspan, "Understanding the Determinants of Debt Burden Among College Graduates," *Journal of Higher Education* 85, no. 4 (2014): 565–98, doi:10.1353/jhe.2014.0020; Lindsay C. Page and Judith Scott-Clayton, "Improving College Access in the United States: Barriers and Policy Responses," *Economics of Education Review* 51 (2016): 4–22, doi:10.1016/j.econedurev.2016.02.009.
15. Erik C. Ness and Molly A. Mistretta, "Merit Aid in North Carolina: A Case Study of a 'Nonevent'," *Educational Policy* 24, no. 5 (2010): 703–34, doi:10.1177/0895904809339165.
16. James C. Hearn and Erik C. Ness, "The Ecology of State Higher-Education Policymaking in the U.S.," in *Toward the Private Funding of Higher Education: Ideological and Political Struggles*, ed. David Palfreyman, Ted Tapper, and Scott Thomas (London: Routledge, 2018), 19–47.
17. Michelle Miller-Adams, *Promise Nation: Transforming Communities Through Place-Based Scholarships* (Kalamazoo, MI: W. E. Upjohn Institute for Employment Research, 2015), doi:10.17848/9780880995061.
18. Gándara and Li, "Promise for Whom?"
19. Kim Parker, "The Growing Partisan Divide in Views of Higher Education," *Pew Research Center*, August 19, 2019, https://www.pewsocialtrends.org/essay/the-growing-partisan-divide-in-views-of-higher-education/; Paul G. Rubin and James C. Hearn, "The Policy Filtering Process: Understanding Distinctive State Responses to the National College Completion Agenda in the United States," *Education Policy Analysis Archives* 26, no. 60 (2018): 1–28, doi:10.14507/epaa.26.3447.
20. James C. Hearn and Michael K. McLendon, "Governance Research: From Adolescence toward Maturity," in *The Organization of Higher Education: Managing Colleges for a New Era*, ed. Michael N. Bastedo (Baltimore, MD: Johns Hopkins University Press, 2012), 45–85.
21. Established in 1974, TSAC administers most of Tennessee's student financial aid programs. See: "About TSAC," Tennessee Higher Education Commission, https://www.tn.gov/thec/about-thec-tsac/tennessee-student-assistance-corporation/redirect-tsac/about-tsac.html.
22. Laura W. Perna and Elaine W. Leigh, "Understanding the Promise: A Typology of State and Local College Promise Programs," *Educational Researcher* 47, no. 3 (2018): 155–80, doi:10.3102/0013189X17742653.
23. Jane Mansbridge, "A 'Selection Model' of Political Representation," *Journal of Political Philosophy* 17, no. 4 (2009): 369–98, doi:10.1111/j.1467-9760.2009.00337.x.
24. Alex Guerrero, "Paradox of Voting and the Ethics of Political Representation," *Philosophy and Public Affairs* 38, no. 3 (2010): 272–306, doi:10.1111/j.1088-4963.2010.01188.x.

25. I appreciate suggestions and input from Jennifer Delaney, Ashley Kuntz, Rebecca Taylor, Joyce Tolliver, and Barbara Wilson. They are not responsible for any of my comments here.
26. James J. Duderstadt, *A Master Plan for Higher Education in the Midwest: A Roadmap to the Future of the Nation's Heartland* (Ann Arbor, MI: The University of Michigan, 2011), 23, http://milproj.dc.umich.edu/pdfs/New_Midwest_Masterplan.pdf.
27. Christopher Cornwell and David B. Mustard, "Merit-Based College Scholarships and Car Sales," *Education Finance and Policy* 2, no. 2 (2007): 133–51.
28. Tuan D. Nguyen, Jenna W. Kramer, and Brent J. Evans, "The Effects of Grant Aid on Student Persistence and Degree Attainment: A Systematic Review and Meta-Analysis of the Causal Evidence," *Review of Educational Research* 89, no. 6 (2019): 831–74, doi:10.3102/0034654319877156.
29. Gándara and Li, "Promise for Whom?"
30. Hieu Nguyen, "Free Tuition and College Enrollment: Evidence from New York's Excelsior Program," *Education Economics* 27, no. 6 (2019): 573–87, doi:10.1080/09645292.2019.1652727.
31. Sarah R. Cohodes and Joshua S. Goodman, "Merit Aid, College Quality, and College Completion: Massachusetts' Adams Scholarship as an In-Kind Subsidy," *American Economic Journal: Applied Economics* 6, no. 4 (2014): 251–85, doi:10.1257/app.6.4.251.
32. Oded Gurantz, "What Does Free Community College Buy? Early Impacts from the Oregon Promise," *Journal of Policy Analysis and Management* 39, no. 1 (2020): 11–35, doi:10.1002/pam.22157.
33. Cohodes and Goodman, "Merit Aid, College Quality, and College Completion."
34. Tatiana Melguizo, "Quality Matters: Assessing the Impact of Attending More Selective Institutions on College Completion Rates of Minorities," *Research in Higher Education* 49, no. 3 (2008): 214–36, doi:10.1007/sl 1162-007-9076-1.
35. Andrew Gillen, *Introducing Bennett Hypothesis 2.0* (Washington, DC: Center for College Affordability and Productivity, 2012), https://files.eric.ed.gov/fulltext/ED536151.pdf.
36. Federick Ngo and Samantha Astudillo, "California DREAM: The Impact of Financial Aid for Undocumented Community College Students," *Educational Researcher* 48, no. 1 (2019): 5–18, doi:10.3102/0013189X18800047.
37. Hosung Sohn et al., "Assessing the Effects of Place-Based Scholarships on Urban Revitalization: The Case of Say Yes to Education," *Educational Evaluation and Policy Analysis* 39, no. 2 (2017): 198–222, doi:10.3102/0162373716675727.
38. Gurantz, "What Does Free Community College Buy?"
39. Recent critics of the meritocratic narrative can be found in Daniel Markovits, *The Meritocracy Trap: How America's Foundational Myth Feeds Inequality, Dismantles the Middle Class, and Devours the Elite* (New York: Penguin

Books, 2020); Michael Sandel, *The Tyranny of Merit: What's Become of the Common Good?* (New York: Farrar, Straus and Giroux, 2020).

40. Laura T. Hamilton, *Parenting to a Degree: How Family Matters for College Women's Success* (Chicago: University of Chicago Press, 2016).
41. Caitlin Zaloom, *Indebted: How Families Make College Work at Any Cost* (Princeton, NJ: Princeton University Press, 2019).
42. Paul Tough, *The Years That Matter Most: How College Makes or Breaks Us* (Boston: Houghton Mifflin Harcourt, 2019), 40–43.
43. Jennifer M. Morton, *Moving Up Without Losing Your Way: The Ethical Costs of Upward Mobility* (Princeton, NJ: Princeton University Press, 2019).

CHAPTER 7

1. The college, communities, organizations, and characters in this case are fictional.
2. "CORIBE," American Educational Research Association Commission on Research in Black Education, http://www.coribe.org/#.
3. Sumitha Hedge, "What Is an Ethical Dilemma?," *Science ABC*, last modified October 10, 2019, https://www.scienceabc.com/social-science/what-is-an-ethical-dilemma-definition-examples-real-life.html.
4. Molefi Kete Asante, *Radical Insurgencies* (New York: Universal Write, 2020).
5. Joyce Elaine King and Carolyn Ann Mitchell, *Black Mothers to Sons: Juxtaposing African American Literature with Social Practice* (New York: Peter Lang, 1995).
6. Andrew Rollins, "Afrofuturism and Our Old Ship of Zion: The Black Church in Post-Modernity," in *Afrofuturism 2.0: The Rise of Astro-Blackness,* ed. Reynaldo Anderson and Charles E. Jones (Lanham, MD: Lexington Books, 2016), 127–47.
7. Kodwo Eshun, "Further Considerations of Afrofuturism," *CR: The New Centennial Review* 3, no. 2 (2003): 288, doi:10.1353/ncr.2003.0021.
8. Carter Godwin Woodson, *The Mis-Education of the Negro* (Washington, DC: Associated Publishers, 1933), viii.
9. Sylvia Wynter, "No Humans Involved: An Open Letter to My Colleagues," *Voices of the African Diaspora* 8, no. 2 (1992): 15.
10. W. E. B. DuBois, *The Education of Black People: Ten Critiques, 1906–1960,* ed. Herbert Aptheker (Amherst: University of Massachusetts Press, 1973), 154.
11. Jessica Gordon Nembhard, "On the Road to Democratic Economic Participation: Educating African American Youth in the Postindustrial Global Economy," in *Black Education: A Transformative Research and Action Agenda for the New Century*, ed. Joyce Elaine King (Mahwah, NJ: L. Erlbaum Associates, 2005), 225–39.
12. Daniel Wildcat, *Red Alert! Saving the Planet with Indigenous Knowledge* (Golden, CO: Fulcrum Publishing, 2009), 5.

13. Adam Harris, "Why America Needs Its HBCUs," *The Atlantic*, May 16, 2019, https://www.theatlantic.com/education/archive/2019/05/howard-universitys-president-why-america-needs-hbcus/589582/.
14. DuBois, *The Education of Black People*, 150.
15. DuBois, 41–60.
16. Samuel G. Freedman, "Parents' Ceremony Serves Up Elements of 'Morehouse Gospel'," *New York Times*, August 21, 2015, https://nyti.ms/1NJSQr3.
17. Shane O'Neil, "'Baptized in Blackness': Why Homecoming Is Vital to the Black College Experience," *New York Times*, October 7, 2020, https://nyti.ms/2Sy1cfA.
18. Marguerite J. Dennis, *A Practical Guide to Enrollment and Retention Management in Higher Education* (Westport, CT: Bergin & Garvey, 1998).
19. Meredith Anderson et al., *Imparting Wisdom: HBCU Lessons for K–12 Education* (Washington, DC: Frederick D. Patterson Research Institute, UNCF, 2020).
20. Benjamin E. Mays, *Born to Rebel: An Autobiography* (Athens: University of Georgia Press, 1971), 196.
21. Shaun R. Harper and Tryan L. McMickens, "Mary McLeod Bethune's Fundraising Success: Implications for Contemporary Presidents of Historically Black Colleges and Universities," in *Models of Success: How Historically Black Colleges and Universities Survive the Economic Recession*, ed. Shametrice Davis and Walter M. Kimbrough (Charlotte, NC: Information Age, 2018), 1–20.
22. Harper and McMickens, 17.
23. Harper and McMickens, 16.
24. Tryan L. McMickens, "Running the Race When Race Is a Factor," *Phi Delta Kappan* 93, no. 8 (2012): 39–43, doi:10.1177/003172171209300809.
25. Ronyelle Bertrand Ricard and M. Christopher Brown II, *Ebony Towers in Higher Education* (Sterling, VA: Stylus, 2008), 13–18.
26. Bobby L. Lovett, *America's Historically Black Colleges and Universities: A Narrative History, 1837–2009* (Macon, GA: Mercer University Press, 2015), 287.
27. Paulo Freire, *Teachers as Cultural Workers: Letters to Those Who Dare to Teach* (Boulder, CO: Westview Press, 2005), 69–79.
28. Felecia Commodore, "The Tie That Binds: Trusteeship, Values, and the Decision-Making Process at AME-Affiliated HBCUs," *The Journal of Higher Education* 89, no. 4 (2018): 397–421, doi:10.1080/00221546.2017.1396949.
29. Mikyoung Minsun Kim and Clifton F. Conrad, "The Impact of Historically Black Colleges and Universities on the Academic Success of African-American Students," *Research in Higher Education* 47, no. 4 (2006): 399–427, doi:10.1007/s11162-005-9001-4.
30. Felecia Commodore, "Losing Herself to Save Herself: Perspectives on Conservatism and Concepts of Self for Black Women Aspiring to the HBCU Presidency," *Hypatia* 34, no. 3 (2019): 1–23, doi:10.1111/hypa.12480.
31. Steve D. Mobley, Jr., "Seeking Sanctuary: (Re)Claiming the Power of Historically Black Colleges and Universities as Places of Black Refuge," *International*

Journal of Qualitative Studies in Education 30, no. 10 (2017): 1036–41, doi: 10.1080/09518398.2017.1312593.
32. Mobley.
33. Krystal L. Williams et al., "Stories Untold: Counter-Narratives to Anti-Blackness and Deficit-Oriented Discourse Concerning HBCUs," *American Educational Research Journal* 56, no. 2 (2019): 556–99, doi:10.3102/000 2831218802776.
34. Steve D. Mobley, Jr. and Leslie Hall, "(Re) Defining Queer and Trans* Student Retention and 'Success' at Historically Black Colleges and Universities," *Journal of College Student Retention: Research, Theory & Practice* 21, no. 4 (2020): 497–519, doi:10.1177/1521025119895512.
35. Mobley and Hall.
36. Commodore, "The Tie That Binds."
37. Raquel M. Rall, Demetri L. Morgan, and Felecia Commodore, "Toward Culturally Sustaining Governance in Higher Education: Best Practices of Theory, Research, and Practice," *Journal of Education Human Resources* 38, no. 1 (2020): 139–64, doi:10.3138/jehr.2019-0006.
38. Rall, Morgan, and Commodore.

CHAPTER 8

1. The college, communities, and characters in this case are fictional.
2. Robert Lee and Tristan Ahtone, "Land-Grab Universities: Expropriated Indigenous Land Is the Foundation of the Land-Grant University System," *High Country News*, March 30, 2020, https://www.hcn.org/issues/52.4/indigenous-affairs-education-land-grab-universities.
3. National Congress of American Indians, *Demographic Profile of Indian Country* (Washington, DC: NCAI Research Policy Center, 2012), http://www.ncai.org/policy-research-center/research-data/bb_2012_november_demographic_profile.pdf.
4. "What Is Native Nation Building?," Native Nations Institute, https://nni.arizona.edu/programs-projects/what-native-nation-building.
5. Megan Bang and Shirin Vossoughi, "Participatory Design Research and Educational Justice: Studying Learning and Relations Within Social Change Making," *Cognition and Instruction* 34, no. 3 (2016): 173–93, doi:10.1080/07370008.2016.1181879.
6. Florence D. Amamoto, "Response-ability in Practice: Discerning Vocation through Campus Relationships," in *Hearing Vocation Differently: Meaning, Purpose, and Identity in the Multi-Faith Academy*, ed. David S. Cunningham (London: Oxford University Press, 2019), 227.
7. Tania D. Mitchell, "Traditional vs. Critical Service-Learning: Engaging the Literature to Difference Two Models," *Michigan Journal of Service Learning* 14, no. 2 (2008): 61 (emphasis mine), http://hdl.handle.net/2027/spo.3239521.0014.205.

8. Robert G. Bringle, Patti H. Clayton, and Mary F. Price, "Partnerships in Service Learning and Civic Engagement," *Partnerships: A Journal of Service Learning & Civic Engagement* 1, no. 1 (2009): 3, http://hdl.handle.net/1805/4580.
9. Mitchell, "Traditional vs. Critical Service-Learning," 55.
10. "Social Change Wheel 2.0," IA and MN Campus Compact, June 16, 2020, https://mncampuscompact.org/resource-posts/social-change-wheel-2-0-toolkit/.
11. Mary Jane Brukardt et al., *Calling the Question: Is Higher Education Ready to Commit to Community Engagement?* (Milwaukee: University of Wisconsin-Milwaukee, 2004), ii, https://community-wealth.org/sites/clone.community-wealth.org/files/downloads/report-burkardt.pdf.
12. See, for example, Steve Dubb, Sarah McKinley, and Ted Howard, *The Anchor Dashboard: Aligning Institutional Practice to Meet Low-Income Community Needs* (College Park, MD: The Democracy Collaborative at the University of Maryland, 2013), https://community-wealth.org/sites/clone.community-wealth.org/files/downloads/AnchorDashboardCompositeFinal.pdf.
13. Ira Harkavy, "Service Learning as a Vehicle for Revitalization of Education Institutions and Urban Communities" (paper presented at the Education Directorate Miniconvention on Urban Initiatives: In Partnership with Education, American Psychological Association Annual Meeting, Toronto, Canada, August 10, 1996).
14. Mitchell, "Traditional vs. Critical Service-Learning," 53–54, 56.
15. Christopher Meyers, "Public Philosophy and Tenure/Promotion: Rethinking 'Teaching, Scholarship, and Service'," *Essays in Philosophy* 15, no. 5 (2014): 58–76, doi:10.7710/1526-0569.1489; Linda Martin Alcoff, "Does the Public Intellectual Have Intellectual Integrity?," *Metaphilosophy* 33, no. 5 (2002): 521–34.
16. Dan W. Butin, "The Limits of Service-Learning in Higher Education," *Review of Higher Education* 29, no. 4 (2006): 473–98, doi:10.1353/rhe.2006.0025.
17. United Frontline Table, *A People's Orientation to a Regenerative Economy* (Climate Justice Alliance, June 2020), https://climatejusticealliance.org/wp-content/uploads/2020/06/ProtectRepairInvestTransformdoc24s.pdf
18. *Governor's Taskforce on Climate Change Report* (Madison, WI: State of Wisconsin, 2020), https://climatechange.wi.gov/Documents/Final%20Report/USCA-WisconsinTaskForceonClimateChange_20201207-LowRes.pdf.

CHAPTER 9

1. Jacob Fay and Meira Levinson, with Elisabeth Fieldstone Kanner, "Engaging with Dilemmas," in *Dilemmas of Educational Ethics: Cases and Commentaries*, ed. Meira Levinson and Jacob Fay (Cambridge, MA: Harvard Education Press, 2016), 211.
2. As first author on this chapter, I (Kuntz) have chosen to follow the June 2020 guidelines adopted by the National Association of Black Journalists, which "recommends that whenever a color is used to appropriately describe race,

then it should be capitalized, including White and Brown." See "NABJ Statement on Capitalizing Black and Other Racial Identifiers," National Association of Black Journalists, June 2020, https://www.nabj.org/page/styleguide.
3. Fay and Levinson, with Kanner, "Engaging with Dilemmas."
4. Joyce E. King, "Who Will Make America Great Again? 'Black People, of Course . . .'," *International Journal of Qualitative Studies in Education* 30, no. 10 (2017): 953, doi:10.1080/09518398.2017.1312605.
5. Meira Levinson and Jacob Fay, "Educating for Civic Renewal," in *Democratic Discord in Schools: Cases and Commentaries in Educational Ethics*, ed. Meira Levinson and Jacob Fay (Cambridge, MA: Harvard Education Press, 2019), 272.

Acknowledgments

This volume is the culmination of our thinking together with numerous colleagues and collaborators over the past few years. While we cannot possibly list each person individually, we are so very grateful to everyone who gave feedback along the way. We do want to extend a special thanks to Jacob Fay for his vital contributions to the project's conceptualization and early development and for his continued support. We are also grateful to Meira Levinson for her insights and support throughout the process. Finally, our collaboration grew out of the Spencer Foundation's 2013 Philosophy of Education Institute, where we also met a number of our contributors; we owe a special thanks to Paula McAvoy and Harry Brighouse for their work in creating such a transformative educational opportunity and for their ongoing support.

We also wish to express individual thanks to those who supported us throughout this project. *Kuntz:* To my husband, Aaron, thank you for being my thought partner and constant encourager. When I said yes to this project, I never imagined completing it across two states and three residences, stretched so thin as parents and partners. Thank you for keeping the faith in me, in us, and in this project. To my children—Anna, Oscar, Oliver, and Micah—thank you for keeping me grounded in the present. You remind me that life is here, now, right before me and all around me. I love you, and I love the way you love each other. *Taylor:* I am grateful to my virtual writing group (and dear pals)—Casey Nichols, Maribel Santiago, and Tadashi Dozono—for their friendship, encouragement, and reliable camaraderie as I navigated multiple cross-country moves and job transitions during the development of this project. Thank you to Ashley Taylor for her generous feedback at so many points throughout the process and to Meg Evans, Daniel Gibboney, Jiyoung Lee, and Joy Mosley for their research and editorial assistance. Finally, thank you to my family for providing the foundation of love and support that keeps me grounded in the joys of living.

We are also grateful to multiple funders who supported this project. Support from the Center for Ethics and Education at the University of Wisconsin at Madison and the Center for Ethics at Emory University made it possible to convene case authors and contributors to workshop two chapters in 2019. A conference grant from the Spencer Foundation funded another workshop for four additional chapters in 2020 and supported our editorial work on the project. The Campus Research Board at the University of Illinois at Urbana-Champaign funded honoraria for our contributors, and Taylor's case development work in the summer of 2020 was supported by a research stipend from the College of Arts and Sciences Committee for Teaching and Scholarly Development at Suffolk University. The opinions expressed in this volume are those of the authors and do not necessarily reflect the views of any of these funders.

About the Editors

REBECCA M. TAYLOR is an assistant professor in the Department of Educational Policy, Organization and Leadership at the University of Illinois at Urbana-Champaign. Growing up in rural Appalachia, she became aware of inequities in our educational and social systems and the challenges of living and learning in community when values conflict—issues she now explores through the study of educational ethics. Prior to joining UIUC, she was an assistant professor at Suffolk University, postdoctoral fellow at Emory University, and research associate in the Stanford Criminal Justice Center. Her work has appeared in various journals, including *Harvard Educational Review*, *Educational Theory*, *Journal of Philosophy of Education*, *Democracy and Education*, and *Educational Philosophy and Theory*. Dr. Taylor holds a PhD in philosophy of education from Stanford University, a master's degree in peace, conflict, and development studies from Universitat Jaume I, and a bachelor's degree in mathematics and philosophy from Washington University in St. Louis.

ASHLEY FLOYD KUNTZ is clinical assistant professor of higher education and director of prestigious scholar development at Florida International University. Dr. Kuntz's experiences as an administrator, professor, and mentor at both public and private universities inform her understanding of and responses to the cases and commentaries in this volume. A first-generation college student from rural Alabama, she received a BA in psychology from Samford University, then worked full-time while earning an MA and PhD in higher education administration from the

University of Alabama. As a graduate student, she benefited from a philosophy of education fellowship through the Spencer Foundation, which complemented and extended her study of higher education. Her work has appeared in *Harvard Educational Review*, *Philosophy and Theory in Higher Education*, and *Emerging Adulthood*.

About the Case Study Authors

MEG E. EVANS, PhD (they/them or she/her), has over a decade of experience as a student affairs educator and administrator, having most recently served as a director in an identity-based center. Their research focuses on racial justice, advocacy, activism, and resistance in higher education.

JACOB FAY is a postdoctoral fellow at the Edmond J. Safra Center for Ethics. His research focuses on normative theories of injustice and their relation to educational policy and practice. Fay is co-editor with Meira Levinson of *Democratic Discord in Schools: Cases and Commentaries* (2019) and *Dilemmas of Educational Ethics: Cases and Commentaries* (2016).

DANIEL P. GIBBONEY JR. is a doctoral candidate at the University of North Carolina at Chapel Hill. His research interests are in the history of psychology, youth studies, and the work of Michel Foucault. Daniel is currently writing a dissertation on the history of childhood and developmental psychology in early twentieth-century America.

AARON M. KUNTZ is professor of research methodology and department chair of counseling, rehabilitation, and school psychology at Florida International University, where he currently holds the Frost Professorship of Education and Human Development. His latest book is entitled *Qualitative Inquiry, Cartography, and the Promise of Material Change*.

NICOLE LINDAHL-RUIZ is senior research associate at the Transformative Justice Initiative at Willamette University. She earned her PhD in jurisprudence and social policy from UC Berkeley, where she studied life histories of men who committed violent crimes, served long prison sentences, and accessed higher education in California.

JOY ELIZABETH MOSLEY currently serves as the director of government relations for the Council for Christian Colleges & Universities. She received her doctor of law from Emory University School of Law, her master of business administration from Belhaven University, and her bachelor of arts from Covenant College.

COREY REED is a PhD candidate in the Philosophy Department at the University of Memphis. He specializes in African American philosophy, critical race theory, and Black existentialism. His master's degree is in comparative humanities from the University of Louisville, and his bachelor of arts degree is from Morehouse College.

ALICE REZNICKOVA is an industry assistant professor and director of the Sustainable Urban Environments Major at New York University's Tandon School of Engineering. Alice teaches interdisciplinary courses in environment and sustainability. Her research interests include sustainability in higher education and sustainable food systems.

JOHN TORREY is an assistant professor of philosophy at SUNY Buffalo State College. His primary research interests are the social, moral, and political limits surrounding Black reparations in America. He has published on the theoretical underpinnings of Black Lives Matter and on doing precollege philosophy. He participated in the UnMute Podcast in 2020.

Index